WHAT'S BEHIND THE RESEARCH?

To Joseph F. Rychlak,
our mentor

WHAT'S BEHIND THE RESEARCH?

Discovering Hidden Assumptions in the Behavioral Sciences

Brent D. Slife
Richard N. Williams

SAGE Publications
International Educational and Professional Publisher
Thousand Oaks   London   New Delhi

For information address:

 SAGE Publications, Inc.
2455 Teller Road
Thousand Oaks, California 91320
E-mail: order@sagepub.com

SAGE Publications Ltd.
6 Bonhill Street
London EC2A 4PU
United Kingdom

SAGE Publications India Pvt. Ltd.
M-32 Market
Greater Kailash I
New Delhi 110 048 India

Printed in the United States of America

Library of Congress Cataloging-in-Publication Data

Slife, Brent D.
    What's behind the research?: Discovering hidden assumptions in the
behavioral sciences / Brent D. Slife, Richard N. Williams.
        p.   cm.
    Includes bibliographical references and index.
    ISBN 0-8039-5862-5 (alk. paper).   —   ISBN 0-8039-5863-3 (pbk.:
alk. paper)
    1. Psychology and philosophy. 2. Psychology—Philosophy.
I Williams, Richard N. 1950- . II. Title.
BF41.S57   1995   95-9376
300'.1—dc20

This book is printed on acid-free paper.

00   10 9 8 7

Sage Production Editor: Gillian Dickens

Contents

Preface

B eing involved on both the applied and theoretical ends of the behavioral sciences (as psychologists), we have been encouraged over the past decade by an increasing level of theoretical sophistication. This book is an attempt to extend this theoretical sophistication to the level of students. Theoretical work in the behavioral sciences has taken place at the professional level almost exclusively, making the work nearly inaccessible to most undergraduate and many graduate students. However, we believe these students can benefit greatly from an increased understanding of this theoretical work, particularly in developing their critical abilities. As Stephen Brookfield (1987) showed in *Developing Critical Thinkers,* two activities are necessary for critical thinking to occur:

1. Identifying and challenging the *assumptions* underlying a person's beliefs and actions
2. Conceiving and exploring *alternatives* to current ways of thinking and living

The purpose of this book is to facilitate these activities in the behavioral sciences. We attempt to address the main assumptions on which theories in the behavioral sciences are based as well as provide alternatives to these assumptions, some of them little known. In increasing accessibility, however, we may have oversimplified some complex issues. Where possible, we have provided footnotes and references to acknowledge the oversimplification and direct readers toward a more complete analysis.

Acknowledgments

We want to acknowledge our debt to a host of individuals who assisted in the writing of this book. We begin with our God, whom we believe sustains us. We also wish to recognize our long-suffering wives, Karen and Camille, whose encouragement and help have been invaluable. Camille, particularly, was a wise and thorough editor of an earlier draft of this book. Our students are, in some sense, the main impetus for the book. We have wanted to provide them with a treatment of the issues contained herein that is readable and yet challenging. Still, we would single out four students: Amy Fisher, Kris Kristensen, and Stephen Yanchar for their conscientious work on the Glossary; and Holly Young for her diligence in putting the manuscript together. Our colleague Emily Reynolds also provided timely and insightful assistance in preparing the final draft.

We are forever grateful to five conscientious reviewers: Constance Fischer of Duquesne University, Jeffrey Lindstrom of Ohio University, Allan Wicker of Claremont Graduate School, Thomas Schwandt of Indiana University, and Jean Maria Arrigo of Claremont Graduate School. In all our years in academia, we have never seen a more helpful set of reviews. The second author wishes to acknowledge the Psychology Department at Georgetown University for help and support during a semester's visiting professorship. The department provided resources and collegial discourse at a critical juncture. Finally, we want to express our gratitude to Brigham Young University for granting us the time to complete this book.

Brent D. Slife
Richard N. Williams

« 1 »

Introduction

Behavioral scientists, by definition, study and explain a broad range of human behaviors. However, if you ask a half dozen behavioral scientists how they would explain a friend's rude behavior, you would likely get a half dozen *differing* replies. As the behavioral scientists consult the theories and models of their disciplines, they would offer explanations ranging from "she's been conditioned by her environment" to "her more selfish id has overcome her more civilized ego" to "she freely and willfully acted rudely toward you."

Explanations from the behavioral sciences can be so numerous that it is easy to get confused or frustrated. You might want to ask, "Just what is the *right* explanation anyway?" Most behavioral scientists would undoubtedly sympathize. Some would respond to your frustration by encouraging you to "tolerate the ambiguity" of behavioral science, because it reflects the ambiguity of life. These behavioral scientists have given up trying to discern the most correct theory or explanation. Other behavioral scientists, however, consider it part of their job to separate the theoretical wheat from the chaff and differentiate the bad from the good explanations. Many theories, they would say, can already be eliminated, because they do not measure up to certain standards. Other theories can be tested to see whether they hold up under the scrutiny of science or practice.

The problem is that these standards and this scrutiny do not typically expose the *implicit ideas* of the theories. All theories have implied understandings about the world that are crucial to their formulation and use. Even if we accept multiple explanations as the "way it is" in the behavioral sciences, this acceptance provides no means of recognizing the assumptions "hidden" in these multiple explanations.[1] As students and consumers of the behavioral sciences, we accept and use theories that have important implications without recognizing those implications.

For example, the explanation you adopt for your friend's rude behavior will affect the way you respond to her. Hidden in any of the differing explanations you can adopt is an assumption about determinism. Did forces out of your friend's control, such as conditioning from her environment or chemicals in her brain, *determine* her actions? If your answer is yes, you might feel sorry for her and want to console her. After all, she could not help herself. If, however, you decide that she could have responded in a more polite manner—that is, her rudeness was *not* determined—you might be angry with her and wish to confront or avoid her. Your answer to this implicit question—whether or not you are aware of answering it—may result in a completely different type of interaction, if not a different future relationship, with your friend.

Discovering and understanding such implicit questions is the purpose of this book. In this book, we attempt to reveal what is implied by these theories so that students, practitioners, and teachers of behavioral science can make informed decisions about its strategies, techniques, and methods. It may be a very long time before behavioral scientists come up with a single theory that explains everything, if indeed this is ever possible. In the meantime, lay persons and professional people alike must adopt in their daily lives explanations and theories that have hidden costs and consequences. Therapists might not realize that the technique they use presupposes that patients are merely jumbles of neurons. Teachers might not know that an educational strategy they use assumes that students have no ability to make choices (even bad ones) in their learning. Managers might not understand that a business practice they employ presumes that clients have no feelings. The point is that all theories and strategies have ideas embedded within them that have very real and practical consequences.

Embedded ideas usually take two forms: assumptions and implications, the "from whence" and the "to whence" of theories. Theories must originate *from* somewhere, and the term *assumption* refers to the historical roots of a theory as well as the ideas about the world that are necessary for the theory to be true. For example, if you consider the environment to be responsible for your friend's rude behavior, you are making the assumption of determinism. Theories must also lead us *to* somewhere. The term *implication* refers to the consequences that logically follow if the theory is put into action. For example, assuming your friend's behavior is determined logically obligates you—for the sake of consistency—to a pattern of interactions that may include consoling her. The relation, then, between assumptions and implications is a logical one, "if_____, then_____." If Assumption A is true, *then* Implications B and C follow.

The difficulty is that in the behavioral sciences, relatively little attention is paid to assumptions and implications. Students are often taught the various theories for understanding behavioral science phenomena, but rarely is this teaching enriched by directly examining the assumptions and implications hidden within these theories. Criticisms of the theories are sometimes offered, but these criticisms seldom do more than scratch the surface. Why? Why have behavioral scientists omitted discussion of implicit ideas?

In our view, this omission has rarely been conscious or deliberate. Rather, the omission has been due to *other* implicit ideas, particularly historical conceptions that have been accepted as true, necessary, and thus not in need of examination. This sense of security about assumptions has obstructed the complete examination of behavioral science theories. Therefore, before we can fully expose these assumptions and implications, we must first begin to understand why the implicit ideas have remained implicit. In other words, we must ask about the conceptual obstructions that have kept practitioners of sophisticated disciplines such as family science, psychology, education, sociology, management, and economics from examining the ideas underlying their most important and respected theories and methods.

OBSTRUCTIONS TO
DISCOVERING HIDDEN IDEAS

As mentioned, many behavioral scientists have downplayed the importance of hidden ideas. Indeed, some behavioral scientists have denied the significance of theories altogether. For several reasons, which we briefly review here, these scientists have assumed that theories and their underlying ideas are secondary or even irrelevant to their professional activities. Your own associations with theories may be similar. For instance, it is not uncommon to hear someone say, "It's just a *theory*," and they say "theory" with a derisive, almost surly tone. What they usually mean, of course, is that the theory is "just" a speculation or an unproven hypothesis.

Scientific Method

This particular meaning of the term *theory* is derived from a widely held view of science. This meaning is important, because many behavioral scientists consider their discipline to be "scientific" in this sense. For them, theory is an educated *guess* about the world that must be held tentatively. The real solutions come only by using their scientific methods. Although many researchers consider this type of guess to be integral to science, theory is still viewed with suspicion until it is grounded in experimental data. Other scientists hope to do away with theories altogether. Their goal is to obtain all their knowledge from the cold, hard facts of science, with no theoretical trappings. This is a major reason that the implicit ideas in psychological theories have not received greater attention. Why spend time on the hidden ideas in guesses and speculations when the cold, hard facts are expected to provide the basis for, if not replace, the guesses and speculations?

One short answer to this question is that science itself is based on theories, or speculations. The method used to support or disprove other theories is itself a theory about how this supporting and disproving is done. Scientific method was not divinely given to scientists on stone tablets. There is no foreordained or self-evident truth about how science is to be conducted, or indeed, whether science *should* be conducted at all. Scientific method was formulated by philosophers, the preeminent dealers in ideas. These philosophers, *not* scientists, are responsible for the package of ideas now called *scientific method*. Scientists may *use* science, but they are often unaware of the ideas formulated by philosophers that lie hidden in their scientific methods. (Chapter 6 describes these ideas.)

This lack of awareness is partly because scientific method cannot itself be experimentally tested. Method has what some philosophers call a bootstrap problem. Just as those who wear old-fashioned boots cannot raise

Table 1.1 Sample of Scientific Data

10	7	9	11	13	6	12	8	8	11
9	10	9	13	6	14	7	7	11	8
14	13	10	7	9	10	6	9	12	9
7	13	6	9	12	10	10	11	5	8
12	8	11	9	5	11	8	13	7	12
8	8	7	11	10	6	9	12	11	7
7	9	6	14	9	11	11	13	12	13
12	8	12	13	7	7	8	6	12	6

themselves into the air by pulling on the straps of their boots, so practitioners of the scientific method cannot use its methods to validate it. Some
people argue that the many successes of science demonstrate its validity.
However, this argument contains the same bootstrap problem. Citing *success*
begs the question of what one considers success and how one verifies it.
Clearly these are speculative, theoretical issues. Moreover, success is not
always an indicator of validity. Hitler's methods of social control were
successful in the view of some people, though few would consider these
methods appropriate now. Success may be in the eye of the beholder. Even
if success were an indicator of validity, another more successful method
might still replace it.

Scientific Facts

There is another reason we should spend considerable time on the hidden
ideas related to science: *The facts of science are themselves theory laden.* A
prominent misconception of scientists is that they are objective observers
of the world. Although researchers use a theory-laden method, many people
assume that scientists conduct their experiments in a way that permits
the objective, nontheory-laden facts about the world to become evident.
We could first ask how a theory-laden method could ever provide us with
nontheory-laden facts. But even if we ignore this issue, we cannot ignore
the necessity of *interpreting* the data yielded by scientific method. Table
1.1 provides us with an example of scientific data. As you can see, these data
have little or no meaning without a researcher's interpretation of them.
We should also note that the source of these data—whether from biological, behavioral, or cognitive experiments—is irrelevant. The data still require
interpretation.

In this sense, data can never be facts until they have been given an interpretation that is dependent on ideas that do not appear in the data themselves. Often these ideas are so hidden that scientists themselves do not know that assumptions are involved in their interpretation, or that interpretation is involved at all. Scientists may be so accustomed to seeing the world through their particular theoretical "glasses" that they forget they are wearing them. Make no mistake, however. Interpretation *is* involved in every understanding of data, and this means that the scientists' unexamined views about the world inevitably enter into the "observed" facts. Even the statistics used to "interpret" data, as statisticians will tell you, have embedded ideas and assumptions. The point is that the so-called facts of science *always* have underlying ideas of the scientists mixed into them.

In sum, then, we cannot escape theories and ideas through science. If theories and ideas are speculative guesses about the world, then scientific method is itself a speculative guess about how one gains credible knowledge, because method is also a type of theory. Because method cannot itself be validated scientifically, it must be evaluated through an examination of its hidden ideas, a task we undertake in this book. Further, the outcome of scientific method—the "cold, hard facts of science"—is not so cold and hard. The data that result from method are interpreted, and *must* be interpreted, by warm, soft human beings, who have biases and beliefs about the world that cannot be avoided. Many behavioral scientists may lament the necessity of interpretation, but there is a positive side. Interpretation brings human meaning to experimental data, tailoring the sterile information of Table 1.1 to the particular context of real life. In this sense, escape from implicit ideas is not only impossible, it is undesirable. Any complete understanding or full use of the facts of science requires awareness of the ideas hidden within them.

Practical Motives

Does this same requirement extend to simple, practical uses of behavioral science information? "I want to help people," one might say, "and I do not see the need for an extensive understanding of behavioral science theories and their hidden ideas. Just have the scientists tell me what techniques work, and I will use those techniques to help people (in education, business, psychotherapy)." This raises the question of the technology of behavioral science. Should the behavioral sciences have technologists—persons who apply its information, but do not necessarily understand its theoretical grounding? A person who repairs television sets typically tests and replaces circuits without a full understanding of how the circuits work. Couldn't a technological psychologist or educator work in much the same fashion? Although there is a sense in which the answer is yes, the difference between an inanimate TV and an animate human should make us hesitant to endorse this approach.

People are, after all, precious and unique. The potential risks and benefits of their "repair" are higher and less straightforward. This means that knowledge of implicit ideas is vital, because unexamined ideas can have important consequences for those to whom they are applied. Remember that any piece of information contains the biases of the information's interpreter within it. Scientists may tell you that their particular ideas about the world stem from "previous research on the issue," but such research itself is not without hidden ideas. Indeed, it is likely that the hidden ideas that led the scientists to interpret the previous research are still active and implicit in the present research. As we demonstrate in Chapter 6, there are *always* other ways of interpreting data, no matter how many data have been gathered.

To some people the task of helping others appears straightforward and simple—no theory seems necessary. Although these people may be well intentioned, the outcome of their "helping" is often less than satisfactory. This is usually due to their underestimating the role of implicit ideas. Often the goal of helping is more complicated than it first appears. For example, there are already ideas underlying their desire to help people. Some people desire to help in order to meet their own needs to be needed, rather than to meet the needs of others. At the very least, this leads to confusion about who is the helper and who is the one being helped. Even the goal of "making a person happy" is fraught with all sorts of theoretical issues. Some therapists claim, for example, that happiness is a poor goal, ultimately damaging many clients.

People with practical motives must therefore know the particular ideas that are concealed in the theories of helping they apply. Indeed, the case could be made that applied behavioral scientists—those in therapy, education, and business—have a *special responsibility* to know the ideas embedded in this information. All people should probably be cautious about the information they use, but those who advise others have a unique responsibility to know the ideas implicit in that advice, whether the ideas originate from science or from the adviser's own sense of things. If certain interpretations are wrong or harmful, then the appliers of these interpretations could harm, or at the very least, waste the time of many who receive these interpretations.

As an illustration, consider those who administered intelligence tests to U.S. immigrants of the late 1920s. At the time, this seemed like a worthy, even altruistic task—preventing the "feebleminded" from entering the United States. Unfortunately, an idea was hidden in these tests that led to some questionable, even harmful, practices.[2] The idea was that intelligence is essentially the same the world over, regardless of language and culture. When some immigrants scored low on the test, the testers assumed that they were feebleminded or mentally retarded. As a result, they were denied access to the United States and often sent back to a country in which they were politically or economically oppressed.

As we now know, however, many of the so-called feebleminded were people with high intelligence but a poor command of the English language and U.S. culture. The hidden idea was basically incorrect (though it continues to exist subtly in many psychological tests). When this idea was finally exposed and subsequently examined, the harmful practice was curtailed. Unfortunately, though, considerable discrimination and prejudice had already occurred. This illustrates the potential harm of such ideas. Exposing and examining them is not an idle exercise, especially for those who actually use behavioral science information and techniques. If anything, the wish to "help people" should also carry with it a lively sense of obligation to be as skillful as possible in recognizing and evaluating the ideas embedded in the information and techniques used.

Avoidance of Theory

Given the potential harm of some theories and ideas in practice, why not avoid them altogether? This seems to be the tack of many mental health practitioners who claim that they do not use or need specific theories to practice effectively (Slife, 1987b, 1995a). Some contend that adherence to a particular theory is detrimental to their clients. These therapists argue that adherents to a theory are biased and less open to clients. Theory causes a therapist to stereotype clients, seeing qualities in them that are products of the theories rather than of the clients themselves. These therapists, then, believe that adopting theories leads them to a close-mindedness and rigidity that is ineffective, if not destructive.

Although open-mindedness of some sort is surely a worthy goal, it is doubtful that this goal can be reached by avoiding theories and their hidden ideas. Indeed, the notion that one should avoid theories and ideas is itself a theory. As Karl Jaspers once put it, "There is no escape from philosophy [or ideas]. The question is only whether a philosophy is conscious or not, whether it is good or bad, muddled or clear. Anyone who rejects philosophy is himself unconsciously practicing a philosophy" (quoted in Valentine, 1992, p. vi). If Jaspers is correct, the desire to be open-minded may lead people to think that they have avoided biases, when all that they have really avoided are the biases that they are aware of—the *non*hidden ideas.[3] The irony is that the ideas that end up guiding educational and therapeutic interventions are the ones that these teachers and therapists know the least. Ideas guide all interventions; behavioral science professionals have no choice about this. There *is* a choice, however, about whether these ideas remain unknown.

A safer type of open-mindedness is based on professionals knowing what ideas are hidden in their theories, including their costs and benefits, and then being theoretically skillful enough to discern what alternate ideas are needed. This is the root of critical thinking (as noted in the Preface). Ideas and biases themselves cannot be avoided. However, a careful understanding of their existence and a sophisticated knowledge of alternatives allow the teacher or therapist to shift ideas when appropriate. Even if it were possible to avoid ideas, we would lose the power that ideas bring to therapy. Ideas guide our actions, enrich our understandings, and fill gaps in our less-than-complete knowledge of the educational and therapeutic issues involved. In this sense of open-mindedness, then, an educational or therapeutic strategy that is supposedly free from biases is not only impossible, it is undesirable.

At this point, three conclusions should be clear. First, we cannot escape theory. Even in wanting to escape theory to be open-minded or wanting to believe that theorizing was unimportant to science, we would be practicing a theory. Second, all theories have assumptions and implications embedded in them. Theories stem from cultural and historical contexts that lend them meaning and influence how they are understood and implemented. Third, these hidden influences have important consequences. They can lead to discrimination, poor science, and ineffective practitioners, just to name a few. We may also simply disagree with some of the ideas implicit in a technique or a method. For any number of reasons—our values, religious convictions, or worldview—we may find some of the ideas unacceptable or wrong. It is therefore vital that we learn about these hidden assumptions and develop skills in evaluating their advantages and disadvantages.

OVERVIEW OF THE BOOK

Presenting these hidden assumptions, along with their costs and consequences, is our task in this book. Whether you are a student of the behavioral sciences, therapist, educator, businessperson, or simply a consumer of behavioral science information, you will need to know the implicit ideas in that information. What are the main interpretations of the data by scientists? What alternative methods are available for gathering knowledge? What ideas are embedded in the usual approaches to abnormality and treatment? Are there other ideas available for generating solutions to human problems? Do conventional approaches to business or education include assumptions about the world or human nature that are questionable or unacceptable to the people who use them? We attempt to answer these and many other questions.

We begin Chapter 2 with a survey of some of the major theoretical approaches in the behavioral sciences: psychoanalysis, behaviorism, humanism, cognitivism, eclecticism, structuralism, and postmodern approaches. These approaches are briefly summarized, and the issues raised in them—though rarely acknowledged or resolved—are outlined. The obstructions to discovering hidden ideas that are described above have kept attention away from the hidden ideas of these traditional "images of humankind." Consequently, the problems inherent in these images have seldom been identified or discussed. In Chapter 2, we attempt to explicate these problematic ideas so that they can be more carefully considered.

The next four chapters reveal and discuss key themes as representative of these hidden ideas: *knowing, determinism, reductionism,* and *science*. A full understanding of these themes may help us to avoid some of the difficult problems. Conventional conceptions of these issues are first described in the chapter as they occur in various behavioral science disciplines. Second, the intellectual history of these conventional conceptions is traced.

Finally, alternative ideas are presented to provide a contrast to the familiar conventions. Such contrasts are vital, because in most cases conventional approaches have so captured behavioral science that they are considered truths rather than points of view. Alternative ideas also help the student to begin thinking about the strengths and weaknesses of each theory. One needs a theory to evaluate a theory. One can never have a perspective on a theory, especially a critical perspective, without alternative theories from which to view and critically analyze the theory.

Conventional and alternative ideas are first considered in Chapter 3, "Ways of Knowing." Behavioral scientists have long been interested in how people know or learn, and have undertaken studies of conditioning and memory. However, one general explanation of this knowing and learning seems to have dominated the disciplines. This explanation says that the object of knowledge is "out there" in the environment and that truly knowing the object means getting the knowledge "in here" inside the head. Many psychotherapists and teachers seem to act on this assumption without full awareness of its consequences. We describe several alternative ways of knowing the world, along with some of the implications of each for therapy and education. For example, one of these alternatives denies the "in here" and "out there" distinction altogether.

Another central tenet of the behavioral sciences—determinism—is discussed in Chapter 4. Behavioral scientists are vitally interested in discovering the "determinants" of behavioral processes. In most of the behavioral sciences, however, the study of determinants has not included alternative ways of viewing determinism itself. Behavioral processes are usually assumed to be either determined or not determined. If these processes are not determined, they are typically viewed as random or chaotic. Randomness, in this sense, is often taken to be the *only* alternative to determinism. Behavioral scientists do not usually think of different *types* of determinism. We explore at least four ways of thinking about determinism, one of which is thought to be compatible with free will. We describe how this is considered possible and outline some of the criticisms of this approach.

Chapter 5 deals with an issue that is particularly relevant to the future of the behavioral sciences—*reductionism*. In the format of the previous chapters, several meanings and implications of reductionism are reviewed. Still, the most common use of the term among behavioral scientists entails the "reduction" of the behavioral sciences to biology—that is, the higher-level constructs and processes of the behavioral sciences are viewed as being reducible to the supposedly lower-level constructs and processes of the biological sciences. In this sense, all the disciplines of the behavioral sciences are little more than provisional structures until more basic, biological explanations are discovered. As we point out, a prominent misconception is that experimental findings support this form of reductionism. However, experimental findings are always subject to the assumptions of the scientist-interpreter. The chapter includes alternative approaches to the problem of reductionism.

In Chapter 6, we explore the ideas implicit in the relation between science and human behavior. The chapter begins with a review of mainstream approaches to science, situating them historically and exposing their underlying assumptions. Behavioral science methods are essentially descendants from the older, natural sciences. Are these methods appropriate for the primary subject matter of behavioral science—human beings? Many philosophers of science, the originators and critical observers of method, claim that natural science methods are not appropriate. These critics contend that humans are qualitatively different from natural objects, such as the particles of physics or the tectonic plates of geology. As a result, alternative methods have been proposed, which we outline and evaluate.

In the final chapter, we anticipate some reader responses to the book. Because we question the assumptions of what is generally taught in the behavioral sciences, readers may find this critical approach a bit unfamiliar. In Chapter 7, we describe three intellectual responses to this unfamiliarity. Understanding these responses should help us address the issues of the behavioral sciences. As a further aid, all the ideas of the previous chapters are summarized and organized into the categories of *necessity* and *possibility*. This organization assists the reader in seeing connections across the chapters and grasping the ideas as a whole. Then, as a springboard for discussion, the authors' own views about the prospects of the behavioral sciences are offered.

Notes

1. By the term *hidden* we do not mean to imply that behavioral scientists *intentionally* hide assumptions in their theories. This term is meant to connote the overlooked, underlying quality to many implicit ideas.

2. Other ideas hidden in these tests have also been seriously questioned, including the assumption that intelligence is basically inborn and the implication that eugenics is the best way to control the "evolution" of inborn intelligence. See Chapter 5 for a discussion of biological reductionism.

3. Obviously, the idea that open-mindedness of this sort is desirable is itself a bias or assumption. Ironically, those who are truly open-minded in this way should be open to the possibility that their strategy of open-mindedness is wrong or less effective than another strategy.

◖ 2 ◗

Human Images

◖ In the first chapter, we introduced the rather simple notion that ideas have consequences. Each of us takes to be true some ideas that we almost never openly examine or recognize. These ideas, however, influence the way we see the world, the way we act, and most important for the purposes of the behavioral sciences, what we assume human beings are like. Because these foundational ideas in the behavioral sciences have such far-reaching consequences, we need to examine carefully their assumptions and implications. This examination will allow us to see whether what they lead us to think and believe seem to be true and necessary ways of thinking about ourselves or our scholarly disciplines.

We have been using the term *idea* very broadly in this book. In one important sense, all theories are ideas, and all ideas are theories about what the world is like. In academic disciplines, such as the behavioral sciences, however, scholars have carefully formulated their explanations of human behavior, formally stating what they think to be true of human beings and why they think these things are true. Furthermore, they have tested some of their ideas (the ones they have recognized and used as explanations) with formal scientific methods to see whether those explanations seem justified and supported by experimental data. Their explanations of human behavior are framed to be universally, or at least very broadly, applicable—when constructing a theory, behavioral scientists want their ideas to be true of a large number of people, over long periods of time, and under a great variety of circumstances. These ideas that behavioral scientists have formulated with such care and tested with their best available methods, and about which there is some confidence concerning their universality, are what are usually referred to as *theories*. Theories, then, can be thought of as "formalized" ideas, constructed from other ideas (assumptions, understandings, observations, etc.) and applied broadly to help us explain a range of phenomena. There is some irony, however, in that for all the care that has been taken in formulating and testing *some* ideas (theories), *other* ideas (underlying assumptions and their implications) often go completely unexamined.

In keeping with the points of Chapter 1, then, we reiterate that theories are ideas and always reflect other ideas. Understanding these ideas is essential to a good education and also to making wise decisions about what to believe. The purpose of this chapter is to present a number of the most important and popular theories in the behavioral sciences, as they are understood today, and some of the ideas underlying them. This will teach us a great deal about how theories are formulated and show us their underlying assumptions and implications—what they ask us to accept as true about human beings.

THE NATURE OF THEORY

Before we begin our analysis of the dominant theories, we should note that the world of theories and ideas moves and changes very slowly. It takes time for people to examine new ideas, subject them to tests, and gain enough confidence in them to use them and espouse them. This is true not only in the behavioral sciences but also in the general culture. For this reason, although the disciplines known as behavioral sciences are more than a century old, only a relatively small number of ideas and ways of thinking have achieved the status of what might be called theories.

We should also point out that ideas, or theories, operate at varying levels of abstraction. Some are applied broadly, employed in explaining a much wider range of phenomena than others. Some of these are of such a general nature that many scholars might see them as *worldviews*, or philosophies, rather than theories. For the purposes of this book, however, because philosophies and theories are, in the most basic sense, ideas, we will use the term *theory* in a very general sense to refer to any idea used in explaining the world. In this chapter we deal specifically with *postmodernism* and *structuralism* as examples of theories that operate on a very broad and abstract level (as philosophies) and have been extremely influential in the behavioral sciences, particularly sociology, family science, and education.

Some ideas are less sweeping, and more focused on particular phenomena. These are what are more commonly referred to as theories. We focus on several theories of human functioning that although most often associated with psychology, have also been widely influential both within and outside the behavioral sciences. These theories, *psychodynamic theory, behaviorist theory, humanistic theory,* and *cognitive theory,* are more specifically focused on images of the human being, and thus are good vehicles for examining the effects of theories on how we understand ourselves.

Some ideas that influence thinking in the behavioral sciences seem more like approaches or attitudes toward theorizing rather than being theories themselves. We focus on *eclecticism* as an example of this kind of attitude. Such informal ideas, however, even ones that claim not to be theories at all, have all the essential features of theories, including a set of assumptions, important implications, and conceptual costs. For this reason we include eclecticism in our discussion of theories.

Because we want to stress that all ideas are built on the foundations of other ideas, and all contain many general and unexamined assumptions, we leave aside the definitional distinctions that might be important for other purposes. Distinctions are often made among philosophies, theories, attitudes, and ideas, but we adopt the general term theory to refer to all of them. We also note in passing that some theories are constructed around such a narrow focus, and are so explicitly tested and examined, that they are functionally different from the theories we have talked about here. They are frequently referred to as *models*. Although we would see these models as theories in the general sense we are using the term, we will not deal with them because they are less well known and less influential outside the particular subdisciplines in which they are used. These models are generally not meant to represent reality, but rather are intended chiefly to simulate or predict specific behaviors. However, proponents of such models tend to forget that they are not meant to represent reality and begin to talk about reality and deal with it in terms of their model. To the extent that this happens, what we have to say about theories applies to models as well. The purpose of the remainder of this chapter will be to examine each of the theories mentioned above to see what assumptions are implicit in them and what implications (conceptual costs) are entailed in accepting them.

A major guiding idea of this chapter—and the entire book—is that all theories in the behavioral sciences make assumptions about people, and these assumptions are most often not explicit. What is more apparent is that even after theories have described what people are like and why they do what they do, there are some problems left over. By problems, we mean assumptions and implications that still need to be dealt with.

These problems generally are of two kinds. First, although all theories explain some things about people, they can never explain everything. There are always some things that any theory has difficulty accounting for. Sometimes this is because the theorist ignores a question; sometimes there is a problem or issue that the theory simply cannot adequately handle. The second kind of problem relates to issues or questions about the assumptions that underlie the original theory. Assumptions should be examined in their own right to see whether they are reasonable or make sense in light of our experience. Also assumptions always lead to implications. We are referring here to the consequences of an idea or theory— the conceptual costs, calculated in terms of other ideas that logically flow from it, that we are logically obliged to accept. For example, we might explain that a person engages in eating behavior because of a hunger drive. However, our explanation has a problem because we are now left with the task of explaining what drives are, where they come from, and how they make a person do something specific, such as eat. We are also left with the question whether a person can choose to eat or not eat if he or she has a drive to do so. This kind of question is very important because it has implications for what we think people are really like.

All this is simply to say that any theory explains some things, but leaves many things still to be explained. These unexplained things and the implications of the theories are important, yet most often implicit, and theorists do not usually deal with them. Only if we become aware of these implicit ideas as problems to be dealt with can we deal with them. In later chapters in the book, we provide other conceptual tools for evaluating the assumptions and implications of theories.

We must offer one final observation before beginning our analysis. Summarizing various theories and families of theories is a daunting, if not impossible task. Theories in the behavioral sciences are often extremely complex and varied, and are constantly under development. Consequently, we do not claim nor attempt to represent all perspectives that may be associated with any of the theories and schools of thought we describe. An even greater problem is to represent particular behavioral scientists who for one reason or another are associated with a particular theoretical perspective. Some scientists who label themselves behaviorists or humanists, for example, may not feel they are adequately represented by the descriptions we present. We have endeavored in all cases to present what we understand to be the core of these theories, at least as traditionally and widely disseminated. These descriptions, however, can only be *versions,* or *readings,* of the particular theories under discussion, and not the all-encompassing, definitive positions of the theories or theorists themselves.

Particularly when descriptions of theories are coupled with criticisms of the theories, as they are here, many behavioral scientists may wish to distance themselves from the descriptions. In some cases, this distancing may be legitimate. However, in many of these cases, the criticisms regarding the hidden assumptions of the theory may apply. Our experience is that some element of the particular theory attracted the behavioral scientist enough for him or her to adopt the perspective, even if it is only the theoretical label. If our description of that theory does not capture some important aspect of a particular version of a theory, this does not automatically mean that the behavioral scientist is exempt from the assumptions of the theory. It certainly does not mean that the scientist is somehow exempt from the obligation of discovering the hidden assumptions and implications of whatever theoretical position he or she espouses. We therefore invite all those who feel that they are "outside" the theoretical descriptions we offer, and therefore immune to the problems we articulate, to undertake for themselves a description of their own hidden assumptions. We urge this particularly because it is often far easier (and safer) to say what one is not—especially when it is under criticism—than to say what one is.

PSYCHODYNAMIC THEORY

In the early 1890s Sigmund Freud was beginning his medical practice in Vienna, Austria. He specialized in what would today be called psychological problems. His way of dealing with his patients was based, of course, on his understanding of the causes of mental disorders, and his view of the causes of mental disorders was, in turn, related to his view of what constituted a psychologically healthy person. From this work, a school of psychology emerged, *psychoanalysis,* which has continued to be influential in psychological practice as well as scholarly work in many other fields. Other thinkers, some of whom were Freud's contemporaries (such as Carl Jung and Alfred Adler), and some of whom followed him (such as Erich Fromm, Karen Horney, and Erik Erikson), emphasized different aspects of the theoretical issues that Freud had articulated, and some contributed new ideas to the movement. It is this broader movement we have chosen to call *psychodynamic theory.* Although much work in the larger psychodynamic tradition differs substantially from Freud's original work, many of the essential elements of Freud's thought (the hidden assumptions) have either been directly imported into later theories or have infiltrated them. As we lack space to discuss the whole of the later movement, we base our discussion of the theory largely on the works of Freud himself. He was by far the most influential figure both within psychology and across other disciplines.[1]

As the term *psychodynamic* implies, proponents of this theory believe that the mind, or psyche, is not a passive recipient of information from the world. Rather, there are a number of dynamic events going on in the mental life of people at every moment. One of the important ideas in this theory is that many of these events occur on an unconscious level, that is, in a way that we are not, and often cannot be, aware of. For Freud, in order to understand a person, the most important thing to understand is the dynamic interplay of unconscious motivations and desires that all people have. These are the real and powerful forces influencing a person's behaviors.

Some scholars have believed that these unconscious forces are strong determiners of our actions, acting rather automatically without our choice or active participation—that is, in spite of ourselves. Others have interpreted Freud's work to mean that although the dynamic processes are real and influential, at some level the person is an (unconscious) agent in determining how the forces are manifested in his or her behavior. Either way, these unconscious forces are considered to be a very important part of understanding and explaining our behaviors.

Freud theorized that the human mind has both conscious and unconscious regions. The unconscious mind is dominated by what Freud referred to as the *id*. The id is quite primitive, carrying out what Freud called *primary process thinking*. This means that it pursues only gratification with no regard for the consequences of its gratification-seeking behaviors. In other words, the id is rather antisocial, in the sense that it cares very little for social conventions and rules of conduct. The conscious mind is dominated by the *ego*. This is basically our conscious identity and awareness of ourselves. The ego carries out *secondary process thinking*. It uses logic and considers the social and moral consequences of its actions. The ego is that part of our mind that is in contact with the outside world—the "I" we most commonly think about when we think of our own self or identity.

There is one more region of the mind that is important to understanding the psychodynamic approach. It is the *superego*. The superego develops as we come to know and adopt the rules and morals of our society, and most particularly, those of our parents. It is often suggested that the superego is our conscience. The superego is, for Freud, very powerful. It uses guilt and anxiety to try to get us to conform to its rules. The superego, at least in Freud's later models of the mind, dwells in both the unconscious and the conscious mind. That way it can stay informed about the unconscious demands of the id, and also help to direct the ego. The ego then is faced with having to direct the person's behavior in such a way that both the id and the superego are satisfied. This, as we may suppose, is not always an easy task.

One of the most controversial aspects of Freud's psychology was his belief that human beings have powerful instincts that motivate them to behave in certain ways. The most important of these, and the only one Freud developed in his theory to any extent, is the sexual instinct. For Freud, the sexual instinct arises in the body and demands gratification. There are alternating cycles of higher and lower arousal of the sexual instinct. When the cycle is at a higher point, it gives rise in the unconscious part of the mind (the id) to the idea of some object that will provide gratification. The id then begins to demand gratification and sets about to obtain the object and carry out behaviors that will result in gratification. It begins to apply pressure for these ideas and desires to become conscious. The superego, of course, at this point opposes gratification seeking in the name of social morality. The ego is very much caught in the middle of these conflicting desires and motivations. This dynamic interaction among the three regions of the mind justifies naming the theory psycho*dynamic*. The struggle to reconcile sexual instinctual urges[2] with the demands of society is the fundamental condition we as human beings find ourselves in. This struggle underlies not only our mental disorders, but our everyday relationships and actions as well.

One other aspect of psychodynamic theory is important to mention here. Freud believed that all people progress through a series of stages as they mature. These stages are characterized by different demands for gratification and different ways of attaining gratification. Unless we receive the proper amount of gratification (neither too much nor too little) at each stage, problems develop in moving through the stages as well as in later life. Freud believed that what happens to us at the very earliest stages of life is especially important. If we do not successfully pass through these stages and obtain the right amount of gratification, we become *fixated*. This means that in our unconscious minds, we continue to have the same desire for gratification that we had earlier in life—when we were properly (chronologically) in that particular stage. To become psychologically healthy, we need to somehow "go back" and deal with the frustration of not being properly gratified. For Freud, adult life can be characterized by how successfully we pass through these stages and get the optimal amount and type of gratification. In summary, this developmental aspect of psychodynamic theory holds that what happens early in life has strong directing influence over what we may do later in life.

This brief summary of psychodynamic theory does not do justice to a rich and varied tradition. The reader should consult other sources for a fuller presentation (e.g., Rychlak, 1981). The sketch presented here is adequate, however, to allow us to bring to light some of the significant assumptions of psychodynamic theory and their implications.

ASSUMPTIONS AND IMPLICATIONS
OF PSYCHODYNAMIC THEORY

One problem brought about by explaining behavior in terms of psychodynamic theory results from the presumed nature of the unconscious mind. The unconscious mind is, after all, unconscious *to us*. If this unconscious mind is capable of having its own instincts and motivations, and of influencing our choices and behaviors, then it follows that our behaviors are influenced by forces that we are unaware of. Furthermore, if we are unaware of these forces, we are not capable of intervening to change or go against them.[3] The main problem with this idea is that if we are really influenced by forces that we are unaware of and cannot control, then it appears that we can have little freedom to direct our own lives. It is important to recognize this implication of psychodynamic theory, because if we believe people are influenced by things they cannot know or control, then we have very different ideas about how and why they behave as they do and, for example, why they might become emotionally disturbed. Such an understanding of human behavior also makes it, in theory, difficult to predict and control even our own behaviors, as we really never know what influences might arise from the unconscious mind at any time. Whether we believe people capable of directing their own lives or largely influenced by unconscious ideas and urges that they cannot control makes a difference in how we understand and react to people (see Chapter 1).

Another problem psychodynamic theory brings to our attention has to do with the hypothesized sexual instinct. It has been quite common for a very long time in our culture to think of people being influenced, or even driven, by instincts of various sorts. This raises a problem similar to the problem presented by the unconscious. Instincts, of course, like unconscious ideas, are things that we don't experience directly—we can "feel" motivated, but we do not ever experience or detect the motivation itself. If we are motivated to do certain behaviors by instincts, then again, we do not have much control over our own motivations because we cannot know or have direct contact with the force that causes them (the instinct).

Perhaps more serious, the contention in psychodynamic theory that sexual instincts are powerful influences on behavior is problematic because it leads us to accept the idea that sexual instincts have some causal influence over *all* that we do. In other words, if the sexual instinct is as powerful and pervasive as Freud said it was, then it is powerful enough to be a motivating force behind any and all of our behaviors. Freud explicitly accepted this notion. If sexual motivations lie at the heart of virtually all our behaviors, then all our relations with other people and all our enjoyments in life are in some sense sexual in nature.[4] This understanding of relationships and enjoyment is quite different from the one our society has usually accepted and the way we normally experience our joys and relationships. The understanding has a real impact on how we understand ourselves and what life means to us. For example, this emphasis on the underlying sexual nature of our motivation means that other people serve the function of objects for our sexual gratification and that we ourselves serve the same function for others. It also means that our motivations, as well as the actions we might carry out, are ultimately driven by a desire for pleasure. This view of the persuasiveness of sexual motivation is one of the truly important assumptions of psychodynamic theory, and one that has real consequences for all who take it seriously as an explanation of their own or others' behavior.

Closely related to the assertion that all human behavior has a core of sexual motivation is the assertion that the sexual motivation itself arises from the body, rather than from the mind. It is the arising of the instinct in the body that sets the mind at work to seek out objects of gratification. What is assumed here is that the body can do things to affect the mind—that is, psychodynamic theory is based on the assumption that the body and mind are related in such a way that events in one can cause events in the other. It should be noted that this is a very old idea and has been the subject of much philosophical work. Nevertheless, it is an issue that has never been satisfactorily explicated—the problem of the relationship between the mind and the body has never been solved in a way that doesn't leave other problems and assumptions still to be dealt with. The implication of psychodynamic theory is that bodies do cause minds to do certain things and that minds cause bodies to do certain things. However, we are left wondering how this might be possible, especially because there are obviously some things we cannot get our bodies to do, no matter how much we might try, and there are some bodily responses that we ignore with relative ease.

One other problem should be mentioned here. Psychodynamic theory holds that things that happen to us early in life leave a genuinely lasting impression. These things, especially the effects of the amount and type of gratification we receive, supposedly never go away. If we take this theory seriously, then to a great extent, we are victims of the past. Our past experiences are still with us in the form of fixations. It may seem obvious that past experiences are somehow important, but according to psychodynamic theory, these experiences not only are important, but directly cause our present behaviors. The idea that we are not consciously aware of the way past events are still alive (as fixations) and exerting influence on us—because this all happens unconsciously—is another way in which psychodynamic theory requires the assumption that people are influenced by powerful forces outside their own awareness and control.

The psychodynamic view of development also brings problems for our understanding of therapy. If people's problems are due to events that happened in the past, and if we assume, as psychodynamic theory would, that the past cannot be changed, then it follows that what we do now can have little impact on the past that is causing our behaviors. If it is true that problems originate and are maintained in the past, then the question arises about how psychotherapy, which after all occurs in the present, can have any impact on people's problems. In fact, if the past is in such control of our lives, we might wonder whether any genuine change in our behaviors is possible. Framed in more general terms, the problem is that psychodynamic theory leads us to question how people can change and escape their pasts at all. Psychodynamic theorists believe, and even take for granted, that therapy does work, helping people resolve their psychological problems. However, claiming, or even showing, that it works and explaining (theoretically) how it works are two very different things. If the theorist has no theory to explain how therapy is able to work on people's problems the way the problems are understood and defined within the theory itself, we have cause to question what the therapy is actually doing, and whether it is doing what the theorists think it is doing.

What we hope to show in the following chapters is that the problems we have articulated here arise because of certain key ideas that are implicit in psychodynamic theory. The solution to the problems demands that we recognize these embedded ideas and become aware of their implications and assumptions. Once we can see the ideas and the problems they entail, we will, perhaps, be able to modify theories to avoid the problems or formulate theories that don't encounter these same problems or choose alternative theories that don't get us into the problems in the first place.

BEHAVIORIST THEORY

Behaviorist theory offers a stark contrast to psychodynamic theory in many important ways. The term *behaviorism,* applied to a school of psychology, is usually traced to a paper published in 1913 by John B. Watson, titled "Psychology as the Behaviorist Views It," although Watson was by no means the originator of the ideas of behaviorist theory. Behaviorism rose to importance over a period of years as a very broad response to the question of human nature and the proper approach to studying it. Behaviorism is rooted in several disciplines—psychology, philosophy, and biology, especially evolutionary theory. Watson was able to popularize these ideas, and thus, he gets much of the credit for founding the movement.[5] What we present here is a brief summary generally descriptive of behaviorist theory;[6] for a fuller and more detailed account, the reader should consult other texts of personality or learning theory (e.g., Hilgard & Bower, 1975).

One of the central ideas of behaviorism is that people are essentially biological organisms, and like other biological organisms, innately capable of responding to the environment in which they live. Although organisms are capable of making very complex responses to the demands of their environment, such complex responses are in fact combinations of simpler responses. At the most basic level, responses are automatic—we do not need to carry them out consciously or purposefully; they just happen, much like reflexes and other bodily processes. Because human beings share this capability to respond with all other organisms, there is a similarity or continuity between animals and people. All organisms possess similar capacities for making similar responses, but humans are more complex. This means that humans are capable of making more complex responses, and also that they are capable of being influenced by, or sensitive to, some aspects of the environment that animals would not be attuned to.

In keeping with the emphasis on people as biological organisms, behaviorists adopt a biological process as the fundamental model, or *root metaphor*, for human behavior. That process is the reflex. All biological organisms that have nervous systems are capable of reflex action. Reflexes happen automatically. For example, when a person touches a hot object, he or she will pull quickly away from it. This reflexive response is automatic, and it has been shown that most reflexes happen without the involvement of the higher brain centers. The neural message of heat and the impulse to withdraw do not go any higher up the nervous system than the spinal cord. This means that reflexes happen without our thinking about them or deciding to do them. Behaviorist theory holds that all human behaviors are essentially like this, automatic, and not involving conscious thought.[7]

Although the reflex is the model for all human behavior, behaviorist theory accounts for more kinds of human behaviors than simple reflexes like pulling away from a hot object. To see how it is possible to think of all human behaviors as being like reflexes, we need to analyze a reflex more carefully to see what is involved. There are three essential elements to any reflex. First, there is a *stimulus*. In our example this would be the hot object. The stimulus, because of some quality it possesses (heat), produces the behavior. Second, there is a *response*. In our example this would be the behavior of pulling away from the hot object. In traditional behaviorist theory, stimuli and responses become linked, or connected in such a way that whenever the stimulus occurs (we experience the heat of the hot object), the response follows (we pull away from the object). The third element of the reflex is the *connection* between the stimulus and the response. In the case of a bodily reflex this connection is plain and easy to see—it is the nerve fibers that connect the heat receptor in the hand to the muscle. In the case of other behaviors, the connection is not so easy to see or identify; behaviorists assume that the connection exists. These connections are often referred to as stimulus-response, or S-R, bonds.

Behaviorist theory explains how stimuli and responses get bonded together such that when the stimulus occurs, the response necessarily follows. The process is called *conditioning*.[8] There are three important factors that influence how conditioning proceeds. The first factor is *contiguity*. Contiguity simply means that two events occur together in time or space. A stimulus and the response it produces are contiguous events because they occur at nearly the same time and in the same place. Some conditioning occurs, that is, stimuli get connected to other stimuli or responses get connected to stimuli simply because the two occur together.

The second important factor in conditioning is the *frequency* with which stimuli and responses, or pairings of stimuli and responses, occur. If a certain stimulus occurs and is followed by a response many times, these two are likely to become bonded together, connected in some way. This process is illustrated by the early experiments of the Russian physiologist Ivan Pavlov, one of the most important figures in the history of behaviorism. Pavlov used a device to blow a bit of food powder into the mouth of a dog (held in a harness) at the same time that he sounded a bell. The food powder would, of course, make the dog salivate. After repeating this procedure a number of times, Pavlov showed that the dog would salivate whenever the bell was sounded even if no food powder was given. In other words, the dog "learned" (was conditioned) to salivate whenever the bell sounded. The stimulus of the bell became connected to the response of salivating because they were paired frequently. This process is called *classical conditioning*. In general, the more the stimuli and responses are paired, the stronger the connection between them and the stronger the conditioning (up to a point where fatigue sets in, of course).

The third important influence on the process of conditioning is *reinforcement*. As the term implies, reinforcement refers to a way of making the connection, or conditioning, stronger. In behaviorist theory, conditioning is made stronger in part by the fact that a response results in some pleasing event. If a behavior results in something pleasant to the organism, it is likely to be repeated. If it results in something unpleasant, it is likely not to be repeated. So, some stimuli and responses get linked together depending on whether the response (behavior) leads to, or is associated with, something pleasant. We should note that, in keeping with the principles of behaviorist theory, the response does not actually have to bring about a pleasant result. Because of the power of contiguity, the response simply has to be associated with something pleasant; the pleasant thing just has to occur closely afterward. It is also possible to suppress links between stimuli and responses by arranging things so that the response results in something unpleasant. This is the technical definition of *punishment*. It is also possible to counteract the effects of reinforcement and conditioning by making sure that the conditioned behavior is no longer reinforced when it occurs. This process is known as *extinction*.

One modification of the traditional behaviorist paradigm should be mentioned. Some scholars in the field, notably B. F. Skinner, have suggested that most behaviors people perform are not elicited from them by stimuli. Only the most simple reflex actions are of this sort. Rather, most behaviors are "learned," because no matter the reason for their initial occurrence, they are followed by reinforcement. This makes them likely to occur again. What this means is that behaviors are controlled by their consequences. These consequences and their relationship to the behaviors are called *contingencies*. In this line of behaviorist theorizing, people, and all organisms, have *reinforcement histories,* meaning that we have been reinforced for certain things throughout our lives. We tend to repeat those behaviors, and we do not continue to perform responses that have not been consistently reinforced.

Framed in terms of stimuli, responses, and reinforcements, behaviorism offers a comprehensive view of all learning, and thus, an explanation for all behaviors. The simplest and the most complex behaviors we perform have their origins in a common set of very simple processes. Further, behaviorist theorists assume that the same processes of learning and reinforcement operate in essentially the same way in all species. The processes of learning and behaving that govern human behaviors can be seen to operate at a simpler level in simpler organisms. This assumption provides a justification for studying the behaviors of animal species with the hope of understanding humans.

The same assumption also leads behaviorists to pursue their studies in much the same way as other natural scientists. If the same processes can be found in all species, it makes some scientific sense to study them in their simplest form—in simple species in carefully controlled environments. Behaviorist theory also recommends the use of recognizably scientific methods for the study of human behavior because of its concentration on observable aspects of the environment (stimuli, responses, and reinforcements) rather than unobservable and mentalistic constructs. The ultimate goal underlying most behaviorist theories is the scientific control and prediction of human behaviors.

ASSUMPTIONS AND IMPLICATIONS
OF BEHAVIORIST THEORY

Behaviorist theory is widely recognized as a coherent and internally consistent way of explaining human behavior—that is, it offers a clear and plausible account of virtually all human behaviors without internal contradictions. Further, behaviorist theory is recognized as being very *parsimonious,* in that its explanations are simple. Behaviorists do not invent complex mental constructs to explain why behaviors happen. However, this does not mean that behaviorist theory lacks problematic ideas and hidden assumptions. There are, in fact, a number of such assumptions, and they have important implications for how we explain human beings and their behaviors.

First, behaviorist theory is strongly deterministic. According to behaviorists, human behaviors do not just happen; rather, they are produced by stimuli or reinforcements that become associated with the behaviors in very precise and lawful ways. The determining power behind behavior is in the stimuli and reinforcers, which are in the external environment, not inside us where we could control them. In other words, behaviorist theory holds that our behaviors are controlled in a very strict way by environmental events, and not by our own wills. Behaviorists hold this strongly deterministic view in common with psychodynamic theorists.[9] One of the important implications of this theoretical position is that as individual human beings, we are not responsible for our actions. Rather, our behaviors are produced by forces over which we have no control. Thus, deliberate control of people's behaviors (by others) is quite possible according to behaviorist theory. And in a larger sense, the "control and prediction" of human behavior is often held out to be a legitimate goal, and perhaps, the most important reason and justification for psychology (see, e.g., Skinner, 1971). Most of the controlling and predicting goes on in laboratory settings, as behaviorists study behavior, but the methods for controlling behavior in real settings are also frequently and widely applied in homes, schools, and other institutions.

Some behaviorists argue that once the environmental causes of our behavior are known we can, in fact, use that knowledge to control our own lives. The problem is, however, that the decision to control and the choice of what behavior to control are both products of forces we do not control. It seems that if behaviorism is true, all "self-control" is superficial and ultimately rests on automatic conditioned responses.

One of the guiding concerns of behaviorist theorists has been the scientific status of psychology. Behaviorists have criticized other approaches to studying human behavior for not being scientific enough. One of the assumptions of behaviorist theory is that human beings can be adequately studied by the methods of natural science, just as other natural organisms and events are studied. Further, behaviorists hold that psychology (or any behavioral science) should restrict itself to talking about things that are observable, because only observable things can be studied scientifically. In other words, for behaviorists, scientific explanations are the best and most useful explanations of human behavior. This implies, however, that anything that cannot be observed should not be studied or used to explain human behavior.

A potential difficulty for behaviorism is the fact that stimuli, responses, and reinforcements, although essential for any behaviorist explanation of behavior, are never actually observed directly. It is possible to observe something that happens in the environment, but it is not possible to observe whether the event is really a stimulus—whether it has the powerful properties of a stimulus, and thus whether this event actually produces the response. Similarly, it is possible to observe a behavior, but it is not possible to observe whether that behavior was really caused by a stimulus. Any connection between a presumed stimulus and a presumed response can only be inferred by the researcher—never observed (see Chapter 4).

Another problem with restricting ourselves to observable phenomena in the name of science is that many of the things most important to us as human beings are not readily observable, such as our emotions and values. Some have even questioned whether the scientific method can appropriately or effectively be used to study human beings, given that human beings are so unlike the objects of the natural world. Moreover, the behaviorist's commitment to scientific methods can be questioned: Can the scientific method in fact produce the kind of certainty and confidence that behaviorists assume it can? This question will be taken up more completely in Chapter 6.

The heavy reliance of behaviorist theory on environmental causes of behavior carries with it the implication that human actions are never really creative or original. In other words, if our behaviors are determined by the environment, then they are in a sense "put into us" by the environment, and we can only do what our past experience in that environment makes us able to do. Simply put, if we have already learned something, then we can do it. But if we have not already learned it, we cannot do it.[10] In simple terms, then, we can never do something truly creative or original where we might "go beyond" what we have learned. For example, as the two of us are writing this book, we can only use sentences (and ideas) we have already learned and cannot create any really new or original ones. By the same token, as you read the book, you can only think of ideas or thoughts that you have already learned, but no truly new ones.[11] The problem of creativity, and behaviorists' inability to account for it, have been ongoing concerns for theorists in the behavioral sciences.

The concept of reinforcement also brings with it a host of implicit ideas. The point of reinforcement is that if a behavior results in something pleasant for the organism, then the organism will tend to repeat the behavior—the bond between the response and whatever stimuli might be present will be strengthened or "learned." This makes a good deal of intuitive sense, in that experience teaches us that people do indeed tend to do things that make them feel good and avoid things that do not. However, there are some conceptual consequences that result from considering this the most important factor controlling human behavior. If we do whatever we do because it brings pleasant consequences, then it would be very difficult for us to do something that is genuinely self-sacrificing. Whatever seemingly selfless behavior we may do, behaviorist theory suggests it is in fact (below the surface) just the behavior that brings us pleasant or positive consequences in that particular environment. This idea has important consequences for our relationships with others. If reinforcement is the fundamental motivator of all our behaviors, then it is also the basis of all the relationships we form with others. Having reinforcement as the basis of all our relationships implies that we relate to people only so long as they provide us with the opportunity of obtaining pleasant outcomes for ourselves. This casts all our relationships in a light that makes altruistic acts and selfless relationships impossible.

As we have noted, behaviorist theory emphasizes looking at human beings as biological organisms, having much in common with other biological organisms (animals). The idea that human beings are fundamentally like all other species also has some serious implications. Because of this cross-species similarity, it is assumed that the processes of learning and reinforcement, and thus, the causes of behavior, are essentially the same for all species. When there are differences in the processes, they are due to greater complexity of the organisms. This means that all organisms basically learn in the same way and for the same reasons. Human learning is just a more complex form of the way rats, pigeons, and apes learn. This, of course, provides a good justification for comparative psychology, as we can observe the processes of learning in simpler forms in animals and then generalize to human beings. However, there are important implications of the assumption that humans learn in essentially the same way as animals. These implications affect how we structure educational materials and situations, and even how we treat students.

The implications can be more clearly seen when we consider something other than learning. We might use loving as an example. First, behaviorist theory reduces the experience of loving to "loving behaviors." It is a clear implication of behaviorist theory that "loving behaviors" will come about in all species because of the same conditioning processes and environmental forces. Under this view, maternal behavior in animals has the same form, function, and origin as parental affection and care in human families—they are all the result of stimulus-response connections and reinforcements. Similarly, we would be led to believe that humans and animals both engage in sexual behavior because of the same types of environmental and biological demands and processes.

From these two examples, it can be seen that the behaviorist assumption that humans are biological organisms like all others, and that the same processes of conditioning and reinforcement work to govern all behavior has a conceptual price. The price of accepting behaviorist accounts of our behaviors is giving up the idea that our behaviors mean anything different from what the behaviors of animals mean. In other words, if we human beings act as we do, loving each other and caring for our children, simply because of biological and conditioning processes—like other animals—then our loving and caring do not mean what we have always thought they did. Human acts of love and caring are meaningful precisely because we *mean* them. We choose to do them because of what they mean to us, and what they *do* mean is partly a matter of our choice. If we have no choice, and like animals our acts are produced by biology and conditioning, this meaning is an illusion. This makes a difference in the way we see ourselves, our relationships, and the meaning of our behaviors and our lives.

HUMANISTIC THEORY

Humanistic theory is a term applied to a group of related theories that have been developed in opposition to the two theoretical approaches that we have talked about—psychodynamic theory and behaviorism. Because humanists have deliberately taken positions opposed to these two schools, humanism is often referred to as the "third force." The best-known theorists in this movement are Carl Rogers (e.g., 1959) and Abraham Maslow (e.g., 1968). These theorists, and others who share their concerns, have explicitly rejected what they perceive to be the negative view of human beings that both psychodynamic theories and behaviorism offer. At the heart of their concern is the hard determinism that characterizes both approaches. Psychodynamic theory suggests that people are driven by sexual and aggressive impulses and unconscious ideas that they cannot consciously control. Behaviorism holds that we are completely controlled by the external environment. Humanists have felt that these views failed to capture what is most human and essential about us, holding out little hope for the progress and development of human beings in general.

Essential to humanistic theory is the idea that every human being is unique. Part of that uniqueness is an innate potential that suggests, and holds out as a goal for us, what we can become if we develop fully. This potential constitutes an inborn sense of identity that can also serve as a guide for us in making decisions about how we should act, what we need, and what we should become. Rogers (1970) refers to this sense as an "organismic valuing process." Simply put, it means that we each know what is best for us individually, and we should be true to that knowledge in order to maximize our growth and development. If we do develop properly, following the dictates of our potential, we can become what Rogers (1959, p. 235) calls "fully functioning" persons. A more commonly used expression for this same process, taken more from the work of Maslow (e.g., 1954), is *self-actualization*. Self-actualization is the state of having fulfilled our innate potential and become fully the people we really are (and should be).

Humanistic theory is based on the contention that human nature is basically good, or at the very worst, neutral. By reason of this fundamentally positive and optimistic view of our human nature, humanistic thinkers feel free to advocate that we all should strive to fulfill our natures and become self-actualized. In other words, because there is nothing to fear within us, we should be encouraged to pursue what we find fulfilling. In fact, if we do not fulfill our potentials, the result is often psychological illness and unsatisfactory relationships.

It is, of course, one thing to suggest that we have a guiding potential within us, and quite another to understand how we can recognize and fulfill it. Three things are important in what humanistic theory has to say in this regard. First, to fulfill our unique potential, we need the freedom to pursue our development. It is for this reason that humanistic theorists oppose both psychodynamic theory and behaviorism so strenuously. If we are determined by negative instinctual impulses as psychodynamic theorists suggest, or if we are controlled by environmental contingencies as behaviorists posit, we would not have the freedom to pursue our own identities and fulfill our potential. Some humanists therefore reject hard determinism and hold that individuals have the freedom to make choices about what they value as well as how they behave. Humanists thus conceive of human beings as unique selves who have the freedom to choose and direct their actions. This freedom to choose is essential to becoming self-actualized.[12]

A second important aspect of becoming self-actualized is fulfilling our needs. Maslow (1954, 1970) suggests that human needs can be arranged in a hierarchy. Some needs are lower or earlier in the hierarchy, and others are higher and become influential later. At the bottom we have the most basic needs, the biologically based needs for food, shelter, safety, and other such essentials. Next above these are the *belongingness needs*. These refer to our need for love and acceptance from others. The highest are the needs for esteem and for self-actualization. Because these human needs are hierarchical, the higher ones will generally not arise in people until the lower ones have been satisfied. Currently active needs that are unfulfilled exercise directing power over behavior, motivating people to act in ways that address the needs. The need for self-actualization will not become salient and motivating until all the lower-level needs are satisfied. Because self-actualization is one of the most important goals or purposes of life, and one of its most satisfying aspects, it is important for people to fulfill their needs in order to become self-actualized and fulfill their potential.

The third important aspect of the process of achieving self-actualization relates to how people can understand their needs. As we noted above, humanistic theorists suggest that people have an inborn capacity to know what they need for their own growth and actualization—what Rogers (1970) referred to as an "organismic valuing process." This process is not usually conscious, but rather is experienced as a feeling, or what might be called an intuition or a gut reaction. To stay emotionally healthy, develop properly, and become self-actualized, a person needs to tune into these feelings of what is best for him or her, and then act on them. Often, because of the society we live in, and the demands and expectations forced on us by our parents and others, it is hard for us to be true to our own feelings. Rather, we tend to behave in accordance with other people's desires and expectations. When these expectations are not the same as what we personally feel is right for us, we become *incongruent*. This incongruence is a state of conflict between what we feel we need and the demands and expectations of others. Incongruence occurs when we pay too much attention to others. To achieve our potential and self-actualize, we need to resist the pressures to live out others' demands and expectations, recognize our own true needs and feelings, and act on them. Further, we should grant everyone the opportunity to do the same thing. Humanistic theorists place great emphasis on recognizing and "owning" our own feelings, and being true to them as guides to our needs and potential.

Most humanists suggest that individual people have personal needs and values, and that they should be encouraged to pursue them, even if they seem wrong to others.

ASSUMPTIONS AND IMPLICATIONS
OF HUMANISTIC THEORY

To many students of the behavioral sciences, humanistic theory seems like a breath of fresh air after the more pessimistic and deterministic outlooks of psychodynamic theory and behaviorism. As we stressed in Chapter 1, however, all ideas have assumptions and implications associated with them—conceptual costs—due to the ideas embedded within the theories. Humanistic theory is no exception to this.

Although humanistic theory makes a point of avoiding the kind of hard determinism seen in psychodynamic theory and behaviorism, arising from unconscious instincts and environmental conditioning, it cannot avoid the issue of determinism altogether. In humanistic theory, a person's inborn potential, or identity, exerts considerable influence over his or her behavior and needs, and especially over whether he or she is healthy and integrated, or incongruent and emotionally unhealthy. The question remains as to where this potential (and our sense of what we need) comes from, and how it influences our behavior. Some humanistic theorists, including Maslow (1968), root this growth potential in our biology. Maslow (1968) refers to it as being "instinctoid," that is, like an instinct, but not as strong. If, however, our potential and sense of our own needs are based in biology, they are not things we can do much about. Although we might be able to do something in *response* to them, we cannot do much about *having* them and their attendant influences in the first place. To the extent they are thought to be rooted in something outside our control or experience and form important sources of influence in our lives, humanistic theory is deterministic in the same way that psychodynamic theory and behaviorism are. Most humanists point out that the determining influence of growth potentials and organismic valuing processes are not as strong as those of instincts and conditioning. However, weak determinism is still determinism, especially if it is rooted in some source outside our own conscious control. Humanistic theory is faced with the dilemma of explaining how and why our inborn tendencies toward actualization are powerful influences, and yet not as deterministic as Freudian instincts and environmental conditioning.

Another assumption in humanistic theory is that each individual has a special ability to know his or her own nature, and what is required for growth and actualization. Seldom, however, is this knowledge explicit and conscious. It is, rather, a special type of knowledge, unavailable to anyone other than the particular individual who has it. Furthermore, it is most often the case that a person cannot wholly and accurately communicate to anyone else his or her sense of self and needs. Often we cannot articulate it fully even to ourselves. This knowledge, then, is always extremely subjective. It seems not different in kind from the type of unconscious knowledge postulated by psychodynamic theorists. Although most humanistic theorists reject unconscious determinism, something very much akin to it seems hidden in the assumptions of their own theory. Humanists, for the most part, maintain that people have the capacity to choose their actions, but to the extent that influences from needs and potentials are strong, and failure to act on them results in psychological problems, the capacity for agency and choice is compromised—or at least in need of explanation.

As we have already shown, implicit in humanistic theory is the idea that people have individual needs and that it is important to fulfill them. In fact, following Maslow, a person's growth and development is dependent on the extent to which his or her needs are fulfilled. Unfulfilled needs bar the way to self-actualization. This emphasis on the fulfillment of individual needs has a conceptual cost. If we take the idea seriously, the clear implication is that each person is justified in fulfilling his or her own needs. In fact, fulfilling our own needs is not only justified, it is the right thing to do. There seems to be a clear warrant for seeking our own satisfaction. Most humanistic theorists strenuously maintain that no one should pursue his or her own fulfillment at the expense of others, but there is, in humanistic theory, no construct nor argument to explicitly prevent this kind of selfishness. In fact, most attempts to regulate a person's behavior, especially behavior aimed at fulfillment and growth, run the risk of stifling the person and bringing about incongruence and emotional problems.

There is an irony in humanistic theory that becomes apparent when we consider another of its implications. Humanists strive to recognize our relations with other people as important factors in our personal growth and actualization. They value genuine, intimate interpersonal relationships; however, the hidden ideas in the theory imply that intimacy is extremely difficult to achieve. If each person has a unique potential, a unique self, and a unique set of needs, and if individuals are the ones best able to know their own needs and what is right and best for them, then the path to health is the path of self-fulfillment and individual development. In this process, others serve only as means to the end of personal development and satisfaction. People may relate to others out of what looks like a genuine concern for them and may establish what appear to be intimate relationships, but if humanistic theory is taken seriously, the concern is always based in the pursuit of self-actualization and the fulfillment of the personal needs of one or both parties. It is difficult to see how a genuine and selfless intimacy could ever develop under these circumstances.

Furthermore, moral relationships with others and moral judgments about our own behavior are also affected by the emphasis on individual selves and needs found in humanistic theory. If we, as individuals, are the ones who really know what is good for us, then we are the only ones in a position to judge the rightness or wrongness—the morality—of our behavior. If our needs ought to be pursued, and if they are unique to us, then we ought to be judged and held accountable only for whether we are acting true to our own needs. Because every person's needs and potential are different, and the right thing to do is to pursue these things individually, then everyone's morality is unique and applicable only to individual persons. This leads us to a position of moral relativism. What is right or wrong can only be judged in light of individual needs for fulfillment and actualization.[13] Furthermore, because only as individuals can we know what is best for us, we are led to a position of relativism in knowledge as well. No one can know for certain what is true for another individual. The result of this relativism in morality and knowledge is a picture of an individual in some sense locked into his or her own life and needs, unable to establish truly intimate relations with other people. Only relationships that satisfy needs and further one's own development are desirable or possible.

COGNITIVE THEORY

Cognitive theory is perhaps the broadest of the names we use to refer to the prominent theories that have influenced the behavioral sciences. It is a term widely used for a large body of work cutting across many disciplines and subdisciplines. Cognitive theory brings together under a shared perspective disciplines as varied in interest and focus as psychology, education, computer science, philosophy, instructional science, communications, and psychotherapy.

For purposes of this book, cognitive theory is broader than some might take it to be, broad enough to be considered a general view of human nature; that is, a theory of how people learn, know, and behave and what they are capable of. The essence of the theory is that human functioning can be thought of as being similar in many ways to that of a computer or some other "information-processing" machine. Just as psychodynamic theorists took the instincts, and behaviorists took reflexes as their root metaphors, the computer is the root metaphor for cognitive theory. In its most basic form, a computer is a device that takes in information from its environment, organizes the information and processes it through various stages—each stage performing its task based on how the previous stages were performed—and then achieves some end product or conclusion relative to the information that had been put in. By analogy, human beings are seen as taking information in from the world (input), organizing and processing it according to some orderly sequence of operations, and reaching conclusions that result in some sort of behavior (output).

It is no coincidence that cognitive theory rose to occupy a prominent position in the behavioral sciences in the late 1960s just as the modern computer was entering a revolutionary stage of development and coming into wide use in a number of applications.[14] The field of artificial intelligence is the area of research where the analogy drawn between computers and human thought is most explicit and clear. Researchers in artificial intelligence assume, either literally or for research purposes, that computers can be built that mimic, if not literally replicate, human thought and problem solving. Some in the field accept the further implication that if machines can be created to think like humans, then it must be the case that humans think or act like machines. Many have investigated the possibility of building computers and programming them to perform tasks so well that a human observer cannot detect whether the task is being done by a human being or a computer. This challenge—to tell whether it is a machine or a person doing the task—is known as the Turing test after A. M. Turing (1950).

Although the modern computer played a significant role in the development of cognitive theory, another important impetus was what many scholars perceived as the failure of behaviorism to adequately account for human behavior. Behaviorism holds that all behaviors are basically like reflexes—they occur automatically without involving conscious thought processes. For behaviorism, human beings are *black boxes*—that is, what happens inside the mind is of little importance in predicting and understanding human behavior. To many behavioral scientists, however, this seemed like an inadequate and misleading picture of human behavior. Cognitive theorists, therefore, attempt to open up the black box and examine what goes on within the mind, believing it is important in understanding how we behave.

Within the black box, according to cognitive theory, we find an information-processing mechanism. This mechanism takes information from the world into the box, and transforms or processes it. The processing is governed by the nature of the information that is taken in and by the structure of the processing devices and the rules by which they operate. The end result of the process is a behavior or cognition that responds adequately to the input information. Most cognitive scientists concentrate on one or another of the processes or processors inside the cognitive system in order to learn of its capacity, its structure, and its function.

Perhaps the best place to see the contrast between behaviorism and cognitive theory is in their differing accounts of language acquisition and language use. Many psychologists point to the problem of language as the important test case in which cognitive theory proved its worth and demonstrated its superiority, at least over behaviorism. The theoretical confrontation took place historically in the works of the behaviorist B. F. Skinner (1957) and the linguist Noam Chomsky (1957).

Behaviorists must maintain that language is learned primarily, if not exclusively, through a simple process of reinforcement whereby children's noises are slowly shaped into recognizable sounds, then words and sentences. Chomsky (1957) showed rather convincingly (in the minds of most scholars) that language is not learned in this way. Rather, it seems that human beings have an innate capacity to learn and use language, a capacity that unfolds naturally rather than being shaped. Learning and using a language is more like following rules than being shaped by reinforcement. Cognitive accounts of language provide better explanations of how people create sentences they have never heard and how children seem to develop their language ability in orderly stages. It was felt that if cognitive theory could account so well for something as basic as language use, then it might have something important to say about all human behavior.

Cognitive theory has been applied to a wide range of human behavior. Virtually all human behaviors (except purely physiological responses) are seen as outputs of cognitive processes. Human actions are understood as resulting from a flow of information. Cognitive theorists construct models of how the mind (or person) works when dealing with the information. We can consider an example from the subdiscipline of social cognition, such as a decision about whether to pursue a relationship with another person. The decision is seen to result from a series of decisions made on the basis of what information is available to the person, such as his or her expectations about the outcome of the relationship, the ratio of potential rewards and costs of the relationship, and other options or relationships that might be available elsewhere. This information is then processed in some way that is governed by the person's information-processing system and the result is a behavior or decision to act in some way about the relationship. Similar analyses might be given for group dynamics, psychotherapy, business negotiations, learning, and other important human phenomena.

Clearly, cognitive theory is the dominant view in contemporary psychology and education. It is common in these fields to refer to the *cognitive revolution*—that period of time from the late 1960s to the mid- to late 1970s when cognitive theory gained strength in these disciplines, began to offer important insights and explanations of an increasing number of complex human behaviors, and replaced behaviorism as the most influential theoretical point of view. In the minds of many, cognitive theory freed the behavioral sciences from the hard determinism of behaviorism and the unseen "mystical forces" used in psychodynamic theory. It was also much more scientifically credible than humanistic theories. Seen in this way, cognitive theory seems a compelling response to some of the most pressing philosophical problems faced in the behavioral sciences, allowing the disciplines to continue as sciences and yet operate from a point of view more faithful to our experience as human beings. The influence of cognitive theory in all the behavioral sciences is substantial and continues to grow.

ASSUMPTIONS AND IMPLICATIONS
OF COGNITIVE THEORY

Although cognitive theory began, in part, as a reaction to behaviorism and the rigid determinism that it imposes on our understanding of human behavior, it is not clear that cognitive theory escapes the problems inherent to behaviorism. Nearly all cognitive models of human behavior begin with input from the environment (see Chapter 3 for a fuller treatment). The input is most often thought of as consisting of stimuli that enter the cognitive system through sensory experience. This notion is not substantially different from behaviorism. The end result of a cognitive process is a response. The response depends in large part on what stimuli were received. At this most basic level, the cognitive explanation of behavior is not radically different from the behaviorist one.

It is true that behaviorists look at stimuli as having some sort of power to directly produce responses whereas cognitivists look at stimuli as containing information. However, because the cognitive processing system works only on information put into it—either in the present or from past experience—the information (stimulus) is largely in control of the response that will ultimately be made to it. To a great extent, the information drives the processing. If this is the case, cognitive explanations are as deterministic as behaviorist ones. The information comes in from the environment; people do not exert much influence over its coming in, nor can they modify it to any great degree.[15] The response is determined by the information, and its properties basically dictate how it is processed by the cognitive system. Whether we consider general models of the entire cognitive processing system that researchers constructed in the 1970s or the more limited models of specific processes that are now more common in the literature, determinism seems to be intact. What comes into the system produces what goes out.

Some cognitive theorists would clearly disagree with this characterization of cognitive models of behavior. They would suggest that information does not simply come into the person (or system) and produce responses automatically. Rather, they would say, the cognitive processes are at work at every stage of the larger process, modifying and selecting what information gets through each stage. This is often called *mediation*. Cognitive processes mediate the effects of the stimulus information. If we accept this argument, the processes are in control of our behavior and the responses we make. This move shifts the determining power from the information itself to the processes that work on it. The question then becomes whether the processes are automatic or whether we have some influence over how they work and what they ultimately do. Clearly, in many cognitive models, there is a strong sense that the cognitive system is somehow inborn—given to us as part of our nature. Its functions and processes are built in. If this is so, then they determine how we process information, and thus, how we behave. If it is not so, then the likely explanation is that previous information (past experience) is the determining factor in how we process information, and thus, how we behave. In either case, cognitive theory is every bit as deterministic as behaviorism or psychodynamic theory. However, many cognitive theorists believe human beings, as persons, can intervene in the cognitive system in ways that soften or modify the determinism. It is unclear how people can do this if they are like information-processing machines, neither aware of nor in control of their cognitive processes at the level where information processing occurs (Williams, 1987). It is questionable whether cognitive theorists escape the kind of determinism they want to escape. Determinism seems to remain hidden within the theory.

The question of the origin of the information-processing system points to another implication hidden in cognitive theory. Recall that psychodynamic theorists suggest that all causes of human behavior are ultimately found in instincts. Behaviorists suggest the causes are in automatic conditioning processes. Cognitive theorists propose that the causes of our behaviors are in the way we process information. The system itself, and how it operates, is the cause. Because we do not choose our cognitive system or the way it operates, we can reduce all questions of why people behave as they do to questions of how the cognitive system works. In this way cognitive theory *reduces* all questions and explanations to an innate, determined structure—the cognitive system (see Chapter 5). Where this system comes from is not really dealt with in most cognitive theories. Many assume that it is a by-product of our biological makeup—the makeup of the nervous system. Others attribute it more directly to evolutionary processes. Assumptions about the nature and origin of the cognitive processes that produce human behavior remain hidden, but they are crucial in understanding the explanations of human behavior that cognitive theorists offer us and their account of what it means to be a human being.

Another important idea that underlies cognitive theory is the nature of information itself. Cognitive theory is based on the assumption that people somehow take in information from the environment and that this information guides the response they ultimately make. However, the nature of this information is not clear (Slife, in press). In some situations, it is easy to see what information is and how it might work. Morse code is an example of how messages can be sent in small pieces. Every part of a Morse code message is either a dot or a dash—it cannot be anything else. The dots and dashes (the bits of information) are combined into a pattern to produce the message. Digital computers work on this same principle. Everything put into a computer is put in as a pattern of "on" and "off" electrical impulses. Information is represented at every stage of the process in basically the same way. When we move from computers to human beings, or from a type of Morse code to real language, it is not nearly as clear what information is and how it can be represented. For example, if a child asks, "Who wants to play with me?" what information does this message contain? How does the information get conveyed to the parent that the child is feeling neglected, that she is much happier playing some things than other things, that she wants to play a game she can win rather than one that is too hard for her, that she is remembering her parents' promise the night before to play with her, or that she is putting off her bedtime? All of this information—which may very well be present in any such simple question—is not encoded in the verbal utterance of the child. Rather it is in the whole context and history of the relationship between the parent and the child. It is difficult to conceive how all of this might be built into a verbal input that can then go into (or come out of) an information-processing system.[16]

A further difficulty with the information-processing approach relates to the definition of information in any real-world human situation. If, for example, a child returns home from school, drops his books on a chair, grabs an apple, runs out through the front door, jumps on his bicycle, and heads toward his friend's house, does the parent watching this series of events receive six bits of information or just one? Whichever answer is given to the question, it is quite clear that whenever anything is designated as a bit of information, it can always be broken down further into smaller bits. For example the books had particular titles and were dropped on a particular chair, from a particular height, with a particular effect. The dropping required particular muscle movements and occurred at a particular place and time. It seems clear that looking at the world we live in as made up of information leads us to a long string of simpler and simpler bits, and calling any one of them information is rather arbitrary. Moreover, as we can see, the farther back we go in the search for bits of information, the more automatic and mechanical they become. Both parent and child will likely experience the event and describe it in terms of dropping books, not in terms of muscle movements. Both will likely interpret the *meaning* of the act as dropping books. Muscle movements are more automatic and mechanical than dropping books and thus less meaningful.[17] This illustrates how thinking of human beings as information-processing machines and thinking of information as composed of bits implicitly leads to deterministic explanations through which agency and meaning are hard to account for.

Another idea hidden in cognitive theory is the assumption that human beings are essentially rational and logical. The whole idea of humans as information-processing mechanisms points in this direction. Part of the reason the computer is the root metaphor of cognitive explanations is because it is the best example we have of a purely logical and rational device. Human cognitive processes are seen to operate in rational, or at least consistent, logical, and understandable ways. Otherwise, the information could not be accurately traced through the processing system and we could not predict or explain the behavior that results from it. The question then arises: How does cognitive theory account for things about us that do not seem so logical and rational, such as emotions or creative endeavors? Human beings quite often seem to be irrational, or at least not wholly driven by logical and consistent processes. The tension between the logical and rational aspects of human beings on one hand and their irrational and creative tendencies on the other is an important one, widely recognized in the behavioral sciences (e.g., in education and psychotherapy) and in popular literature. This tension has led many to question whether an information-processing model as proposed by cognitive theorists can offer an adequate explanation of what human beings do or ought to do.

In summary, many people have questioned whether cognitive theory is significantly different from behaviorist theory (e.g., Russ, 1987). Looked at in one way, cognitive theorists simply propose that there are mental processes that act on stimuli and affect how those stimuli produce responses. Nevertheless, the argument goes, the stimuli are still producing the responses. The cognitive processes simply "mediate" how this is done. Cognitive theory may very well give better explanations of how complex human behavior really is (more complex than simple stimulus-response reflexes). However, if the cognitive processes themselves are innate and operate automatically, or the mediation is determined by previously stored stimuli, all of the conceptual questions and problems we saw in behaviorism are also relevant to cognitive theory. All of the ideas and assumptions that are implicit in behaviorism are also embedded in cognitive theory. Cognitive theory in psychology began as an attempt to isolate particular cognitive functions—things people did while performing mental tasks. There was little interest in the larger theoretical and philosophical questions underlying psychological theories. Nevertheless, as cognitive theory has become more generally applied both in psychology and in other disciplines, taking on the status of a comprehensive theory of human behavior, the need to deal with these issues is becoming clearer.

ECLECTICISM

In the earlier decades of the behavioral sciences, it was common for scholars in many disciplines to identify with one theoretical orientation or school, which they used broadly as a theory of human nature, applying it to a very wide range of behaviors and situations. In psychology, for example, the theoretical perspectives we have presented thus far are general and comprehensive enough to offer explanations of nearly all types of behaviors in which behavioral scientists are interested. However, as the various theories came in direct competition with one another for scholars' allegiances and more research was carried out testing the adequacy of the theories, increasing numbers of behavioral scientists became more and more uncomfortable about allying themselves with a single perspective. In more recent years there has been a substantial tendency within the disciplines to refrain from endorsing any one theory as the correct, or even the best, theory of human behavior. Many, if not the majority of behavioral scientists, now feel that the best strategy for understanding human behavior is to borrow ideas or constructs from all reputable theories, using any that seem like good explanations.

For example, in attempting to explain love, or interpersonal attraction, a psychologist might say that psychodynamic theory explains *some* phenomena of attraction, because people do have a strong sexual instinct that they seek to gratify. He or she might also believe, however, that people are sometimes conditioned by reinforcements to be attracted to some people and not others. Further, the psychologist might believe that some, but not all, conditioning occurs automatically, and that sometimes cognitive processes intervene to determine just how stimuli and information produce attraction responses. And finally, the same psychologist might believe that people are also motivated in their loving and attraction by a need or desire for self-actualization. All these theories may be seen to be in operation at once, or alternatively in particular persons in particular situations. This approach to explanation we refer to as *eclectic*.

The eclectic approach has been increasing in popularity over the past few decades. Many applied behavioral scientists seem drawn to eclecticism because their major concern is trying to help people and to solve particular problems rather than producing good theoretical accounts of behavior. Students are often drawn to an eclectic position regarding explanation because all the theoretical positions they are exposed to make such convincing cases that they are inclined to believe that all are in some sense true. The opposite is sometimes also the case; none of the theories seem completely convincing, so a viable theory must be constructed from the bits and pieces of established theories that are convincing. Eclecticism allows one to believe in all the positions (or embrace parts of them) and thus not run the risk of missing some truth or value they may have.

One other intellectual force in contemporary behavioral science seems to be moving people toward an eclectic strategy of explanation. Contemporary scholars place great importance on openness and withholding judgment, on refraining from making definitive judgments about the truth or value of ideas. Eclecticism allows one to value, and to some extent, to validate all positions, and thus remain intellectually uncommitted. Although these seem like good, and even perhaps compelling, reasons for adopting an eclectic position, as we have stressed in this book, all ideas have hidden ideas within them, and thus, have costs and consequences. Eclecticism, because it is also an idea, is no exception to this.

ASSUMPTIONS AND
IMPLICATIONS OF ECLECTIC THEORY

Although taking an eclectic approach to theory may seem to imply suspending belief in any given theory, it should be kept in mind that eclecticism is itself a theoretical position. Those who hold this position say, among other things, that it is desirable to suspend theoretical judgment and commitment. This suspension is not a given, an obvious fact of intellectual life, but rather, it is a theory about how our theorizing and scholarship should be carried out. There are advantages and disadvantages of this view of theorizing. For example, it may be much better scholarship to pursue a single position, investigate it ferociously, and keep doing this to all positions until we find one that passes muster as a comprehensive theory of human behavior. Eclecticism is not an obvious and necessary answer to the question of how to do good theorizing, but rather a theory of how to do it, and as such, it has strengths, weaknesses, and intellectual consequences.

Another problematic implication of eclectic theory is that it often leads us to believe in theories that are mutually contradictory.[18] For example, if behaviorism is true, then psychodynamic theory cannot be. The fundamental constructs of behaviorism do not allow it. Behaviorism and psychodynamic theory are in competition for exactly the same role and power in explaining human behavior. They cannot both be believed simultaneously. Some eclectics might say that it is not necessary to hold both theoretical views at the same time—under some circumstances one view is true, under other circumstances the other is true. However, again using the example of behaviorism and psychodynamic theory, if behaviorism is true, there will never be circumstances where psychodynamic theory might apply. In other words, people cannot both be entirely products of their conditioning and reinforcements, and sometimes products of their inborn instincts. If they are products of one, there is never a time when they can be products of the other. Although eclectic theorists appear to take all theories seriously, in fact they fail to take any of them seriously, because they refuse to recognize the fundamental claims underlying the approaches.

Some eclectic theorists believe this attribute of eclecticism is their greatest strength—that they fail to take the various competing theories seriously. An eclectic theorist often attempts to stand apart from, or outside, all the various theories and remain uncommitted to any. However, in borrowing from the theories and accepting their explanations of some behaviors, the eclectic theorist is actually standing inside the theories—all at the same time. To be outside the theories, the eclectic would need to accept none of them, but in accepting parts of any or all of them, the eclectic behavioral scientist is drawn into them. For example, a therapist may help a client "gain insight" into a problem, borrowing a point from psychoanalysis. However, this presupposes that insight is helpful and that the client needs help getting insight because the problem is somehow hidden, or unavailable. This, in turn assumes that there is indeed an unconscious realm of mind where the roots of our problems can be found.

Very quickly, the therapist who simply wanted to borrow a good point from psychodynamic theory is drawn into the whole of psychoanalysis. Borrowing seemingly simple points leads us to operate within a whole set of assumptions.

What we wish to stress is that by accepting part of a theory, we also accept all of the assumptions and implications that a theory brings with it, most of which are never acknowledged or carefully examined. In trying to avoid some of the mistakes any one theoretical perspective might bring with it, the eclectic opens him- or herself to the mistakes of all of them at the same time. Ideas *never* come without assumptions and implications; the eclectic strategy of borrowing some of the ideas of a theory involves ignoring the fact that every part brings with it the whole of the host of hidden ideas that any theory always has.

One other consequence of eclecticism deserves mention here. Some eclectic theorists believe that borrowing constructs and explanations from various theories makes explanations easier and richer, because we are not bound to any one theory and the necessity of "stretching" it to fit all the things we want to explain. There is one important sense, however, in which an eclectic strategy makes explaining more difficult and complex. If an eclectic theorist claims that sometimes one theory applies and sometimes another, then he or she not only must defend the particular theory that applies in some situation, but requires another, overarching theory to explain *why* one theory applies here and another applies there. In other words, to produce a coherent theory, an eclectic needs a theory to explain when theories apply and why. Eclectic theory is complicated further by the implication that human beings are subject to all or most of the causal forces of, for example, psychodynamic theory, plus all or most of the causal forces of behaviorism, and so on through all the theories that the eclectic wants to use. This view of human behavior seems hopelessly complex, and this complexity has its hidden ideas and intellectual costs as well as moral consequences.

STRUCTURALISM

The theories we have discussed to this point—psychodynamic theory, behaviorism, cognitive theory, humanism, and eclecticism—have been relatively narrow in their scope. As we pointed out earlier in the chapter, some theories with important implications for the behavioral sciences are more general in focus, so much so that we might refer to them as worldviews or philosophies. Structuralism is such a theory. More appropriately, the term *structuralism* refers to a family of theories and approaches with important common elements that are found in a great many of the behavioral science disciplines. Our discussion focuses on what is common in the assumptive bases of the various theories that makes it reasonable to classify them as structuralisms and on the common implications to which these theories lead.

The term structuralism will likely be more familiar to readers from sociology, family science, family therapy, and philosophy than to those from other behavioral science disciplines. However, some theories known by other names in the various disciplines can also be seen as examples of structuralism. Examples include systems theory, Marxist theories, many feminist approaches to behavioral science, and a number of developmental theories, including that of Jean Piaget.[19] As the name implies, the defining feature of a structuralist theory is the idea that the phenomena (things or events) we observe in the world arise from some underlying structure that we cannot observe. The existence and the characteristics of these structures are not available for direct observation and thus must always be inferred. According to structuralist theorists, however, such inferred structures offer the best explanations of observable phenomena, and phenomena cannot really be understood until they are understood in terms of the structures that produce them.

Perhaps the most obvious example of a structuralist theory with which readers may be familiar is *Marxism*. Marx proposed that the most important influence on how people live their lives, as well as how governments and cultures work, is the economic structure that determines who controls the means of production in a society. He argued further that such a structure has existed throughout history, and although it has taken various forms, it has always been the primary influence on how governments and societies have run. Further, this structure has had extremely broad influence. It has influenced not only economic matters, how people make things and earn money, but how they structure their family lives, what ideas they think, what kind of art they produce, and even what religions they develop. The underlying structure is the primary cause of virtually all human activity. If indeed this structure or others like it do exist, it is easy to see why they would be of great interest to behavioral scientists.

For Marxists, the underlying economic structure is not easy to "see" or understand. Although it can be seen and understood, people are most often unaware of it, even though their lives are strongly influenced, or even determined, by it.[20] According to Marxist theory, seeing the underlying structure and understanding its effects requires being educated or made aware. Once properly educated, one can see the structure at work in human affairs and use it as a means of interpreting the world and explaining events. The result of this educative process is a properly Marxist analysis of behaviors and events.

In the minds of many, if not most, behavioral scientists, Marxism is an extremist theory. It is, nevertheless, a good example of structuralism and the sort of explanations of human activities that structuralism offers. Other types of structuralism are found in the mainstream of many behavioral sciences. Sociology, for example, has been heavily influenced by various theories that can be classified as structuralisms, many by name.[21] Students of sociology will affirm that the field has long been interested in *social structures* of various sorts. One of the defining purposes of sociology has been to identify social structures, study them, show how they work, and make clear the influence they have in people's lives. In one sense, social structures are the primary explanatory constructs employed by sociologists.

Another example of structuralism, *systems theory,* has come to be an important explanatory perspective in family sciences; family therapy; and branches of education, psychology, and sociology. The fundamental notion of systems theory is appealing. It is that the behaviors of people cannot be understood without paying attention to the social "system" in which they live. The entire system must be understood and its influence accounted for if human behavior is to be adequately explained. Systems theorists make analogies to ecological systems or to living organisms to show how it is that all parts of complex systems must function together and how the organism can only be understood as an entire system. The system itself, *as a system,* is largely unseen; like other structures found in society and in Marxist analysis, it lies beneath the surface, not directly accessible, but powerful in directing the observable phenomena that make up the system.

Stage theories have become very influential as explanations of human development. The best known of these is probably that of Jean Piaget. According to these theories, all human beings develop in childhood and beyond through an orderly series of stages. Each stage "sets the stage" for the next. The orderliness and generality we perceive in development is due to the operation of a stage structure that is not explicitly observable. This structure lies beneath the surface of behavior, but it guides and produces the characteristics that typify each stage. Consequently understanding development requires understanding the structure of stages and processes that govern it.

Feminist analysis[22] has in recent years become increasingly important in all behavioral sciences. Its influence has been felt directly in women's studies programs and less overtly in theories about women's alternative voices, sex differences, and gender roles and identification, among many other things. Although feminism is a multifaceted perspective, it seems, in very many of its manifestations, to be essentially structuralist in approach.[23] Many feminists have acknowledged the close intellectual link between feminism and Marxism. That link is structuralism. For most feminist perspectives, much of what we observe in human action is determined by an underlying structure of gender relations (not unlike the structure of economic relations a Marxist would recognize). This structure of gender relations is a sort of "invisible hand" influencing interpersonal relations, family structures, values, art, and even religion. Feminist critiques of society and culture have been every bit as broad and effective as Marxist criticisms, owing to the very broad scale on which the underlying structure of gender relations has been presumed to operate. Feminists posit that this structure has been powerful and has lasted for centuries in large measure because it is not readily seen and thus not easily overcome. To recognize it requires being educated or trained to recognize it. This process of becoming sensitive to the structure and its effects is referred to as *consciousness raising*.

There are many other manifestations of structuralism in the behavioral sciences, far too many to deal with in this chapter. We have outlined the important defining features of a structuralist approach to explanation and illustrated several manifestations of it in various disciplines. Many theories that do not contain explicit reference to structuralism can nonetheless be shown to be essentially structuralist in approach.

ASSUMPTIONS AND
IMPLICATIONS OF STRUCTURALISM

By its very nature structuralism offers a good example of the sort of hidden or implicit ideas that we seek to uncover in this book. The issues raised here are meant to stimulate thought and aid recognition of the implicit assumptions and implications of structuralism; some of the issues will be more directly relevant to some structuralist theories than to others. One issue relates to the capacity of structuralism to foster critical self-analysis. The structures structuralists invoke as explanations are always implicit. For most structuralists, there is nothing more funda- mental than the structure, and thus there is no alternative to the structure. It is just there. It seems reasonable to ask, however, on what grounds the structuralist claims that understanding stops at this, or any, particular structure. Why are there are no alternative explanations for behaviors or for the existence of the structure itself? For example, on what basis can a Marxist claim that the structure of economic relations is *the* most impor- tant structure or that there is no other movement or structure of greater importance that produces the structure of economic relations? On what basis can a Marxist claim that the end result of the structure will be an acceptably Marxist state rather than some other social arrangement? The conceptual problem of many structuralist theories (such as Marxism and feminism) is justifying the existence and importance of some structure as the ultimate explanation of phenomena, when the arguments and analyses used in justifying it are the products of the very structure they are meant to justify and explain. By definition there are no independent means of verifying the existence of the structure.

Another important question that might be raised concerning structu- ralist theories involves the inherently hidden and implicit nature of the structures that determine human phenomena. The behavioral sciences have a long history of rejecting explanations for human behaviors that are based on powers that operate on some level other than the natural world and which cannot be observed or tested empirically. Religious explana- tions, for example, are often rejected for just this reason. Structures invoked by structuralists as explanations, however, have characteristics very simi- lar to those we might expect religious explanations to have. On a philo- sophical level it might be argued that there is considerable similarity between the "invisible hand of God" and, for example, the "invisible hand of the structure of gender relations." Both operate on an extremely broad scale, both do their work "behind the scenes" of human history, and both do so without being observed, at least without our conscious awareness. Given this similarity, we might expect the behavioral sciences to be as skeptical of structuralism as they have been of religion and to subject structuralist theories to careful scrutiny.

Structuralist explanations of human behavior are strongly deterministic. Although most structuralist theorists have tried to avoid some kinds of determinism, especially mechanistic kinds such as we find in behaviorism, they may have substituted another kind of determinism that is just as strong and just as far-reaching in its consequences for our view of human beings (see Chapter 4). If powerful structures operate to direct our lives on a level where we cannot clearly "see" them or have conscious awareness of them, then it would seem that we are not able to do much about them. They seem to be uninfluenced by our acts of agency. In fact, if there are structures such as these, it is questionable whether we are in control of our actions at all. All of the questions we raised regarding the determinism inherent in psychodynamic theory and behaviorism seem relevant to structuralism as well.

There is one additional aspect of this question that many structural theories raise. If it is possible for some people with specialized education or raised consciousness to become explicitly aware of the structures that have in the past determined their behavior, and by this awareness to become free from the structures' influences, then it seems reasonable to ask whether those structures are really as fundamental and as strong as structural theorists normally claim. For example, if becoming sensitive to the structure of gender relations that so strongly influences so much of our culture can leave us free of its effects, we might question whether that structure is really all that fundamental or powerful. It might be asked whether the supposed structure is anything more than a bundle of simple habits elevated to the status of explanation when they are things waiting to be explained themselves.[24]

One final and related conceptual issue concerns the nature of the structures themselves. Simply put, we might ask: What are these structures? Are they real? Our intellectual tradition has tended to divide reality into two fairly broad categories, material things and ideas (ideal things). This division became important in the work of the 17th-century mathematician and philosopher René Descartes, but is also found in the earliest Greek philosophies. It is clear that the structures used to explain human behaviors are not made of matter. They do not constitute a material reality. However, they do not seem to be ideas either. In fact, the structures spoken of by Marx, many feminists, and Piaget are supposedly what *determine* our ideas; they make ideas possible. If something is more fundamental than ideas—because it determines them—it seems doubtful that it could be an idea. The question then becomes: What is a structure? We are not suggesting that there are only two categories of "real" things—material and ideas. However, structuralist theorists have not given much attention to the fundamental nature of the structures they identify and invoke as causes. To name them—as structures—is not the same thing as doing the careful work necessary to give some idea about their nature. Unless some attention is given to this, the adequacy and coherence of structuralist theory should be questioned by behavioral scientists.[25]

POSTMODERNISM

Postmodernism is another theory that is broader than what we usually call theories. Like structuralism,[26] it is so broad that many of its proponents would not want to call it a theory at all. In fact, postmodernism—like structuralism—is perhaps better described as a family of theories and perspectives that have something in common. We concentrate on that common perspective in our discussion here.[27]

Postmodern theories in the behavioral sciences grow out of postmodern philosophies, deriving their ideas and insights from the criticism postmodern philosophies make of what is referred to as the *modern tradition* (i.e., virtually all Western philosophy since the time of Descartes in the 17th century). One of the central ideas of this criticism is that contrary to what has been central to our intellectual tradition, there are no metaphysical absolutes; no fundamental and abstract truths, laws, or principles that determine what the world is like and what happens in it. Applied to behavioral science, this idea means that human behavior is not caused by absolute laws, principles, or causes that exist or operate independent of human beings themselves. This position rejects at once psychodynamic instincts and unconscious minds, behavioristic laws of learning and conditioning, humanistic needs and growth potentials, and cognitive structures and processes. Indeed postmodernists tend to be suspicious of structures and abstractions of any sort that can be invoked as explanation.

We are left with a world composed of human beings engaged in behavior. However, the behavior will never be understood by looking for laws and principles, because it is not the product of such things. Rather, behaviors must be understood by being involved "authentically" in the world in which the behavior occurs. For example if we wish to understand the behavior of a child in a classroom, we do not look for principles of learning, past conditioning, or social structures that might be determining the child's behavior. Rather we become engaged in the world of the child both within and outside the classroom. We participate with the child in the meanings that make up the child's life and actions.

A postmodern perspective suggests that human behaviors reflect a broad, rich, changing, and open-ended context, much as the plot of a novel reflects the whole of what has gone on earlier in the novel. Just as the plot of a novel can only be understood by reading the novel and making sense of the whole of it, human behavior can only be understood by "reading" the broader context of life and history within which the behavior occurs.

This view of human life is not deterministic in the way that most prominent behavioral science theories are.[28] Postmodern theory *begins* with the assumption that people are not determined by instincts, laws, needs, or systems. They are seen as being involved in the creation of their own lives and meanings from their earliest entry into life. However, we are not free to make meaning and create our lives individually, all by ourselves. We are constrained by conditions of the world as well as by the actions of other people. Still, whatever conditions exist in the world must be interpreted by us, and then it is our interpretation of the world that to a great extent fleshes out the role it will play in our lives. The actions of other people are also important in the way we create our lives and meanings. We get our language from other people, and we share it with them. Through this language we obtain the categories with which we understand the world and the ways to make it meaningful. One dramatic implication of our dependence on language for the power to create life and meaning is that we are dependent on others for our identity. Because all language is social and infused with meanings that only exist as shared meanings, the language with which we understand ourselves and create an identity is not our own, but shared with others as well. This should not be understood as a return to behaviorism. The influence others may have on us is not the product of their stimulus properties or their reinforcing us, but rather the product of their creating with us a life we live together and a language of meaning we share.

Postmodern theory, with the emphasis that all meanings come from language rather than from absolute laws or principles, suggests that knowledge is a creation. What this means is that postmodern theorists reject the idea that human beings can arrive at certain truth or knowledge by logical reasoning or scientific method. Rather, for most postmodernists, knowledge and truth are creations of groups of people who share a language and a perspective. Truth and knowledge are thus constantly open to revision and even to negotiation as we come in contact with others and our language and context become broader and richer.

The root metaphor for postmodern theory is a text (such as a book). Postmodernists want to look at human beings as texts or stories. Just as a story must be interpreted, and good stories are open to many interpretations and are in some sense never finished, human beings and their behaviors also need to be interpreted; they are open-ended and unfinished. Just as there is no one final reading of a book, but rather a good book is somehow different every time we read it, there is no one final explanation of a human behavior. Just like a book, a behavior "takes on a life of its own," and if it is an important behavior, its meaning is never final.

An example of such a behavior might be a divorce. The meaning of a divorce cannot be determined at the time it occurs. Further, the meaning and nature of the event can only be understood in the context of a long history of families and kinship relations, and moral and societal obligations. What the divorce *means* is yet to be determined. We must wait and see what ultimately becomes of the couple involved, their children, and perhaps, their children's children. Any decision about (or explanation of) the nature and meaning of the divorce will likely change as the event continues to unfold and to undergo interpretation. In other words, our understandings and explanations of events must change and grow as the events (people, contexts, and languages) do. This principle applies not only to behavioral scientists trying to explain why people behave as they do, but also to us *as people* trying to explain—in our everyday lives—why people, including ourselves, behave as they (we) do. Human lives are open-ended, changing, and creative. We will never be finished. Both our knowledge and our natures are being created and laid down in the very acts of our living.

ASSUMPTIONS AND IMPLICATIONS
OF POSTMODERN THEORY

Postmodern theory presents a serious challenge to traditional behavioral science. The nature of the challenge, like the nature of postmodern theory itself, is just emerging in the disciplines. We want to emphasize, however, that postmodern theory is not without hidden ideas and implications that need to be considered and confronted if the theory is to be taken seriously and if it is to have an effect on the field. One important implication of postmodern theory, at least as it is presented in many disciplines, is that it leads to relativism. Postmodernism seems to suggest that there is no way for us to arrive at a truth that will not at some later time be abandoned and replaced by another seeming truth. This aspect of the theory is particularly relevant for behavioral scientists because they have tried to establish their disciplines as sciences. If there is no truth that can be established once and for all, is science possible? In Chapter 6, we explore more fully whether science is able to establish the type of truth we have believed it could, the type that gives us certainty. For now, however, we simply raise the question because postmodernism offers such a direct challenge to that whole notion.

As postmodernists reject the possibility of establishing unchanging truth and certainty, another kind of relativity seems to creep into our explanations of behavior. If truth cannot be established with certainty, we have a difficult time passing judgment on the morality of any behavior. Some theorists are not concerned about this type of moral relativity; however, it must be remembered that moral relativity is not a suspending of all theories. Rather, it *is* a theory. It is not an obvious and necessarily true theoretical position, but merely a possible one. Such relativity has hidden ideas, implications, and conceptual costs. It also may not be congruent with the experience of many or most human beings. Theorists in the behavioral sciences must account for people's moral judgments even if they do not want to pass moral judgment themselves. In some species of postmodernism, there seems to be little basis for either making or explaining moral judgments.[29]

Although postmodern theorists reject the kind of determinism espoused by most traditional theorists in the behavioral sciences, they are faced with the problem of explaining human behavior without determinism. In other words, determinism is a conceptual aid in making sense of people's behaviors. We feel like we understand behaviors if we have some idea of what causes them. If there are no such causes—as most postmodernists would claim—then we have to understand behaviors without causes. It seems a mistake to assume that behaviors are random; people do behave consistently. Postmodern theorists are faced with explaining the origin of human behaviors without making them products of hard determinism, and at the same time, without suggesting that they are random and unrelated to the world in which people live. In other words, postmodern theorists must find a way to acknowledge that the world in which we live is important, and that it impacts our behaviors, without making the environment the cause of our behaviors. Similarly, postmodernists must find a way to acknowledge that we *experience* ourselves as having impulses and needs without making such needs, or some "inner nature," the "real" cause of our behaviors in the way more traditional theorists do.

CONCLUSION

Our survey of the prominent theories of the behavioral sciences leaves us with a host of unresolved hidden issues. Some of the issues are assumptions that the theorist must presume are true and necessary for the theory to be valid or helpful. Other issues are implications that the theorist must follow if the theory is carried to its logical conclusion. In either case, the difficulty and complexity of these issues should not be underestimated. Indeed, their difficulty and complexity are perhaps the reasons why the behavioral sciences have not dealt with them before. Because there are no obvious and easy ways of addressing the issues, the behavioral sciences have to a great extent proceeded as if such problems did not exist.

Unfortunately, however, they do exist and they do affect what behavioral scientists do. Hence, we must find some means of at least beginning to understand the issues involved. Fortunately, our survey has revealed several commonalities, or repeated themes, among the hidden assumptions and implications of the various explanations offered by behavioral scientists. We concentrate on these themes in the next four chapters. The first theme, *knowing*, involves the way in which the particular theory relates persons to their world. In behaviorism and cognitivism, for example, the assumption is that the environment is constantly coming at people with stimuli and information that cause their thoughts and behaviors. The prominence of this kind of knowing is easily seen in behaviorist and cognitivist theories of learning and memory. All theories postulate *ways of knowing*, some way in which the world and the person are related.

A second theme revealed in our survey is *determinism*. Deterministic assumptions involve those aspects of a theory that explain what is responsible for the particular effect under study. When students of the behavioral sciences are first exposed to hidden ideas, they are often struck by the prevalence of deterministic assumptions. All explanations in the behavioral sciences entail some sort of determinism. This is true even for those theorists who have attempted to escape determinism, as in many humanistic conceptions; they still retain it in some implicit way. Many postmodern theories explicitly reject familiar varieties of determinism. However, this raises many questions, particularly if science itself is thought to require determinism.

It is also commonly assumed that science requires *reductionism*, the third theme in our survey. Reductionism is the notion that simpler explanations are better than more complicated ones. "Simpler" has frequently meant "biological" to many behavioral scientists, hence the emphasis of many theories on biological processes and metaphors. Psychodynamic theorists emphasize the biological instincts of an organism; behavioral theorists focus on the pleasure seeking and pain avoidance of biological organisms; and humanists often rely on the natural and biological tendencies of people to heal themselves. Although the other theories of the behavioral sciences are less explicitly reductionistic, each of these theories involves explanations that "reduce" the factors involved in human behavior to those deemed most important. Because of this, all theories include assumptions about why the factors they can be reduced to, such as biology, are fundamental or important.

The fourth and final theme in our survey of behavioral science theories is science itself. Repeatedly in these theories—even in the case of the other themes considered here—the justification for many assumptions and implications is that science requires them. What is science that it should command such respect? Science is a set of beliefs about how knowledge is advanced. For the most part, behavioral scientists have adopted their beliefs about how knowledge accrues from the natural sciences. However, each theory we have surveyed includes a position on how this science should be carried out. Behaviorism, for instance, is noted for rigid adherence to natural science methods, whereas postmodernism is noted for criticisms of natural science methods. Whatever is the case, understanding the assumptions that each theory makes regarding science is crucial for understanding and addressing the hidden ideas of the theories.

The next four chapters are devoted to these four themes. In each chapter, we place these themes in their historical contexts. This allows us to better understand the nature of the problems, particularly as they affect the behavioral sciences. We also expose the most common understanding of the theme at hand—knowing, determinism, reductionism, or science—as well as important alternative understandings that can serve as contrasts. In every case, we refer back to the various behavioral science theories summarized in this chapter to illuminate the issues and problems entailed in the theoretical themes.

Notes

1. A number of the terms used by Freud and other psychodynamic theorists have found their way in our everyday vocabulary although their history is not known and the assumptions built into the terms themselves are not examined. Thus we use terms such as *ego, libido, unconscious,* and *repression* in referring to ourselves and others as though they were part of the human reality. This phenomenon has provided us one of the motives for writing this book. It is, at least, an interesting example of what we mean when we say that ideas have consequences.

2. We recognize here that it is also proper to say that people are motivated by pleasure. Some theorists prefer to use the general term *pleasure* to describe our fundamental motivation, rather than concentrating on its sexual nature. This is in part because Freud interpreted sexuality as much more than genital sexual behavior, including many desires and behaviors that do not seem to us to be truly sexual. Although it is true that for Freud the sexual instinct was so general and pervasive that it could be equated with pleasure in general, careful reading of his theory also implies that all pleasure in general can be equated with sexuality. Theorists who emphasize that when Freud said "sex" he really meant "all pleasure" must deal with the other side of the theoretical coin—when he said "pleasure" he really meant "sex."

3. Some would suggest that this concern reflects too narrow a view of the self or agent. They would argue that consistent with some interpretations of psychodynamic theory, we have an unconscious self or ego that is capable of intervening in the internal affairs of the mind and making decisions fully aware of the intrapsychic situation. It still seems nonetheless the case that we, as persons, are unaware of both the influences and the intervention made in our behalf by our unconscious selves. Discussing whether this is an adequate response to the problem of the unconscious and determinism is beyond the scope of this chapter.

4. Even if "sexuality" is broadly defined as "pleasure," the problem is the same.

5. Some scholars (e.g., Leahey, 1992) suggest that Watson deserves only a small part of the credit he is usually given.

6. Although some authors (e.g., Leahey, 1992) make distinctions among various terms, such as *behaviorism* and *behavioralism,* and it could be argued that *behaviorism* is different from *behaviorist theory,* we will not concern ourselves with these distinctions nor with the reasons for them. We adopt the term *behaviorist theory* to refer to a general approach to understanding and explaining human behavior, emphasizing that by the definition put forward in the book it is, indeed, a theory. Sometimes, to avoid too-complicated phrasing, the shorter term, *behaviorism,* will be used interchangeably.

7. Obviously, behaviorist theorists recognize that people do think and that they are conscious. To say that all behaviors are *essentially* like reflexes is not to deny that people can and do think. Rather it is to claim that thought and conscious awareness are not necessary to *explain* the behaviors. Behaviors are learned first in a fairly automatic way by means of processes that are reflexlike. Later on, however, people also learn to think and talk about their behaviors by means of the same processes by which they learned the behaviors themselves. Because of this learning, thought and consciousness are taking place while people behave, but they are more the results or correlates of the behaviors than they are essential causes. Consciousness and thinking are themselves behaviors learned in a basically automatic way. This issue becomes even more complex when we turn to behaviorist theories that have moved toward more cognitive approaches, such as Bandura's (1977) social learning theory. However, the issues raised in any careful analysis of behaviorist theory apply to such modifications because they do not require repudiating their essentially behaviorist groundings. More often, they are open to all the theoretical questions raised by cognitive theory as well.

8. The term *conditioning* is used in behaviorist theory in place of *learning* to describe what we would normally refer to as learning. Learning is generally defined as a change in behavior attributable to changes in the environment. The new term conditioning has been invented and is preferred because it carries fewer connotations of mental activity and purposefulness, in keeping with the spirit of behaviorism. Note here how unexamined assumptions and implications can be "packed into" a definition. In fact, definitions are often fertile sources of assumptions.

9. Some researchers of psychodynamic theory do not see it as being quite so strictly deterministic, or they suggest that psychodynamic theorists rely on types of determinism other than efficient causes (see Chapter 4). See the discussion of Freud's theory in Rychlak (1981) for a treatment of this issue.

10. This creates a very difficult problem for behaviorist theory itself. If we can only do what we have already learned to do, than how are we to account for the very first bit of learning or conditioning, as by definition, no other learning could have preceded it? The answer for behaviorist theory lies, of course, in the idea that the first "learning" consists of purely reflexive bodily responses that require no prior learning because they are automatic and biologically wired in. The interesting theoretical question that remains, however, is how these simple biological reflexes can ever become complex social and mental behaviors. We are aware of no full and careful account of this in the behaviorist literature.

11. This book, then, can act as a stimulus to elicit behaviors or ideas the readers already know, but it cannot teach them anything new. This is a great discouragement to authors and teachers.

12. The question of how completely humanistic theorists reject determinism and what kind of determinism they accept is more complex than we have suggested here. Although most humanists would certainly reject hard determinism, they do, nevertheless, accept the idea that we have an inner potential that exerts considerable influence over our behaviors and choices. We will deal with this issue in the next section of the chapter. The definition of agency in humanistic theories is also a matter of some debate. Most initially favor a view that holds that people have freedom *to* choose their behaviors, but what most often gets emphasized is that people need freedom *from* environmental influences and pressure from others. These two notions of freedom are not identical in their assumptive basis nor in their implications. Freedom from environmental pressures might still allow for other kinds of determining influences, for example, from biological forces or innate potentials

of some sort. Freedom to choose might still be quite impossible. Here, we have given humanistic theory what we consider to be the most generous reading. However, the reader is encouraged to keep in mind that advocating freedom is not necessarily the same thing as giving a careful theoretical account of what it is or how it is possible.

13. The potential for abuse of this situation is obvious. In principle, if someone were to feel that it was right for them, and necessary for their fulfillment, to harm or destroy another person, we would be hard pressed to mount an adequate conceptual refutation from within most humanistic theories. We grant that this is an extreme example, but theories often show themselves in their most basic and understandable form in the light of extreme cases. Most humanists would defend against this extreme case by pointing out that according to the theory, people have no such violent and aggressive impulses, so there is nothing to fear in letting them do what is fulfilling. It should be noted, however, that the belief that there is nothing to fear in our natures is not supported by sound argument or scientific evidence. It is, rather, a largely unsupported grounding assumption. The more important point is that, in principle, given the grounding concepts of humanist theory, it would be difficult to mount a discussion of the morality of anyone's action. To do so, we would need to step outside humanism and appeal to traditional moral principles—something humanistic theorists themselves suggest may lead to incongruence.

14. It should be acknowledged that there is much more to the story of the development of the cognitive sciences, including the formulation of information theory, a renewed interest in rationalism, dissatisfaction with behaviorist explanations, the work of Jean Piaget, and much important work in linguistics. Some of these will be dealt with in the discussion here and in later chapters. We emphasize the development of the computer because it has been such an effective root metaphor.

15. As we elaborate below, we recognize here that many cognitivists would argue that we can exercise a good deal of influence over the information that enters the cognitive processing system. This is certainly more true in cognitive than in behaviorist models. However, much of the influence over incoming stimuli is a function of attentional processes of which people are usually not aware and over which they can exercise very little volitional control. Another potential influence on the incoming stimulus information comes from past experience called up from a memory store (usually long-term memory, of which, again, we are not consciously in control) and used to make sense of present stimuli. If, however, cognitive theorists maintain that past experience influences current actions and interpretations, once again they seem to be in agreement rather than in contrast with behaviorists.

16. It might be argued that the parent is processing much more information than just the verbal information in the child's utterances. This position would suggest that there is information in the child's body language, intonation patterns, and other things. However, none of these possible alternative kinds of information can stand alone. The meaning of the child's message is in the interplay of all of them. Further, these other kinds of information soon begin to look more like contexts and histories of involvement, in which case the concept of information is superfluous. Context is necessary to make sense of any information and can account for understanding on its own without the need to posit the existence of information at all. This type of argument—that there are multiple sources of information—seems to be mostly an attempt to save the model and betrays a prior theoretical commitment that information must exist, and exist in some sort of linear arrangement (Slife, in press). The alternative is that *information* is simply a metaphor we use to "explain" understanding as we will argue later.

17. One gets the feeling that if we go back far enough, tracing ever smaller bits of information as input, we will get to the point that they are so small and context free as to

be essentially meaningless. The problem then becomes that these bits of information—wherever we may begin—are meaningless, and yet when processed, they yield information. This is a type of getting something from nothing that most would find troubling.

18. Sometimes the ability to simultaneously believe in these contradictions is taken as a measure of intellectual maturity. Many eclectic strategies of explanation suggest that it is not only possible but desirable to sustain mutually contradictory explanations.

19. Some scholars (DeGeorge & DeGeorge, 1972) would also include Freud's psychoanalytical theory and even cognitive theory (Williams, 1987) as examples of structuralism. Although we believe this categorization is essentially accurate, we have chosen not to emphasize the structuralist aspects of the theories because it is not the structuralism that is most recognized and most influential in contemporary mainstream behavioral science disciplines. However, the questions raised about structuralism apply to these theories as well. In broader terms, it could be argued that structuralism of one sort or another underlies nearly all approaches to the behavioral sciences, but making this point would lead our discussion away from what we wish to emphasize.

20. This type of structure operates very much like the sort of unacknowledged or implicit ideas (assumptions) that we have talked about throughout this book.

21. We refer the interested reader to Johnson (1981) for a fuller treatment of the ways in which "structure" and structuralism have been important in the history of sociology. We also recognize that a more particular philosophical movement has emerged in recent years under the banner of structuralism that has been a rather more modern and radical influence in sociology. For purposes of the analysis offered in this book, we want to use the term structuralism very broadly, and so will not deal with the nuances that distinguish various movements.

22. We acknowledge here the great diversity of points of view that have, at one time or another, gone under the name of feminism. Many histories of feminism are available. For a discussion of the history and theoretical assumptions of the movement, see McDowell and Pringle (1992). The early feminist movement, at least in the United States, had its roots more firmly in the liberal democratic tradition than in more explicitly structuralist traditions.

23. Some contemporary feminists, particularly those who identify with the social constructionist movement, are aware of structuralism and some of its assumptions and implications, and attempt to avoid some of the attendant problems. Some feminists refer to themselves as *poststructuralist*. Whether any of these succeed in avoiding structuralism is an issue that cannot be dealt with fully in this volume. In regard to the question we cite Ollenburger and Moore (1992): "The poststructuralist feminists focus on individual solutions even though the key to oppression is often structural" (p. 25).

24. Some might argue that raised consciousness can free someone from a mind-set, or pattern of thinking, imposed by the structure, but that there may be aspects of the structure that are institutionalized, and thus it is impossible to be free from their effects. An interesting alternative possibility is that if raised consciousness were achieved by more and more people, then there would be no one left with a mind-set to continue the institutionalized practices, and the structure and its effects would disappear de facto. This would again suggest that the structures were not self-existent realities, but habits.

25. The explanatory problem facing structuralists seems to be essentially the following. Because structures are construed as causes of ideas, it seems problematic to claim that they are ideas. Some structuralists might say that they *are* ideas, as ideas can cause other ideas. However, if structures are *just* ideas, then it is impossible to be sure that there are no ideas more fundamental than the structures giving rise to them. Thus, the structures are not

necessarily fundamental. Some structuralists would ground the structures in *practice,* but it is difficult to support a claim that such practices are fundamental. Finally, it appears that structures are very similar to Platonic forms. However, most structuralists, being post-modernists, would be very uncomfortable with any return to Platonic explanations and the absolutism they imply. The explanatory task facing structuralists is formidable if structures are to be understood as anything more than rhetorical devices.

26. Some readers might consider structuralism, as discussed in previous pages, to be very much a postmodern movement. We acknowledge that this is true to some extent, but we have chosen to discuss the two as separate "theories." Our major reason for doing so is that we detect some differences between postmodern movements with implications leading to structuralism and postmodern movements lacking such implications. Whether any one postmodern movement is successful in avoiding structuralism is very much open to question. That discussion is, however, beyond the scope of this book. For now, we attempt to show by means of examples and illustrations how some types of postmodern theories can be cast in nonstructuralist forms.

27. For a fuller view of these perspectives and their important differences, the reader is referred to other, more specific texts (e.g., Faulconer & Williams, 1990; Messer, Sass, & Woolfolk, 1988; Packer & Addison, 1989; Polkinghorne, 1983).

28. This a bold claim when stated so matter of factly. We want to emphasize that the claim here is that theories of the sort that we include as postmodern are not deterministic *in the way that other prominent theories are.* This does not mean necessarily that they are not deterministic. We refer the reader to Williams (1992) for a brief discussion of determinism that illustrates that some types of determinism are compatible with postmodern theories and intents. We want to acknowledge that to claim that postmodern theories are not deterministic in the way other theories are is not to claim that this is always clearly established in the behavioral science literature articulating postmodern perspectives.

29. In spite of this, most postmodern scholars do in fact make moral judgments. Few would envision a world, either ancient or future, in which slavery would be acceptable, or in which women should be treated more shabbily than men. Most postmodernists make the moral judgment (and often support its being incorporated into social policy) that one person's or group's moral judgments should not be imposed on others. Most often, postmodern theorists seek a moral grounding by making a final appeal to pragmatism or some supposedly unquestionable truism, such as, "People should not suffer." This may be the most important philosophical dilemma with which postmodernists must grapple.

3

Ways of Knowing

This chapter begins our discussion of the key themes that reveal hidden ideas. Up to this point, we have shown that hidden ideas exist and raise important issues (Chapter 1) and that the many theories of the behavioral sciences do not necessarily resolve these issues (Chapter 2). The present chapter focuses on the theme of knowing. Knowing is vitally involved in every discipline, though not always explicitly. What we mean by knowing is often found in the literature on learning and memory, because learning, memory, and knowing all entail relations between our world and our being—that is, we may learn from our circumstances, remember yesterday's events, or know about our environment, but all require some relationship between ourselves and our world.

Applied behavioral scientists are, of course, particularly interested in this relationship. Educators, by the very nature of their discipline, study and use different approaches to learning and knowing. Therapy also demands that processes of learning and memory be as completely understood as possible. Crucial to clients' problems is what they have learned from their experiences, including childhood experiences. Moreover, *how* clients are thought to learn—the nature of learning—is crucial to helping clients solve their problems. Social, cognitive, and developmental behavioral scientists are no less concerned about learning and knowing. How people become conditioned or "take in" and process information is pivotal to any theory of mind or behavior. Even animal researchers are interested in how animals of all species learn about and process their surroundings.

With so many divergent professionals concerned about ways of knowing, one might assume there are many different theories of knowing in the behavioral sciences. Surprisingly, this is not the case. Although there are various models of learning and approaches to knowing, the assumptions that underlie the majority of these models and approaches are basically the same—that is, the *epistemologies* of these models and approaches—the ideas underlying theories of learning—are essentially alike. In philosophy, epistemology concerns the nature, origins, and limits of knowledge. This term gives us a convenient way of referring to different, very general theories of knowing.

The epistemology endorsed, sometimes unknowingly, by the vast majority of behavioral scientists is *empiricism*. Our first job is to describe this general epistemology and relate it to the tasks of these professionals. Next, we ask the question: Are there alternative epistemologies? Obviously, to identify empiricism as *one* epistemology is to imply that other epistemologies are possible. But are there other epistemologies that are relevant to behavioral science? We believe the answer is unequivocally yes. A small minority of behavioral scientists use other epistemologies.[1] We take a close look at the main alternative to empiricism—*rationalism*—and relate it to the needs and purposes of behavioral scientists.

Our job will not be complete, however, with a description of these two epistemologies. Other behavioral scientists object to epistemologies on postmodern grounds (see Chapter 2). These scientists acknowledge that traditional theories depend on epistemology, but object to this dependence and point instead to *social constructions* and *modes of engagement* as alternatives. We attempt to understand these objections to traditional epistemologies, explain how well these alternatives meet these objections, and then describe how they postulate a radically different relationship between our world and our being.

CONVENTIONAL WAYS OF KNOWING

We have so far lumped together learning and knowing as if they were essentially the same process. In many formal explanations in the behavioral sciences, however, theories of learning are distinguished from models of memory (knowing). Learning theory typically refers to the way the environment conditions and shapes one's behavior across time; memory models usually deal more with cognitive and mental forms of knowledge. This distinction is useful, but it can also be misleading. It is useful, because it helps us to differentiate behaviorism, with an emphasis on learning theory, from cognitivism, with a concentration on models of memory (see Chapter 2 for a description of these two human images). However, this distinction is sometimes deceptive, because it can lead students to think that behaviorism and cognitivism differ fundamentally. As we shall see, both approaches consider sensory experiences to be the root of the learning and knowing process.

This dependence on sensory experience is the reason that both approaches are considered to be empiricist. *Empiricism* is the notion that our learning and memory are primarily derived from our experience of events of the world. Indeed, the Latin term *empiric(us)* means "experienced." Events of the world are considered to impinge on our senses in ways that cause us to experience and learn them. These events are thought to have an organization independent of our consciousness of them. Learning is the taking in of the events and thus their organization. This is not to say that we always learn events correctly, but that whatever we *do* learn is ultimately rooted in our experience of the external world. This external world may consist of the viewing of a scene, the presentation of a lecture, or the touching of a hot stove. Whatever the set of events, knowledge and learning can supposedly be traced to our sensory experience of the external world.

This approach to knowing has a rather long history. One can see empiricist themes as far back as the Greek philosopher Aristotle.[2] Aristotle held that knowledge was available in particular sensory experiences, and we can see famous thinkers picking up this theme through the centuries. In the 14th century, for instance, William of Ockham asserted that the surest knowledge available to us is "intuitive cognition"—direct contact with the objects of the world. Perhaps most influential in the behavioral sciences were the British empiricists, because the British intellectual culture is the heritage of most English-speaking behavioral scientists. British empiricists of the 17th and 18th centuries, such as John Locke, built entire philosophies around the notion that knowledge can be derived from sense experiences. Indeed, these philosophies are considered to form the foundation of most modern theories of personality, education, and cognition (cf. Rychlak, 1981, 1988, 1994).

Locke's version of this philosophy is perhaps the best known. In Locke's view, the human mind at birth can be understood as a *tabula rasa,* or blank slate, on which experience etches representations of the external world. Locke felt that our knowledge originated from two sources: *sensation* and *reflection.* Sensations, such as heat, softness, and bitterness, come from objects of experience that are independent of our minds. Reflections result from an *internal sense* of the mind that attends to its own operations. Simple sensations enter the mind as *atoms* of experience, but complex ideas arise from the reflective operations of the mind as it associates simple and discrete sensations. Although reflective operations are recognized, the ideas on which they operate, and on which they therefore depend, stem from our sensations of a separate and external reality.[3]

This philosophy is so influential today that it is often taken for granted in the behavioral sciences. The basic positions of Locke and Ockham are so familiar to students that it may seem odd to note that empiricism is *an* approach to knowledge rather than the only way to understand it. Indeed, dependence on sensory experience is so common that many students of the behavioral sciences would be hard pressed to conceive of an alternative approach to knowing. Where else, they might ask, could knowledge and learning come from except from our sensory experience? Likewise, in many fields of the behavioral sciences, knowledge has become almost synonymous with information from the external world (i.e., empiricism). Empiricists acknowledge that the external world might shape behavior directly or it might require some processing by our minds. Whichever is the case, our experience of the external world is the starting point for virtually every theory of conditioning or model of memory.

Conditioning principles clearly rely on empiricist assumptions. After all, a person's behavior is conditioned *by* his or her environment. With instrumental or operant conditioning, the behaviors that are ultimately learned and exhibited are those that the environment has reinforced. The case is the same for classical or Pavlovian conditioning. The behaviors that are learned are those that become associated with certain stimuli in the environment. Without those stimuli the behaviors are not exhibited or acquired. The environment in both cases controls the behaviors learned and the behaviors exhibited, without any reference to the mind at all. Sometimes operant behaviors are referred to as *voluntary,* but this term cannot mean that persons purposefully initiate their behaviors. Operant responses are thought to be shaped and maintained by the environment exclusively. Conditioning theory is thus clearly empiricist in its epistemology.

Among the behavioral sciences, it is not uncommon to think about cognitive models of memory as qualitatively different from behavioral principles of learning. This is due, in part, to the histories of these human images (see Chapter 2). When cognitive approaches to learning arrived on the scientific scene, they were hailed as revolutionary (cf. Ashcraft, 1989, p. 21; Ellis & Hunt, 1989, p. 4; Reynolds & Flagg, 1977, p. 4). Unlike the behavioral approach, cognitive theories and methods permitted the *mind* to be included in the learning process. However, the question arises: Did this revolution entail a new epistemology, with a new set of implicit ideas? As we shall see, it did not. Empiricism is, after all, a theory of how mind is related to its world. In fact, all the noted empiricists of old—William of Ockham and John Locke among many others—had "cognitive" models of learning and memory. The crucial issue is whether current cognitive models rely on sensory experience as the ultimate source of knowledge.

Solso (1991), in a widely respected U.S. text, affirms this about cognitivist approaches to learning when he says: "Fundamental to all human cognition is the representation of knowledge: how information, derived *from sensory experiences,* is symbolized [emphasis added]" (p. 9). According to Solso (1991), sensory experiences are symbolized and processed in other ways, but such experiences are nevertheless the root of knowledge, because all knowledge is "derived" from these experiences. An alternative term for sensory experience, given the computer metaphor of the cognitivist, is *input.* Nearly all cognitive models of knowing can be boiled down to this basic formula: INPUT → PROCESSING → OUTPUT. The environmental input with which the formula begins is processed in the mind and then output in the form of behavior. This type of theorizing is clearly within the tradition of empiricism.

Some cognitive models would not seem to fit this simple formula. These models appear to put more emphasis on what it is happening "inside" the mind than what is happening "outside" the mind. In fact, some models of memory seem to assert that processing is not governed by changes of sensory experience or the "data" from the environment at all. Some models appear to allow for knowledge to be generated from inside the mind by the processing itself. These models would, of course, not be empiricist, at least as we are using the term here. Nevertheless, one must be cautious before making this judgment. Many widely used models of memory are ultimately driven by sensory experience, despite an emphasis on internal processing.

Consider, for example, the distinction often made between data-driven and concept-driven models of cognition (e.g., Ashcraft, 1989, pp. 71-74). The data-driven model clearly fits the empiricist mold, because it is driven, or governed, by the data of the environment. However, the concept-driven approach does not seem to work in this fashion. In a concept-driven model, concepts that are already formed in the mind are the driving, or controlling, factors of memory. These concepts are thought to filter, construct, and interpret the data of reality and thus control how they are ultimately responded to. Here, concepts in the mind are at least as important as data from the senses. The dominant role usually assigned to sensory experience in empiricism is reassigned to cognitive processes.

This conclusion, however, is premature. Before we can know whether a concept-driven model is incompatible with empiricism, we must know the origin of the concepts. How did the concepts that supposedly drive the process of knowing come to be concepts in the first place? Most cognitivists are unequivocal in their answer to this question: Concepts ultimately originate from sensory experience (cf. Slife, 1993, chap. 5). Although mental concepts in some sense govern processes of knowing, these concepts are themselves governed by previous sensory experiences. Input from the past is stored in the mind, and then this stored input is used in the form of concepts to process present input. This gives a new twist to our basic formula above, but it does not change it fundamentally. The origin of knowledge is still sensory experience. The new twist is simply that old sensory experience (in the form of concepts) can be used to process new sensory experience. Again, this is quite compatible with empiricism.

The ability of empiricism to encompass several different models of learning (behaviorist and cognitivist) may raise a question we considered briefly above: Isn't it just common sense that knowledge begins with our sensations of the external world? If empiricism is just *one* epistemology, this implies that there is another epistemology that does not rely ultimately on sensory experiences as the governing principle or primary source of knowledge. How is such an epistemology possible? Questions such as these betray how empiricist our Western culture is (Fox & Slife, 1995). Our epistemological heritage, through pivotal British thinkers such as Locke, has ingrained in us this one way of knowing to the virtual exclusion of any other. In this sense, we do not *choose* empiricism because it is correct. For choice to occur, we need to know more than one epistemology from which to choose. Without some alternative, empiricism is merely passed down to us by our teachers, texts, and traditions, often without reflection, because empiricism was passed down to them, and so on.

This point is similar to the one made in Chapter 1. To truly evaluate and understand the ideas behind other ideas, we must have a point of comparison. We must have some contrast with the implicit ideas or they will not look like ideas. They will look like common sense or truth or axioms rather than the points of view that they really are. Some of us, for example, learn about the structure of the English language only when we try to learn a new language. A similar process occurs with theories and unfamiliar assumptions. In this case, an alternative epistemology— *rationalism*—is necessary to learn the strengths and weaknesses of the more familiar epistemology, empiricism. Sometimes one is tempted to reject alternatives, such as rationalism, out of hand. They are so unfamiliar that they may seem outlandish or counterintuitive. Still, we must endeavor to understand and seriously consider such alternatives, or their ability to elucidate familiar concepts, such as empiricism, will be lost. Of course, once we understand empiricism as a point of view, we may or may not consider it the correct point of view. In other words, alternatives serve to present us with options for our consideration.

AN ALTERNATIVE EPISTEMOLOGY

The epistemological root of rationalism is *reason*. Unlike empiricism, which is rooted in sensory experience, rationalism is based on the assumption that the source of all true knowledge is logical thinking or reasoning ability. Even the Latin root of rationalism—*ratio*—means "reason." Rationalists rarely deny that experience is important, but they do deny that all knowledge comes directly and only from experience. The 17th-century philosopher Descartes was famed for showing that sensory experiences cannot be completely trusted. Most people, in fact, have experiences in which their senses mislead them—magicians and illusionists take advantage of our capacity for sensory deception. Although this type of deception may occur relatively rarely, the problem is that we can never know *for sure* at any given time whether our senses are misleading us.[4] Descartes desired a firmer foundation for knowledge, one that he could always trust. But what could that foundation be? What approach to knowledge could lead to certainty and no doubts *at all*?

Descartes used the method of *skepticism* to find his foundation. Skepticism is a rather simple method. One performs it by subjecting a topic to doubt (or skepticism). If the topic under inquiry is found lacking in certainty—that is, it is doubtable—then it cannot be a firm basis for knowledge. Descartes already knew that his senses could betray him, so he knew that his sensory experiences could not be the foundation he sought. Descartes, however, was a religious man. Could he doubt that God existed? Yes, although he *believed* in God, he did not know with certainty that God existed. Could he doubt that he—Descartes—existed? Yes, he could be a figment of someone else's dream, about to wake up and find that he was not Descartes. The only thing that Descartes could not doubt was that he was doubting. Even if he doubted that he could doubt, he was still doubting. He realized that doubting was a form of reasoning, and thus reasoning had to be the foundation of all knowledge. Experience was helpful, but without reasoning, one never knew whether it could be trusted. In this manner, Descartes was the founder of modern rationalism.

Rationalism's historic roots, however, go back even farther than the 17th century. Much like the empiricists, rationalists trace their intellectual heritage to the ancient Greeks. Plato, for example, believed that the best form of knowledge was the kind that people conjured up with their reasoning abilities rather than experienced through their senses.[5] In fact, he "proved" this in a famous dialogue called the *Meno* (Slife, 1992). Here, Plato shows how it is possible for someone to learn and come to know through reasoning without experiencing the knowledge in an empiricist sense. Let us briefly look at Plato's proof, because it illustrates many of the claims of the rationalist.

As in all of Plato's dialogues, the main character is Socrates, who essentially speaks for Plato. Socrates contends at one point in the dialogue that Meno's slave boy can solve a difficult problem in high-level geometry without any formal education or training in mathematics. Through

Socrates's skillful questioning, the slave boy solves the problem and arrives at knowledge that is roughly equivalent to a mathematical theorem. Socrates does not tell the boy this knowledge, and the solution to the problem is not at all obvious. However, Socrates helps this relatively ignorant young man come to know something that only the highest intellectuals of his day knew. And this knowledge is obtained in a very nonempiricist fashion—Socrates helps the slave boy discover the answer in himself. From Plato's perspective, Socrates's questions provide the occasion for the boy's logical reasoning abilities to arrive at knowledge.[6]

Plato's proof illustrates several different aspects of rationalist epistemology. First, perhaps the purest form of rationalist knowledge is the logical reasoning involved in mathematics. As Bertrand Russell (1919/1971) demonstrated, logic and mathematics are virtually identical enterprises. In fact, mathematics can be said to be a precise articulation of logical relations (equal to, greater than, etc.). Logic enables the mathematician to advance knowledge (and learn) without ever referring to sensory experiences. Three apples plus four apples may equal seven apples "out there" in the world of sensory experience, but mathematicians can also advance their knowledge without real-world references, that is, without apples or other material objects. Indeed, many perfectly legitimate mathematical terms, such as the square root of -1, have no referent in sensory experience whatever.

Researchers in many other disciplines claim to advance their knowledge and learning similarly. Certainly, many people in the humanities would contend that their reasoning abilities allow them to analyze and synthesize important concepts and thus increase their knowledge. Similarly, theoreticians in many scientific disciplines would assert that they can increase knowledge in their respective fields without direct need of sensory experiences. Many scientists would insist that a theoretician's ideas be validated experimentally (and thus experientially). However, the reasoning that the theorist does in arriving at these theories is itself advancing the process of knowing in the discipline. Moreover, many theories are never tested scientifically, because the theorist can tell—through logic and reasoning principles—that the theory is not worth the effort. Conversely, some theories gain standing in the scientific community not because they best fit the data of sensory experience, but because they make the most logical sense.

Albert Einstein could, in this manner, be considered a theoretical physicist. Although he certainly considered experimental data and his sensory experiences related to physics, the advances he made in his discipline stemmed from his prodigious ability to reason. In fact, many of his advances in physics could be said to be a rejection of the "common sense" of his disciplinary experiences in favor of what his intellect told him. To accomplish this, Einstein used *gedanken,* or thought, experiments almost exclusively. Mathematics was sometimes involved in these experiments, but often Einstein simply reasoned through the implications of various concepts. Once, for instance, he imagined that he was on an object moving at the speed of light. At this imaginary speed, he realized that certain physical factors would be relative to that speed, and thus he arrived at his famous theory of relativity.

Another form of rationalism is represented by the 18th-century philosopher Immanuel Kant. Kant held that at least some human knowledge results from mental activity that is a priori. The term *a priori* has come to have many connotations in theory and philosophy. We focus primarily on the term's use in Kant's rationalism, where a priori factors are mental factors *prior to* experience. Contrary to the empiricists, Kant argued that experience does not simply come into our minds directly from experience with the outside world. Kant contended that our minds are naturally prepared to organize and give meaning and interpretation to the sensations we experience. Indeed, if the mind were not so prepared, the many sensations of our world would overwhelm and confuse us. We are not overwhelmed and confused, because we selectively attend to some sensations, organize them, and thus endow our experience with meaning. In short, *we* make sense of the world; it does not make sense of itself.

But where does this organization of our sensory experiences stem from? (The reader may recall that we asked this same question of the cognitivists above.) The organization cannot originate from the experiences themselves, because the experiences are the things being organized. Kant asserted that our minds have innate *categories of understanding* that structure and color our experiences. These categories are so natural to us (being innate) that we employ them unconsciously and automatically. Indeed, these categories and their operations seem so much like givens that we assume they are "out there" in the world rather than "in here" in our heads. In other words, we have assumed that the a priori mental structures that we use to organize the world "in here" are properties of the world as they exist "out there."

Two of Kant's a priori structures are time and space. Empiricists in the behavioral sciences and the larger culture presume that time and space are "out there" organizing our sensory experiences. From Kant's perspective, however, this is the same mistake that persons with rose-colored glasses make when they forget they are wearing the glasses and presume that the world is basically rose colored. Time and space, just like the rose color, stem from a type of mental "lens" that we all look through and use to organize our world. Actually, the nature of the mental lens we "look through" is a matter of debate among rationalists. The main point is that we all have some type of a priori factors that organize our experience, and thus this experience is not simply a matter of the world etching itself on a tabula rasa (Locke's conception). Rather, our experience is always a combination of the a priori organization and the world itself, without our necessarily recognizing which is which.

Rationalist epistemology has profound implications for modern science (see Chapter 6). Many behavioral and natural scientists today assume that *data*—a more formal term for empirical experience of the world—are the final and primary source of knowledge. As we mentioned briefly above, we tend to evaluate theories and validate or confirm them with data. This, of course, is the epistemology of empiricism applied to science: Data, or experience, are taken to be the primary source of knowledge. The rationalist, however, turns the scientific tables a bit. The rationalist reminds us that the data must always be interpreted—that is, data, just like sensory experience, are just confusion without some way to organize them (see Table 1.1 in Chapter 1). The rationalist reminds us that experimental data are not experimental *findings* without the organization imposed on them by the scientist. This organization comes at least in part from the reasoning abilities of the rationalist, including the rationality of mathematics and statistics.

Data, then, can never provide the primary source or final confirmation of knowledge. Although data are important to experimental findings, the a priori abilities of scientists are also important. In fact, one could argue that a priori factors are *more* important. Like Descartes, one could question whether data by themselves can be the firm foundation required by science. Data in themselves cannot "tell" us anything, because they are specific to the particular conditions under which they are collected and require interpretation. A priori factors, on the other hand, allow data to *mean* something (through interpretation) and permit us to reason through generalization beyond the individual case of these data to other cases with similar conditions.

The developmentalist Jean Piaget was a modern rationalist in this Kantian tradition. We spoke of Piaget in Chapter 2 as a structuralist, because he argued that the mind itself uses structures to organize and give meaning to experiences. In this sense, Piaget was a structural rationalist. Similar to Kant, he felt that we impose our own organization on sensations from birth, and we never stop imposing a priori structures. These structures are incorporated into Piaget's *stages of cognitive development.* Indeed, Piaget called his theory genetic epistemology, because he was quite aware not only that his theory was an epistemology but also that it posited genetic factors that were innate and universal (Rychlak, 1981). We could rightly change the name of his approach to genetic rationalistic epistemology. Piaget, like all rationalists, valued experience, but the rationalist notion of experience is not the same as the empiricist notion of experience. Experience for the rationalist is the natural combination of a priori cognitive structure and events of the world that Kant called *phenomenal experience.*

Both Kant and Piaget accepted the existence of an external world outside our consciousness. Indeed, this external world (termed by Kant the *noumenal world*) was for them essential to phenomenal experience. However, both also believed that we never have direct access to that external world, because our experiences are always combined with our a priori organization. At the level of science, this means that a truly objective science—in the sense of having direct access to the properties of objects outside of our consciousness—is not possible. Scientists are no different from other human beings; their experiences with their data are always interwoven with their interpretations, as guided by their a priori organizing. Therefore, the facts of science always have the scientist's a priori, nonempirical structuring mixed into them.

Are there rationalists other than Piaget in the behavioral sciences? As Rychlak (1981) notes, Kantian rationalism underlies most psychodynamic and humanistic views of personality and education (see Chapter 2 descriptions). Most psychoanalysts and humanists postulate innate ways in which experience is organized and endowed with meaning. Even Freud's id can be viewed as an innate organization of experience and thus a priori

(Rychlak, 1981). What about models of memory? Recall that many cognitive models place considerable emphasis on the internal workings of the mind, but are ultimately data driven. For a memory model to be rationalist, the "internal workings" must be more than a passive channeling of external information through encoding stages, storage banks, and feedback loops.[7] The mind must be integral to the experience itself, not something that *follows* or simply processes experience. If the workings of the mind follow or depend on experience, then the explanation is better understood as an empiricism, with the objective world dictating and governing the mind, rather than the mind organizing and structuring the phenomenal world. For the rationalist, sensory experiences and mental operations cannot be meaningfully separated. The mind is active right from the start, at the point of experiencing itself.[8]

POSTMODERN WAYS OF "KNOWING"

Although postmodern behavioral scientists are probably more in sympathy with the rationalist a priori than the empiricist sensory grounding for knowledge (Gelven, 1989), there are important ways in which both epistemologies are rejected. For postmodernists, the focus of attention shifts altogether from the mind to social processes. Traditional epistemologies consider social processes to be derived from more basic individual principles, such as learning and cognitive processes. Postmodern approaches, on the other hand, consider such individual principles to be derived from social processes, such as language use and interpersonal relationships.

We review two postmodern ways of knowing: *social construction* and *hermeneutic modes of engagement*. Although these two approaches differ in important ways, both reject empiricism and rationalism as universal ways of knowing that supposedly apply to all or most situations. Consequently, in postmodern theories no "principles" of learning are sought, as in the case of the empiricist, and no logically necessary categories of mind are postulated, as in the case of the rationalist. As we shall see, both postmodern approaches remove ways of knowing from the private mind entirely, placing them more within the sphere of social activity and discourse. Indeed, many postmodernists consider the whole concept of the mind a type of social myth that is perpetuated by the behavioral sciences (Coulter, 1979; Gergen, 1985).

Social Constructionism

Social constructionists are principally concerned with explaining how people experience and describe the world in which they live. Social constructionists look for common forms of understanding, common "constructs," or views of the world, that are created and shared by most people in a society—hence the term *social construction*. These common understandings are often compared to the common understandings of other societies, either in other cultures existing at the same time or in the same culture at earlier historical periods. Are these common understandings the same or different? Such comparisons can give us some idea whether the social constructions of cultures pertain to a particular culture or all cultures universally. This type of comparison also allows us to postulate which understandings are created by the culture and which understandings are perhaps more necessary and essential (Fox & Slife, 1995).

The results of these comparisons are often quite surprising, especially when our own society and era are compared with other societies and eras. For example, Western conceptions of personality vary greatly from Eastern conceptions. Westerners tend to endow people with traits and attributes that remain the same, even when the person is in differing situations. Most Asians, however, tend to identify people with their situations and do not consider them to carry around their traits from situation to situation. In Western culture, for instance, John's honesty is thought to be a trait that John has in numerous, if not all, situations. In many Eastern cultures, by contrast, John's honesty is linked to his situation, such as "John's honesty at the bank" (Schweder & Bourne, 1982). It is more accepted in Eastern cultures for such personality characteristics to vary from situation to situation.

Many other behavioral science conceptions differ markedly from culture to culture (see Heelas & Lock's 1981 edited volume). Explanations of emotion among the Ifaluk (Lutz, 1982), identity among the Trobrianders (Lee, 1950), knowledge among the Illongot (Rosaldo, 1980), and the self among the Maori (Smith, 1981) challenge conventional understandings in Western behavioral science. Even conceptions considered to be crucial to behavioral science as a science are often found to be bound to particular "cultures" (Kuhn, 1970), and many pivotal scientific concepts —such as causality, time, and space—have been shown to be socially constructed (cf. Slife, 1993). Traditionally, many behavioral scientists have dismissed these differences by claiming that Western culture is more advanced. Because the notion of progress has come to mean closer to the truth, any conception that is deemed more advanced is automatically thought to be more accurate as well.

Increasingly, however, cross-cultural researchers are challenging this type of thinking (Fox & Slife, 1995). More than ever before, claims of advancement and correctness are being viewed as cases of ethnocentrism. The term *ethnocentrism* is similar to the term *egocentrism*. Just as egocentric persons assume incorrectly that they—the ego or "I"—are the center of the world, so too ethnocentric persons assume incorrectly that their ethnic group is the center of the world. Increasingly, differences between cultures are being viewed as just that—differences—rather than as more or less correct. In any case, the mere fact that many behavioral science conceptions are not found to be universal leaves us with the distinct possibility that they are cultural constructions instead of logically or empirically derived truths. (We do not rule out the possibility, of course, that empiricism and logic are themselves cultural constructions—see Chapter 6.)

Historical comparisons of social constructions result in much the same conclusion. Understandings of the world that seem to be truths today differ not only across cultures but also across time—societies and their social constructs change over time. Consider our Western understanding of romantic love. Today it is common to view romantic love as the basis for enduring interpersonal relations, such as marriage. Consequently, behavioral science theorists who seek to understand and explain relationships must reckon with romantic love as though it were a natural part of such relations. The problem is that romantic love is considered to have been "invented" during the medieval period (11th and 12th centuries) of Western civilization (e.g., Averill, 1985; Leahey, 1992). Few if any relationships before the medieval period required romantic love in order to endure. Most marital relationships were arranged, and personal feelings about the mate were not considered relevant even by the persons in the relationships.

But what does all this have to do with ways of knowing and epistemology? A leading social constructionist, Kenneth Gergen (1985), notes that neither of the traditional epistemologies is useful for explaining these cultural differences. Gergen (1985) specifically disputes the empiricist assumption that sensory experience dictates the way in which the world is understood.[9] Are not reports of one's experiences grounded in language conventions and the very words that one might use to describe the world a product of social agreement? If so, the experiences of the empiricist do not directly access the world as it is. These experiences access the world as it is mediated by language, which is itself socially derived. This mediation means that our thoughts and descriptions, including our interpretations of our world, are socially constructed. Empiricists rightly emphasize the importance of our experiences, but wrongly assume, according to the social constructionist, that the experiences themselves are not socially constructed.

Here, the social constructionist draws heavily on the later work of the linguistic philosopher, Ludwig Wittgenstein. Wittgenstein's (1953) work is important because he was one of the first to study how people actually use language, both in ordinary talk and in more formal scientific discourse. Early in his distinguished career, Wittgenstein was considered an empiricist. He contended that words obtain their meaning from their correspondence to the objects of reality. Language was constructed by experience rather than experience being constructed by language. The word *chair,* he felt, received its meaning from its association to the object chair. This seemed to work pretty well, and indeed, because most Westerners are informally (and perhaps unconsciously) empiricists, this is often the lay person's understanding of how language acquires meaning. Problems, however, occurred when Wittgenstein moved to less concrete terms. The word *pain,* for example, does not necessarily have an "object" to which it corresponds. Pain does not seem to be associated with any certain outward behavior. We may notice people holding their chest and moaning, and conclude that they are in pain. However, we do not always conclude that we are in pain just because we hold our chest and moan. (Some of us may be singing the national anthem.)

Perhaps there is an "inner" object of pain. Wittgenstein studied this hypothesis very carefully, from several perspectives that space prohibits our describing here. One aspect of his investigation should give the reader a sense of why Wittgenstein eventually rejected this hypothesis. It concerns the spatial location of this inner object of pain. All objects or referents for words, whether they are inner or outer, should be susceptible to being located in space. With most objects, assigning a spatial location is relatively straightforward. If I hold a jelly bean in my hand and then pop it in my mouth, its spatial location is straightforward: The jelly bean was once in my hand and is now in my mouth. The spatial location of pain, however, is more difficult. If I cut my finger, I can say that the pain is located in my finger. However, if I put my cut finger in my mouth (as I did the jelly bean), it is not correct to say that the pain is in my mouth. Wittgenstein decided that *pain* and many other less concrete words, such as *sadness, education,* and so forth, are not assigned locations like ordinary objects. Thus, in contrast to his early empiricism, Wittgenstein was forced to conclude that many words do not have objective experimental referents.

What then is the origin of word meaning? Wittgenstein's later work suggested an alternative approach to language that undergirds the contentions of the social constructionist. Statements about pain are not descriptions of objects; they are *expressions*. Moaning expresses pain; moaning does not refer to the pain. Wittgenstein asserted that sentences such as "I am in pain" are the language equivalents of moaning, expressing the pain, but not objectifying it. Why is the sentence "I am in pain" the equivalent of moaning? This sentence is the social *convention*—one might even say the social construct—for the linguistic sound that one makes when one is in pain. If society deemed *mudget* to be the linguistic word for pain, we would be saying "I am in mudget" without thinking twice. The point is that the social agreements we have with others are the controlling factors in language. Even when we refer to our experiences, we must use language expressions that are not tied to objects. These language expressions are tied to common, social understandings that cannot be explained through empiricist epistemology, because they cannot be tied directly to our sensory experiences of objects.

Social constructionists are more in sympathy with the epistemology of rationalism and are sometimes referred to as *sociorationalists* (Gergen, 1982; Gergen & Morawski, 1980). After all, if Gergen and Wittgenstein are right, the people of a society must have the rational capacity to go beyond sensory experience to *construct* their understanding of the world. However, unlike the conventional rationalist, social constructionists do not believe that understandings come directly from an individual person's mind. Rather, understandings are derived from within the social aggregate. What is "rational," then, is the result not of some individual's reasoning process but of "negotiated intelligibility" (Gergen, 1985, p. 272). This term means that what makes sense or seems reasonable within a culture—what is "intelligible"—is "negotiated," or agreed on, by people within the culture. Often, cultural understandings seem to make no logical sense, particularly to people outside the culture, but make all sorts of sense to people within the culture. This is because logical "sense" is bound, according to the social constructionist, to the cultural conventions of the society that constructed them.

The upshot is that the social constructionist proposes a radically different way of knowing. This way of knowing does not occur simply through sensory experiences, such as observations or experimental data, nor through logical reasoning, such as thought experiments or mathematics alone. This way of knowing does not occur *within* an individual at all. It occurs in the *relations among individuals* as they converse and negotiate and share their world with one another. Just as the whole can be greater than the sum of its parts, the social whole as a social construction can be greater than the sum of its individual members. What we "know," in this sense, is how we understand, and how we understand is a product of historical and social discourse. It makes considerable sense, then, to suggest that human beings and their behaviors should be understood in terms of socially constructed knowledge.[10]

There are two issues, however, that social constructionism must deal with in order to offer a comprehensive alternative to the behavioral sciences. The first issue is relativism. It is one thing to say that social reality and knowledge are constructed, and quite another to say these constructions are true, that is, right, good, or adequate. Unlike empiricism, which appeals to common experience, and rationality, which appeals to "common sense," social constructionism has no firm standard for validating its epistemological and moral claims. Most social constructionists ultimately appeal to pragmatism—what seems to work effectively within a culture. This appeal, however, has its own problems. One is that pragmatism itself can be seen as a social construction, and if it is not, how does this conception somehow transcend cultures when others do not?

The second issue is whether social constructionism affords any unique or important way of knowing about the so-called real world. Natural objects, for the most part, seem unaffected by our social constructions and language games. Rain, for example, gets us wet in spite of how we might talk about it. The question, then, is whether social constructionism is relevant for our understanding of the natural world and our place in it. There are responses to these issues in the social constructionist literature, but what they are and whether they are successful are issues beyond the scope of our discussion here.

Hermeneutic Modes of Engagement

We cannot leave the topic of postmodern ways of knowing without a discussion of *modes of engagement*. Although these modes are similar to what we find in social constructionism as a basis for knowledge, their connection to *hermeneutics* sets them apart. Hermeneuticists agree with social constructionists that behavior is not determined by empirical laws, rational principles, or environmental causes that operate independently of the human being. As we noted in our description of postmodernism (Chapter 2), this leaves us with humans in relation to one another and their historically situated world. The term *hermeneutic* comes from the Greek word *hermeneuein,* meaning "to interpret." Just as Hermes—the messenger of the Greek gods—supposedly helped humans know the meanings of divine messages, hermeneutics is intended to help humans know the meaning of various kinds of messages, including the "message" of human actions. Therefore, hermeneutics is a way of knowing that is different from social constructionism.

The first formal use of hermeneutics seems to have been in religion. Biblical scholars were vitally interested in the original meaning of the various authors and works of the Bible. Wilhelm Dilthey is the person normally credited with bringing hermeneutics to the world of the human sciences (Dilthey, 1900/1976; Polkinghorne, 1983, p. 218). Because the meaning of human actions is not always apparent, he felt interpretive methods were necessary to make them understandable. Dilthey (1900/ 1976) took the hermeneutic procedures that produced an understanding of ancient biblical texts and applied them to the human realm of both verbal and nonverbal acts. Hermeneutics is now applied in many behavioral science disciplines to study meaningful human phenomena on the basis of "practical understanding." It is this practical understanding that is our primary concern here.

What we are calling practical understanding is a mode of engagement with the world that differs qualitatively from the modes of engagement employed by the rationalist or empiricist. Both traditional and hermeneutic modes were described by Martin Heidegger, an influential 20th-century philosopher. Heidegger distinguished between what he called *present-at-hand* and *ready-to-hand* modes of engagement, the first characterizing empiricism and rationalism, and the second signifying practical understanding. The rather cumbersome terms for those modes are a result both of their translation from German and the lack of comparable terms in English.

According to Heidegger, our Western intellectual tradition—with its traditional epistemological base—has taken as the standard of knowledge a present-at-hand mode of engagement. This mode is entered when we detach ourselves from ongoing practical involvement in the world. On these occasions, we "step back," reflect, and consider a more general and abstract understanding of the things of the world. This mode of engagement is usually so detached from things and events in the world that it is separated entirely from the "content" of the world and considered to be a "process" or a "method" for understanding. Examples include the logical or mathematical process of the rationalist and the experimental method of the empiricist. Whether rational or empirical, such methods are implemented by assuming that persons seeking to know the world are separate from and independent of the full context of the world they are seeking to know.

This reflective, detached mode of engagement, Heidegger noted, leads to a reflective, detached understanding of reality. History, culture, and everyday living are supposedly independent of the detached and reflective work of rationality. They become objects of study and reflection. Rational beings contemplate and experiment with reality as though it were separate from them. This separation suggests that reality consists of two separate "worlds": the subjective and the objective. The subjective is the inner world of the person, consisting primarily of an individual's consciousness and rationality, including a priori mental processes. Thoughts and feelings can take place only within this subjective world, the world existing supposedly within the boundaries of each person's skin. The objective world, on the other hand, is the world of things or beings as they really exist, independent of our own subjective thoughts. The objective world is found mostly "outside" the skin. The present-at-hand mode, then, requires that our reality be split into these two worlds.

This mode of engagement, it can be argued, has given rise to our traditional epistemologies. With two worlds—the subjective and the objective—it seems only natural to ask how the two worlds relate to one another. Empiricism and rationalism are essentially the two main ways in which this question has been answered. With empiricism, the objective holds sway over the subjective, whereas with rationalism, the subjective holds sway over the objective. Empiricists basically assert that the objective world of things, as experienced through our senses, controls and determines our knowledge and thus our subjective world. Conversely, rationalists contend that knowledge derives from our subjective abilities to reason and organize experience.

As popular as these ways of knowing are, they are not the most fundamental or even the most basic ways of knowing, according to Heidegger. He describes a ready-to-hand mode of engagement that denies subject/object distinctions and rejects the idea that methods of attaining knowledge of the world are independent of cultural and historical context. This is the mode we are in when we are actively engaged with the things of the world in practical activities. Practical activities are the everyday activities that occupy most of our nonintellectual (and nonpresent-at-hand) lives, whether they be verbal or nonverbal. Heidegger claims that when we engage in such everyday activities, we do not experience our world as a separate objective world. We experience the world as "ready" (to hand), because the world is prepared for us to use it. Indeed, the world is so ready (and we are so ready for it) that the world and our engagement with it become fused. The world becomes, in a sense, an extension of our bodies, though we are mostly unaware of this. This is because we are most focused on the outcome of our project and not aware of our fusion with the world that allows for this outcome.

Let us illustrate with some mundane examples, because the ready-to-hand is often the mundane. Consider Clara's lateness to a college examination. She lives off campus, so she must drive her car. Clara has all sorts of ready-to-hand engagement with her world as she comes to class. This is because her concern and her awareness are primarily focused on "getting to class." This is her engagement. The countless little things she does—opening the car door, shifting the gears, and turning right or left—are so overpracticed and familiar that they occur almost without her knowing they occur. Indeed, when we say "she turns right toward campus," our reference to "she" in this phrase could as easily include the *car* as the person. In a very real, ready-to-hand sense, Clara and the car—as they make the turn—are one. She does not experience the car as a separate, present-at-hand "thing" with certain physical properties, such as a fuel-injected engine and rack-and-pinion steering. She experiences the car turning as *her* turning toward her class.

In this instance, the car is not unlike our bodies. When a person grabs a hammer, that person rarely says, "My hand just grabbed a hammer." Although this may be true in a present-at-hand sense, we usually experience our bodies as extensions of us: "*I* grabbed the hammer." At these times, we do not think about ourselves as subjective beings "inside" our bodies, commanding the objective world of our arms and legs. When our legs operate properly, *we* are the people who are walking somewhere, rather than our legs being the objects taking us somewhere. In this ready-to-hand sense, all aspects of our environment can become extensions of our body-mind (because body and mind are not separable). If our task is to drive a nail, we focus on the nail moving into the wood as we strike it. The hammer as an *objective* entity (e.g., with metal of a certain tensile strength) is simply not in our awareness. Indeed, it can be said that the hammer does not *exist* that way. The hammer has become an extension of our arm, just as our arm is an extension of us.

Our awareness, in this sense, is holistic rather than split. While we engage in the ready-to-hand mode, we are aware of one world rather than the two worlds of the present-at-hand. This fusion of mind-body-world is vital to many activities, because it enables us to perform complicated sets of actions as though they were one action. Indeed, when we do move into the detached, reflective mode of the present-at-hand, we often feel overwhelmed by complex actions. We become self-conscious and find that our piano performance or our hammer striking is noticeably deteriorating as we leave our fusion with the world. This is because these complex actions are ready-to-hand wholes. To regard objects (hammers or pianos) *as objects* being manipulated by a subjective being (present-at-hand) is for them to lose their ready-to-hand identity. To regard the activities themselves objectively is for them to lose their purpose and their "natural" existence. The activities lose the meaning they once had for us.

At this point, Heidegger's two modes of engagement should be apparent. Now we must consider some practical implications of these modes, as well as Heidegger's assertion that the ready-at-hand is usually more important and, in some sense, the more basic mode of engagement. The hermeneutic distinction between the physical universe and the lived (or practical) world should be helpful here (Dreyfus, 1979; Packer, 1985).[11] The physical universe is the realm that traditional epistemology and the present-at-hand mode seek to understand. As we shall see, the lived world of practical understanding is the realm that hermeneutics and the ready-to-hand mode are intended primarily to understand. Let us begin with analogies of these two worlds, and then attempt to be more explicit about why this analogy is important to ways of knowing.

Consider the difference between a map of a city and an informal account of the same city from a friend who lives there. Objective reality is analogous to the map, whereas the lived world is analogous to the same city as interpreted by the person who inhabits it. We should note that the map is a result of detached, present-at-hand description. Although different maps emphasize different aspects of a city, all maps are abstract formalizations—using standardized formats and symbols—that depict only those features of the place that would be unchanged *if no one lived there* (e.g., pattern of the streets, layout of the buildings). This is why we are calling maps "abstract." The professional mapmaker must regard the city as a pattern of physical objects, without regard to the people who may live and work there.

The city as a lived world, however, is quite different. An interpretation of the city as lived in can be informative too, but this interpretation is not abstract, formal, or objective in any conventional sense. Indeed, it is necessarily personal, incomplete, and biased. This is because it is an account of the city from the practical and ready-to-hand perspective of someone who lives there: the best routes to take (for scenery or efficiency), the parts of town to avoid, the best restaurants, and so forth. This account of the lived world is admittedly biased and omits considerable information, but then that is why it is so useful and practical to a stranger. It gives *meaning* to the town, from a native's point of view. It also endows the city with a richness and flavor that no map could ever provide. In fact, this sort of practical account can be useful to people who already know the city. Unlike the map, which becomes useless once the pattern of the city is known, someone else's lived account of the city can give even natives a fresh perspective and an enriched understanding of their town.

The friend's account of the city is, of course, not the only account. Other accounts are possible, so there must always be something *beyond* the friend's account. However, this "beyond" is not some city in itself, some Kantian noumenal city that exists apart from our interpretation of it. In other words, the reason for the other interpretations is not that the uninterpreted city is waiting to be interpreted. The "beyond" in the hermeneutic sense is other possible interpretations of the city. The context of the city always exceeds our interpretation of it. The reason for the other interpretations, in this sense, is that no one interpretation exhausts that context.

According to the hermeneuticist, this lived world is the more basic and significant source of our knowledge. This claim may immediately strike some readers as odd. Most Western thinkers have been trained to think of objective reality (the map) as the less biased and thus more important source of knowledge. In addition, most Western thinkers have been led to assume that objective reality, including the environment, is the realm that governs and determines the lived world.[12] For a hermeneuticist, however, so-called objective reality is an abstraction much like the map. Although this abstraction clearly has its uses, it is but one conception of reality and a very biased conception at that. The hermeneuticist reminds us that a seemingly neutral and objective reality (like the map) is itself a point of view that has become popular for historical reasons (see Chapter 6). Its popularity is not a problem as long as we do not *reify* this view, that is, as long as we do not believe this interpretation of reality is *the* reality "out there." We do not want to treat the map as somehow the *real* city.

If we avoid reifying, then we have to admit that the supposed objectivity of reality is not its independence from interpretation and bias. So-called objective views of the universe are themselves a *type* of bias, a type of interpretation, similar to the map. The map, after all, is not the city itself. It is just one view of the city and doesn't even include its inhabitants (surely a necessary part of most cities). Likewise, what we take to be objective reality is one of many possible interpretations, all of them stemming from an interpreter. In this sense, interpreters are more "basic" than any one interpretation, because they create the interpretations. Similarly, it is the mapmaker who created the map in the first place. If the interpreter had had no use for the interpretation (the map or objective reality), no interpretation would have been given. It is the lived usefulness of objective reality that is the reason for its existence as an unacknowledged interpretation of our lived world. From this perspective, understanding the world of usefulness—the lived world—is primary to our understanding any interpretation of that lived world, even a so-called objective interpretation.

Consequently, when hermeneuticists study human behavior, they want to study it from the perspective that affords the *most basic knowledge* available, our ready-to-hand engagement with the lived world. To study human action from an "objective" perspective is to study it as an abstraction from the lived world. It may be an abstraction that has some usefulness, but we cannot evaluate this usefulness until we know the lived world in which the abstraction is to function. Of course, it is an interesting human action that creates an objective map that is populated only with lifeless things such as buildings and streets. Still, this action would be impossible to understand without first understanding the lived world for which it was created.

We should note before closing that the lived world of the ready-to-hand is not a subjective world. To have a subjective world is to imply that there is an objective world, and the hermeneuticist specifically denies that the world can be divided so neatly into these two realms. This denial is important because the existence of the two realms separates meaning (subjectivity) from objects in the world (objectivity), and the hermeneuticist views both as tied together in a whole—the lived world.

Consider the friend's account of her city. As she describes the city, she is not just talking about subjective feelings, as a subjective reality in her head. She is talking about *her city,* as a lived and practical place. Her understanding, and thus her description, stem from practical engagement with the city. When she talks about a particular restaurant, she might mention that it is inexpensive and yet has great food. This restaurant is not a representation of the restaurant in her head, that is, a subjective impression of the restaurant. She is talking about the restaurant as the restaurant itself. It is true that her interpretation of the restaurant could differ from someone else's—it is not unbiased. However, there is *no* interpretation that is unbiased, including the interpretation of the restaurant that considers it merely part of objective reality. The point is that interpretations are always *and* already interpretations *of* something.[13]

CONCLUSION

We have described in this chapter several different ways of knowing. We began with the most prominent explanation in the behavioral sciences—empiricism. Empiricists consider the ultimate source of knowledge to be the objects of reality, as experienced through our senses. The number of variations on this epistemological theme is very large. Empiricism encompasses most types of behavioral and cognitive approaches to learning and knowing, including many models of memory that are purported to be concept driven.

Empiricism also has implications for how scientists learn and advance knowledge. The objects of reality are again the focus and source of knowledge. As manifested in the "data" of experiments, these objects are thought to dictate the findings and theories of science. This epistemology of science has been so influential that the term *empirical* has become almost synonymous with *scientific*. However, science and empiricism are not the same. Empiricism offers one particular approach to science, and the other ways of knowing offer their own alternatives.

Historically, the chief intellectual alternative to empiricism has been rationalism. Both epistemologies can be traced back to the early Greeks, with Aristotle seen as an early empiricist and Plato an early rationalist. Rationalists call attention to our innate abilities to arrive at knowledge through reason. Perhaps the epitome of this type of knowledge is mathematics. In mathematics, knowledge can be advanced without reference to sensory experience. However, a priori abilities—those abilities that are prior to experience—are most often used in conjunction with sensory experience. Indeed, according to rationalists, such as Kant and Piaget, although sensory experience is necessary for knowledge, it is the a priori abilities that make our experience possible and sensible. These abilities supposedly give order and structure to our experiences.

Rationalism also has implications for advancing science. An emphasis on the rational is an emphasis on the theoretical, both as an end in itself and as a means of testing hypotheses against data. As an end in itself, rigorous theoretical thinking, such as that performed by Einstein in his *gedanken,* or thought, experiments, can advance science. Careful theorizing is also invaluable for scientific method. Rigorous reasoning can reject some theories without the expense of a scientific test. Rigorous thinking can also refine other theories to produce the most pertinent hypotheses for experimentation. In either case, abilities to think and theorize prior to the experience or data of reality are viewed as the centerpiece of scientific knowledge by the rationalist.

Postmodern approaches challenge both epistemologies. Although proponents of these approaches may be more in sympathy with rationalism, postmodernists do not consider our knowing to be determined by either rational principles or empirical laws. Postmodernists look to the relations among people and their world. This implies, in particular, that postmodernists do not maintain the traditional distinction between subject and object that is so important to rationalism and empiricism. It also implies that the focus is not on the mind, as the center of sensory experiences and reasoning processes, but rather on the social world of practical activity.

The postmodernist seems to be pointing to not only a different way of knowing but a different conception of the world that one is to know. Both of the postmodern approaches described here view traditional epistemology—rationalism and empiricism—as dealing with the physical universe as rendered in a present-at-hand form of knowing, because both approaches believe the physical universe is best understood as an abstraction. The social constructionist considers the more basic world to be the world of social discourse. Social discourse has two vital characteristics: It is constructed and shared by the people who live in it, and its language is constrained and created by social convention. Science is thus advanced by comparing the cultures and languages of different societies, both in the past and in the present.

The hermeneuticist views the lived world as more meaningful than the physical universe. The hermeneuticist accounts for common conceptions of the physical universe by noting how a present-at-hand mode of engagement—with its detached and reflective thinking—leads to a sterile and abstract understanding of the world and its objects. This world is considered one important means of interpreting reality. However, it is not the most significant nor the most fundamental interpretation. Indeed, the meaning and significance of even this physical world is thought to be found in another world—the lived world. In this lived world, objects and the people who interpret and use them are not independent in any meaningful way. The world is ready-to-hand in the sense that the world is ready-made to fit with our concerns, even to the point that this world seems to be an extension of our concerns. This lived world is a world of interpretation, a world in which meaning and the objects that are meaningful cannot be separated.

Notes

1. Some may question whether rationalists really do make up only a small minority in the behavioral sciences. We would acknowledge that aspects of rationalism have been

incorporated into cognitive and psychoanalytic theories. However, our experience is that thoroughgoing rationalists are relatively rare. They are so rare that their theorizing is often viewed as outside the mainstream of the behavioral sciences. The logical learning theory of Joseph Rychlak (1994) is a case in point.

2. Although Aristotle felt that knowledge begins with sensory experience, and in this broad sense can be considered an empiricist, he differed greatly from many modern empiricists, especially those in the behavioral sciences (Robinson, 1989).

3. Locke's legacy, through the empiricists who followed him, is perhaps more radical than the philosophy he espoused. We contend that this radical legacy is most visible in contemporary behavioral scientists and the way they look at ways of knowing.

4. Another problem we encounter if we rely entirely on sensory experience as the direct cause of knowledge is that sensory experience is constantly changing as things in the world change. Thus, knowledge that comes directly from experience is quite likely to change as experience changes. Empiricists argue we can easily be misled by our senses because any next experience can refute a previous one. At least we have difficulty claiming our knowledge is final. David Hume's work raised similar issues.

5. This rationalist simplification of Plato does not do his extensive philosophy justice, nor does it acknowledge the many readings and interpretations of his dialogues that are possible. For a more extensive treatment see Gulley (1962).

6. This interpretation of Plato's *Meno* is not exactly accurate, at least regarding Plato's intentions. Although a modern rationalist would probably interpret Socrates's demonstration in this manner, this interpretation reaps the benefit of the modern development of logic, which occurred *after* Plato and Socrates. Plato was instead attempting to demonstrate his *doctrine of recollection*. This doctrine held that Meno's slave boy was re-collecting what was already available—taught by the gods—before the boy's birth.

7. These more passive, innate capacities are more compatible with Locke's passive tabula rasa than Kant's active categories of understanding. In general, the rationalist view of innate capacities is more active and self-controllable than our usual notion that innate and genetic capacities are automatic and essentially uncontrollable.

8. To see how different this type of theorizing is from the more traditional empiricist theorizing, the reader is referred to the rationalist learning theory of Joseph Rychlak (1988, 1994).

9. We do not explicitly take up the issue of rationalism here, but we do discuss the possibility of logic itself being a social construction in Chapter 6.

10. In one sense, this claim is not radically different from that of certain species of behaviorism, particularly what is known as radical behaviorism. Just what differences might exist between social constructionism and this type of behaviorism is an interesting question with important theoretical implications. We suspect that the differences are significant. We do not, however, have space to pursue them carefully, and they are beyond the scope of this book.

11. We are not suggesting here—nor would most in the hermeneutical tradition suggest—that there are literally two separate realities. We hope the succeeding discussion makes clear that this distinction refers to two ways of interpreting a single reality, namely, the world. The discussion we pursue illustrates the attempt by hermeneutic thinkers to address the question we asked earlier about social constructionism: How is the world affected by our language-based conception of it? The nature of reality and its relation to human activity is one of the more important problems addressed by hermeneutic thinkers. The suggestion that the world and our interpretation of it are not separable, much less independent, is intriguing. However, we lack space to do justice to the issue here.

12. Part of the objective reality we could include here is the physiology of the brain. Traditional accounts or theories of brain physiology, in terms of objective properties and constructs, are usually seen as the most real accounts of the brain and its function. The physical brain, as objectively described, is taken to be the more basic realm that governs the lived world. Because the present-at-hand view of the body may not be the essential or fundamental view, the ready-to-hand emphasis of the hermeneuticist has important implications for materialistic reductionism (see Chapter 5).

13. This statement is a variation on the phenomenological notion of intentionality derived from the work of, among others, Franz Brentano and Edmund Husserl.

❦ 4 ❧

Determinism

❦ It is difficult to overestimate the importance of determinism in the behavioral sciences. Discovering the determinants of socialization, learning, group dynamics, abnormality, and effective management is the goal in most behavioral science disciplines. What if, for example, the determinants of depression were discovered? Although some behavioral scientists might claim that they already know what determines depression, current knowledge is more an educated guess than an exact understanding. What if we knew precisely the determinants of depression? Knowledge of this sort would surely provide a clear-cut comprehension of the phenomenon as well as suggest a surefire treatment of its harmful effects.[1] In other words, we would know the *cause* of depression.

The term cause is italicized here to help us see the intimate relation between causality and determinism. Many behavioral scientists, in fact, use *cause* and *determinant* as interchangeable terms, because each refers to that which is responsible for some effect. Conventional notions of causality are linear, in that causes are thought to precede effects in order to be the producers of the effects. This means that any determinant of

94

a phenomenon must occur earlier in time than the phenomenon itself. How much earlier depends on how far back the chain of causation goes. An immediate cause of an effect can itself be an effect of an even earlier cause and so on, allowing long chains of causes and effects. Such chains are sometimes likened to rows of dominoes toppling as each hits another in sequence. When causes are understood in this way, the primary or most fundamental determinant of any phenomenon must be the first or earliest cause in the cause-effect chain.

This is one of the major implications of conventional notions of determinism and causality in the behavioral sciences—they focus the behavioral scientist's attention almost exclusively on past events. The determinants of depression must, of necessity, exist in this past, because causality itself works in this fashion. Indeed, most people would assume this is just common sense. Where else could the cause of someone's depression exist, except in the past? The present could not be such a cause, because the present is just a fleeting instant of time, itself an effect of the past, and the future is never actually reached. The past is all that we have as a source of explanations and determinants—or so it seems to most people in Western culture. This type of reasoning amply demonstrates just how ingrained this conventional notion of determinism is. It is so ingrained that an alternative may seem inconceivable.

In this chapter, we show that alternatives *are* conceivable. We begin by reviewing the way in which most behavioral scientists understand determinants and determinism. Behavioral scientists, for the most part, follow the reasoning just described and generally reach the conclusion that all entities, humans included, are determined by their pasts. Here we present alternative forms of determinism, some of which are found in philosophy as early as the work of Aristotle and his notion of the four causes. Unlike conventional determinism, these alternative explanations are independent of linear time (Slife, 1993). They do not demand that related events occur in sequences like conventional causes and effects. Further, causes conceived from this alternative perspective do not require any passage of time to produce their effects. This means that the past as an objective set of events does not determine the present. Free will and other so-called unscientific issues are discussed in this light.

DETERMINISM IN THE
BEHAVIORAL SCIENCES

Conventional notions of determinism and causality guide virtually all behavioral science theory and research as well as prescribed treatments. With few exceptions, behavioral scientists limit themselves to studying past events in attempting to understand the present. In fact, there is amazing agreement about the importance of the past among behavioral scientists, who normally disagree about other aspects of their theories. Freud, of course, was one of the first to make the significance of the past salient, and most modern psychodynamic thinkers have not deviated from his emphasis on the past. Other theorists in behavioral science have also tended to regard the past as sufficient to explain present behaviors. Although conflicting with psychodynamicists on virtually every other issue, proponents of most other approaches concur that past events are crucial to understanding the present. There are exceptions to this virtual consensus about the question of determinism, which we will discuss in due course. However, the extensive agreement among these factions is noteworthy.

Most therapists, for their part, accept this popular view of determinism as well. For instance, it is considered routine in most therapeutic quarters to begin therapy by taking a "history" of the patient. This history consists of the patient's own unique experiences as well as important life events (e.g., previous hospitalizations). The therapy sessions that follow this history taking almost without exception revolve around the past. Although the emphasis on the distant or immediate past may vary from technique to technique and therapist to therapist, past events remain the primary topic. This primacy is understandable, given the notion that all disorders are caused by events in the past.

Educators rarely stray far from this common view of determinism either. Learning is frequently considered to involve the storage of past educational experiences or information. When teachers encounter learning problems in their students, they often look to the student's past for solutions. Perhaps this student missed an essential experiential element or piece of knowledge in his or her educational career. Cognitively oriented educators may use computer metaphors (see Chapter 2). If the learning problem is not in the hardware—genetics or the physiology of the body—then it must be in the software—the experiential programming of the student. Just as a computer may not operate properly without appropriate programming, students cannot function properly without appropriate learning experiences in their past.

What about science? We have described how theorists, therapists, and educators rely on past events and conventional notions of cause-and-effect chains in their explanations of behavior. Does behavioral *science* also depend on these notions? Not only can we answer this question affirmatively, but this approach to determinism is viewed as one of the foundations of modern science. In a prominent behavioral science text, for example, Ross (1987) holds that all scientific explanations must consist of proximate and ultimate causes, both of which precede their effects. He feels that "As a psychologist I accept the logic of [this form of] determinism" (p. 160). All behavioral scientists, declares another textbook author, believe that "Behavior is caused by previous events" (Ryckman, 1989, p. 89), and these beliefs have dramatic implications for scientific method. Experimental methods, for instance, attempt to measure phenomena "before" and "after" to discover causes and effects. Nearly all behavioral science investigations are based on this deterministic approach.

THE NEED FOR ALTERNATIVES

At this juncture, the dependence of behavioral science on linear determinism should be readily apparent. Scientists and educators alike give past events a privileged status in explanation. The processes that constitute or explain human behavior, as well as the methods that are used to study them, are considered to be sequential in nature—all because causes and effects are thought to have this temporal characteristic. The dominance of this view of causality is so extensive that it is often not considered a "view" in the behavioral sciences. Causality is seen to be a property of reality, occurring "out there" in the relations among events.

This approach to causality is, of course, another instance of reifying a hidden idea. As noted in Chapters 1 and 3, when notions, such as causality, are held to be the only possible views, it is but a short step to elevating those views to the status of reality itself—"out there." The key to calling behavioral science back to a realization of the "viewness" of this idea of determinism is to demonstrate that alternative views are available.

The major problem lies with certain philosophical ideas, sometimes referred to as *conditions of causality*. These, in the minds of many, are the ways causality *must* be understood. If a potential alternative view of determinism does not meet these conditions, then it supposedly cannot be a cause or determinant. This way of defining causation is itself a point of view. In other words, not only has linear determinism lost its "viewness," but the conditions that supposedly define determinism have themselves lost their "viewness." Only a questioning of these conditions will allow alternatives to develop. The current understanding of the conditions of causality lead inevitably to linear determinism. If the privileged status of these conditions were validly challenged, then alternative conceptions of determinism might be possible.

THE CONDITIONS OF CAUSALITY

Our modern idea of what conditions must be met in order for us to know whether a cause-effect relationship exists between two events comes from one particularly influential 17th-century philosopher, David Hume. Hume argued that there are three conditions for causality: *constant conjunction, contiguity,* and *antecedence* (Valentine, 1992). These three conditions have dominated behavioral scientists' approach to determinism; indeed, most theories are directly based on them (see Chapter 1). When all three conditions of causality are present, most behavioral scientists assume that deterministic or causal relation has been established. The condition of *constant conjunction* means that two events must be continually associated with one another to have a causal relation. Observation of one event would necessarily entail observation of the other. Observation of a particular business technique might constantly be conjoined with improved sales. Hence, it would be likely that the particular technique caused the sales improvement. Needless to say, we would require an extremely high correlation between the two events, perhaps even a perfect correlation, to consider the correlation causal.

The conditions of *antecedence* and *contiguity* specify the conditions of time and space supposedly necessary for causation. Two events must occur sequentially in time (antecedence) and near to one another in space (contiguity). In the case of antecedence, it is considered patently ridiculous for the effect to precede the cause. The cause has to be the producer of the effect. This is the very definition of a cause. Moreover, the *simultaneous* occurrence of two events would rule out any causal relation between them. Without some elapsed time, there is no time for the cause to produce the effect. In the case of contiguity, a causal event cannot occur in a location entirely separate from its effect. Although a chain of causes and effects can operate over some distance, the causes and effects *within* the chain must be contiguous or near to one another. A cause must be able to reach its effect directly.

Interestingly, prevailing theories in the behavioral sciences have tended to overlook Hume's contention that these conditions by themselves do *not* allow inferences about causality with certainty. Hume felt that we tend to infer causality—subjectively—using these three conditions as clues. However, these three conditions are not sufficient in themselves for us to know that two events are causally related to one another. Many events meet these conditions without being causally related. For instance, the hands of two independent clocks can be arranged so that they follow one another constantly (constant conjunction), are near to one another in space (contiguity), and move to all time positions one before the other (antecedence). Yet these hands are not causally related. This means, of course, that any set of events that meet these three conditions could be similar in nature—correlated events rather than causally related events.

Information about the correlation between two events—even perfect correlation—tells us only that when one event appears, the other event appears. Causal relation, however, must meet a fourth criterion also found in Hume's work. Hume posited that in order to know that A is the cause of B, we must know that there is no other possible cause of B; he referred to this principle as *necessary conjunction*. Some behavioral scientists contend that such knowledge is possible because experimental method allows for all other possible variables or potential causes of an event to be ruled out. Experimental method supposedly is able to control all but the hypothesized cause, so that if some (second) event occurs, we can safely conclude that it must be caused by the (first) cause we are studying.

Hume directly challenged this contention. How can we ever be assured, Hume asks, that *all* possible causes of the effect have been ruled out? We cannot.[2] The history of science is full of instances where one supposedly certain piece of knowledge is later found to be questionable and ultimately replaceable. As we demonstrate in Chapter 6, there is always, in principle, more than one way to interpret the data of any experiment, and therefore, more than one possible causal event. This means that the knowledge needed to infer causality—that one event produces another—is unattainable.

Some scientists have challenged this contention that true causal knowledge is unattainable. They argue that sometimes causality can be established through contiguity. They acknowledge that correlation does not necessarily mean causation, but they argue that a perfect correlation *and* a firm, contiguous contact between two events is a causal relation. They might claim that the two sets of clock hands in our example above are not truly contiguous. Because they are hands from independent clocks, the hands are separated. Causal events, however, must have no separation, because some sort of direct (and contiguous) contact is required for the effect to be produced. Therefore, the example of the clock hands might not be a true test of Hume's conditions, because the two objects (the clock hands) are not truly contiguous.

Are there examples of events that meet Hume's three conditions of causality, including clear contiguous contact, but the events are not causally related? Consider the head and handle of a hammer. The parts of the hammer are not only contiguous in space, they are firmly attached to one another. Astronauts could be orbiting the earth in such a manner that the head of the hammer first enters the lens of their telescope and then the handle (antecedence). Now if the astronauts were not already familiar with a hammer, they could mistake this antecedence for a causal relation, because at each orbital pass of the spaceship the head and handle would be constantly conjoined and clearly contiguous. The head, in effect, would be the cause of the handle. Given that we do not normally consider the head of a hammer to cause its handle, it is clear that even when Hume's first three conditions are met, we cannot distinguish causal connections from correlated events. Hume's three conditions, then, cannot be sufficient for objective inferences of causality, as Hume himself explained.

THE ANTECEDENCE OF CAUSALITY

Many behavioral scientists have proceeded as if the conditions of causality were the only conditions necessary to establish causality among events. The condition of antecedence has been viewed as particularly significant in establishing causality in the behavioral sciences. Antecedence has become so important that the presence of this condition alone is sometimes thought to be sufficient for inferring causality (Williams, 1995). If, for example, a behavioral science professional—a teacher or a therapist—knows that a child has been sexually assaulted, he or she is likely to assume that the assault will cause emotional problems in the child's adulthood. The other conditions of causality are often ignored. The child abuse and adult problems as cause and effect are not constantly conjoined, nor are they contiguous in time or space. The antecedence of the assault is all that seems necessary to many professionals to make all types of causal inferences about the distant future.[3]

As the physicist and philosopher Mario Bunge (1959) pointed out, this confounding of antecedence and causation is extremely widespread: "The confusion between antecedence and causation is so common that philosophers have found it necessary, very long ago, to coin a special phrase to brand this fallacy, namely, *post hoc, ergo propter hoc* (after that, hence because of that)" (Bunge, 1963, p. 189). Most behavioral scientists acknowledge this fallacy. They readily admit that the mere chronological ordering of two events does not make them causal. Although therapists, teachers, and business consultants appear to forget this occasionally, few challenge the fallacy in this practice.

A more important issue, perhaps, is the widespread notion that antecedence is *necessary* for causality. Behavioral scientists may admit that antecedence is not sufficient for causality, but most would assume that antecedence is necessary for causality. As we shall see, this assumption is common in the behavioral science disciplines. It restricts all disciplines to one type of determinism, ruling out many other potentially productive options. Therefore, some loosening of these conceptual restrictions is necessary before proceeding to alternative approaches to determinism.

Bunge's (1959) careful work on causality is again helpful. He has conscientiously reviewed the prominent formulations of causality and found, perhaps surprisingly, that "None of them contain the idea of temporal priority" (p. 63; see also Brand, 1976; Rakover, 1990). None seems to require that the cause occur prior to the effect. The reason is, as he demonstrates, "The principle of antecedence and the causal principle are independent of each other" (p. 63; cf. Bunge, 1963, p. 189). This independence does not mean that the cause can follow the effect, but it does imply that cause and effect can occur simultaneously. As Bunge (1963) puts it:

It is not physically possible for the effect to precede its cause, since the cause is supposed to give rise to, or to produce, or to contribute to the production of the effect, e.g., by means of an energy transfer. But it would be logically possible for the cause and the effect to be *simultaneous* [emphasis added] in a given frame of reference, particularly if they occurred at the same place. (p. 189)

Bunge (1959, 1963) is clear that the cause must be present in order for the effect to occur. This is true by definition, because the cause must be the producer of the effect. Nevertheless, this definitional requirement does not mean that the cause must occur *before* the effect. Occurring before the effect is admittedly one way to be sure that the cause is present, but its presence is not required before the effect. Its presence can be wholly *simultaneous* with the effect. Indeed, the cause *has* to be simultaneous to some extent with the effect for the cause to make contact with the effect. If the cause merely precedes the effect (and does not overlap with it in time to some degree), it would be separate from the effect and unable to produce it. The cause, in this sense, has a logical (or a definitional) priority in that it must be present for the effect to occur. Still, this does not require any chronological priority. The cause need not occur before the effect in time.

Unfortunately in our time-conscious world, a logical priority often becomes a chronological priority. What is supposed to be merely present (as opposed to absent) becomes before (as opposed to after). This misunderstanding is unfortunate because it rules out what Bunge (1963, p. 189) calls "instantaneous links." Recall from our discussion above that behavioral scientists have considered the simultaneity of two or more events to be evidence of a noncausal relationship, because some passage of time is thought to be necessary for the causal event to produce its effect. Although this elapse of time makes some sense in a causal chain, where the beginning cause of the chain is separated from the ending effect by time, a single cause-effect "link" in the chain cannot operate in this fashion. Indeed, as mentioned, some type of instantaneous (or simultaneous) contact is necessary between each cause and effect for the cause to have any impact on the effect.

Most researchers view simultaneous connections as an indication that events are *not* causally related. The personality theorist Carl Jung, for instance, was particularly troubled by this practice. He noted many events that he felt were pivotal to science and therapy, yet they were simultaneous (or not contiguous). He called these relations *synchronistic,* because many of them were simultaneous (or synchronous) (see Slife, 1993, pp. 81-83, for discussion). Nevertheless, behavioral scientists have felt that these relations could not be important, at least in any ultimate sense, because they did not meet Hume's three conditions, particularly the condition of antecedence. If, however, antecedence and the other conditions are not necessary to causal relation, then it is possible that a multitude of significant, synchronous relations are being overlooked, merely because one variable is not observed to precede the other in time.

THE FOUR CAUSES

The possibility that cause and effect are synchronous is seen most readily in the work of those philosophers and behavioral scientists who contend that antecedent causation is just one of several forms of causation. There are a number of theories of causation, one of which is antecedent causation; the remainder are rarely used in behavioral science (Brand, 1976; Bunge, 1959; Faulconer & Williams, 1985; Overton & Reese, 1973; Rakover, 1990; Rychlak, 1981, 1988; Slife, 1981, 1987a, 1993). As far back as Aristotle, many scholars have distinguished no fewer than four general categories of causality. The only one really compatible with antecedent formulations of determinism was called *efficient causation,* because it required movement (*efficiens*) across time. The work of Hume and the wide acceptance of the notion of linear time narrowed intellectual focus from the four causes to one: efficient causation (Bunge, 1959, pp. 62-64; Rychlak, 1988, chap. 1; Slife, 1993, pp. 16-18). Antecedence became a requirement of causation, and all behavioral science processes were then presumed to be the effects of linear chains of events across time.

Aristotle viewed all four causes as necessary conditions for the production of any effect.[4] When a carpenter constructs a house, for example, all four causes are involved in, and necessary for, the effect—the completed house. The *efficient cause* is the piece-by-piece construction of the house across time. First one pours the foundation, and then one erects the frame, and so on. The *material cause* is the material or substance of which the house consists. If the house were made of gelatin, for instance, it would be a different house altogether. The *formal cause* is the form or blueprint of the house. Without a specific form of the house in mind, the materials and construction process could not proceed or effect the particular house ultimately constructed. The *final cause* concerns the end or "finality" of the house. Undoubtedly, there is a purpose or goal associated with the house. If there were no purpose for the house, no materials would have been gathered, no blueprints would have been produced, and no construction would have occurred. In this sense, all four causes are necessary to account for any phenomena, including the phenomena of human behavior.

Behavioral scientists, however, have all but forgotten the last three causes. The reason for this forgetfulness is straightforward. These three causes—final, formal, and material—do not meet Hume's conditions of causality.[5] Perhaps most important, none of the three causes involve antecedence in their causal relations. The purpose, form, and material of the house do not *happen* across time, they just *are*. All three causes establish their effects through synchronous connections rather than the sequential links demanded by efficient causes. Furthermore, these other three causes can produce effects that are not contiguous to one another: Causes can determine events that are located some distance from the events. As Bunge (1963) puts it:

> Even if the cause and the effect took place at different regions in space, one could imagine that a physical agent might traverse a distance in no time—as has been held by most theories [in physics] of action at a distance. And such an *instantaneous* [emphasis added] action at a distance would be perfectly compatible with causality—Hume and Humeans notwithstanding. (p. 189)

This noncontiguous, simultaneous action may seem counterintuitive at first. Many Western thinkers have been taught, implicitly or explicitly, that Hume's three conditions of causality are necessary to causal relations. We must remember, however, that these conditions are not scientific facts, but philosophical biases formalized by Hume and shared by many behavioral scientists. These biases may be very familiar to us, but they are biases nevertheless—indeed, very questionable biases, even by Hume's standards. Consequently, we review each of the alternative causes or ways of talking about determinism in turn. Each type of determinism has evolved historically from its role as a necessary condition in Aristotle's original formulation to its role as philosophical assumption. No longer are the four causes employed as simply categories of principles that account for the makeup of a thing. They have become different assumptions about how the world operates and thus different ways of understanding how events in the behavioral sciences are determined.[6]

Formal Causality

In tracing the evolution of these causal constructs, we begin with formal causality. Formal causes are causes in the sense that what things are, or what they do, is in large part determined by what form they have. Another way to think of formal cause is as an "essence." It makes sense to say that the essence of a thing—its fundamental nature—exerts considerable influence over what it does. In this way, an essence is a cause. One could even say that the formal cause determines, in some sense, the efficient cause. After all, the blueprint, or pattern, of the house (the formal cause) guides its piece-by-piece construction (the efficient cause). The formal cause, however, is a static entity occurring simultaneously with its effects. It guides the carpenter *as* the construction takes place, rather than before. Although the carpenter can break the pattern of the house into separate steps for purposes of performing the construction, the formal cause demands all the parts of the pattern be together at the same time to form the pattern. The carpenter, for example, would not know where to place the living room (or know that it is a living room) without its simultaneous arrangement with the rest of the house. Seeing the various parts of the house in sequence (like an efficient cause) does not tell the carpenter the overall plan and position of the parts.

The formal cause, then, can only "work" or "determine" entities that are wholly present at the same time. How is this simultaneous determinism possible? Formal causation does its work through the relationship, or *gestalt,* of the various parts of the pattern or whole. The term *gestalt* has implied traditionally that the whole is more than the sum of its parts. In a sense, this "more than" is formal causation. The change that a whole undergoes when it moves from the "sum of its parts" to the "whole of its parts" affects the parts within the whole as well as the whole itself. When a blueprint rectangle becomes a living room because it is placed within a house pattern, this is an example of formal causal determinism. It may take time for an architect to place the rectangle on the paper within the pattern of the whole house. However, the determinism that results in a new meaning of the rectangle—such that it becomes the living room—stems

Figures 4.1 and 4.2. An Illustration of Formal Causality, as the Symbol for Female Changes to the Head and Upper Torso of a Stick Figure

from the rectangle's simultaneous relationship with the rest of the house pattern.

Formal causation also violates Hume's condition of contiguity. Events (or parts) can determine other events (or parts) without making physical contact with them. Because the relation among the parts determines the whole, and the whole determines the gestalt of each part, it is possible—perhaps even required—that some parts are changed or determined without any causal event being contiguous (or having any contact) with them. Consider the common kaleidoscope. When viewed through the eyepiece, the position of the colored rocks in the kaleidoscope sets up a colorful pattern. If just one rock is repositioned—for example, it moves as we turn the scope—the *entire* pattern is changed. This shift in pattern not only affects the rock that moved, but also the other, unmoved and untouched rocks (as seen through the eyepiece). The gestalt of the other rocks has changed (or been formally caused) even though they are not in physical contact with the rock that moved.

Consider as another illustration Figures 4.1 and 4.2. The symbol in Figure 4.1 has a form that, in some contexts, represents a female. Each portion of this figure can also be said to have gestalt properties. The top portion, for example, is typically seen as a circle—the simultaneous arrangement of a set of ink fragments (if the reader looked through a microscope). However, once another part is added to the bottom of this figure (see Figure 4.2), the other portions of the figure are changed for most perceivers. No longer is the gestalt of the top portion a circle. For many perceivers, the figure as a whole is now a stick person and the top portion is a head. The bottom portion does not make direct contact with the original circle—indeed, the top portion remains some distance from the bottom portion—yet the addition of this bottom portion formally causes the circle to be perceived as a head. Although adding the bottom portion may itself take time, the change from circle to head occurs simultaneously with our realization of the additional part. As soon as this part is added, a simultaneous change in the gestalt of the whole and the meaning of the other parts occurs.

This also implies that simultaneous change not only occurs all at once, but also can be observed "all at once." Unlike efficient causal change, it does not require two or more observations to track the beginning and ending of a change process, because the change "process" is instantaneous. "Before" and "after" observations can, of course, pick up instantaneous changes (if the observations are positioned correctly). Indeed, there *is* a type of sequencing involved in such change, as the circle perception shifts to a head perception. Still, this particular type of sequence is not efficient causal in nature. It involves no priority of the "before" (i.e., antecedence), no period or "length" of time, and no physical contact. From the formal causal perspective, the designation of "before" and "after" merely implies the order of the differences observed.

We may be tempted at this point to say something like: "Well, it is true that the 'appearance' of the circle has changed, but it is also true that the circle itself has not 'really' been affected." (A similar statement can be made about the change in the unmoved rocks of the kaleidoscope.) This distinction between appearance and reality is familiar to most people in Western culture. It is itself an embedded assumption that we could question, at least in terms of its status as "the way things are." However, we will not directly challenge this hidden idea here. We only note that the explanation of our experience of things—their appearances—is itself an important task. Moreover, some theorists would contend that we only have access to our experience of things. The original circle (or rock arrangement) is itself an appearance, that is, our perception of the circle requires our experiencing and thus our interpreting the appearance of its parts as the appearance of a whole. Even scientists, as we noted in Chapter 1, must interpret their data, relating the various data points into some meaningful whole. From this perspective, formal causal determinism is simply another way of interpreting the data of experience.

Formal Causal Interpretation

Formal causality may at times be the *preferred* interpretation, even in the natural sciences. Although we review some of the formal causal explanations of behavioral scientists, it is sometimes helpful to know that natural scientists have many findings, the understanding of which seems to require instantaneous change and noncontiguous determinism. Many quantum physicists, for instance, hold that electrons move from one orbit to another instantaneously (Wolf, 1981, pp. 83-84). Electrons simply disappear from one quadrant and reappear in another quadrant. This is very difficult to explain with sequential forms of causality. Further, this phenomenon should not be dismissed as merely an issue of the appearance, as opposed to the reality, of things changing. Although the "quantum leap" is the *interpretation* of these physicists, it is a widely accepted interpretation of "hard" scientific empirical findings.

The physicist David Bohm cites other empirical findings for which formal causality seems to be the preferred explanation (1980, pp. 71-72). He describes, for example, the disintegration of a molecule into two atoms. This disintegration essentially separates the two atoms and sends them flying off in different directions. While the atoms are in flight (and potentially separated by great distances), any attempt to measure the spin of one atom is *instantaneously* registered in its counterpart. No time has occurred in which to allow any "transmission" from one atom to the other, yet the two are somehow instantaneously related. Again, theorists who favor efficient causation are hard pressed to explain this.[7] Bohm and other physicists have clearly moved to formal causal determinism in attempting to understand these atomic events.

What about the behavioral sciences? Have there been theorists in the behavioral science tradition who preferred formal causal to efficient causal determinism in their conceptions? We have already mentioned Carl Jung in this chapter. Jung cited several examples of formal causal determinism both in science and in his own clinical practice. He tells of one patient who was in the midst of describing a dream that involved a scarab (Jung, 1960, p. 438). At the time in which the patient was describing the scarab—the most crucial element of the dream—an odd tapping occurred at the window of the therapy room. Jung turned around to see a flying insect knocking against the window from the outside. He opened the window and caught the creature—a scarabaeid beetle. The scarab had apparently felt an urge to enter a mostly dark room—in contrast to its usual habits—at the very moment the patient described the scarab in the dream.

Jung was quite aware that most people would dismiss this as merely coincidental. Nevertheless, Jung asked us to consider whether this is really "mere coincidence," or the Western thinker's need for an efficient causal (and therefore contiguous) connection between the two events. Jung would probably contend that the formal causal relation between the beetle and the dream is no different, at least in principle, from the relation between the two atoms (above). Their simultaneous and noncontiguous relation does not mean that they are not related. It just means that their relation is not efficiently caused. Formal causality allows for the two sets of events to be parts of a larger whole and thus simultaneously and noncontiguously related. Jung felt that such synchronistic relations are fundamental to all components of personality and self.

Gestalt theorists have also preferred formal causality for understanding their "laws" of holistic relations. None of these laws, it should be noted, works across time. Figure and ground, for instance, are always simultaneously related. The movement of a teacher (the figure) against a blackboard (the ground) is simultaneously determined by the nonmovement of the blackboard. If the blackboard moved with the teacher, the teacher would not appear to be in motion. The gestalt theorist Kurt Lewin exemplifies this formal causal tradition. He held that only events of the present can influence present events (formal causal simultaneity). He based his entire theory of personality—his theory of the "life space"—on this premise. As Lewin (1936) put it: "We shall strongly defend the thesis that neither past nor future psychological facts but only the present situation can influence present events. . . . In representing the life space therefore we take into account only what is contemporary" (pp. 34-35).

Structuralists have often explained their structures in gestalt or formal causal terms.[8] These structures, including the relations among economic and societal factors (e.g., Marxists), group or family members (e.g., systems theorists), and between genders (e.g., feminists), have been understood to be simultaneous with and yet causes of the effects they are presumed to bring about. These relations are not material causal because the structures are not palpable and substantial; this is the reason they are rarely observable. Moreover, these relations are not final causal because the structures are not presumed to "act for the sake of" a purpose or "higher" objective; they just *are*. For example, from the structural perspective, the qualities of an individual family member must be understood as emerging from that member's role in the family system. A "bad" father in one system might be a "good" father in another system. The qualities of bad and good, then, are not inherent in the father, but rather are formal causally determined by his simultaneous relationship with other family members.[9]

Some developmental theorists, many of whom are also structuralists, have contended that moves between stages of development are instantaneous. If such stages are different gestalts—different wholes that give meanings to each of their parts—then transitions between stages would require abrupt, instantaneous shifts. Piaget (1973), for example, recognized that each stage would not be a "stage" without its qualitative difference from the previous stage; stages depend on different qualitative states that change discontinuously, as a whole. If each "state" were continuous with the preceding state—that is, on a continuum—there would be one continuous whole. Stages would be distinguished only by their quantity (position, or point on the continuum) rather than being discrete wholes qualitatively different from one another. Piaget (1973) clearly affirmed qualitative differences between stages and therefore the requirement that change be instantaneous.

The formal causal influence of these theorists—Jung, Lewin, Piaget—has continued in the behavioral sciences, particularly in therapy. Many existential therapists, for example, differentiate themselves from the more antecedent-oriented theory of Freud (e.g., Yalom, 1980). If anything, these therapists focus more on the "future-becoming-present" than on the past as recommended by the therapies based on efficient causation. This is the reason many group therapists focus on the "here-and-now" interactions of their group members (Yalom, 1985). These therapists feel that the determiner of individual qualities is the simultaneous whole of the group dynamics—which can change from moment to moment—rather than each individual's past (Slife & Lanyon, 1991).

Material Causality

Much of what we have learned of formal causality is helpful in understanding material causality. Like a formal cause, the material cause of an effect does not occur across time (in a cause-and-effect sequence); the material cause just is. For example, wood-carvers may carve their material across time, whittling it down (the efficient cause) and shaping it into a specific form (the formal cause), but the wood as a piece of wood does not essentially change through this process. It is ostensibly the same wood before and after the carving. This means that the aspects of the wood—its physical properties—occur simultaneously. This also means that the wood's effect on the carving is simultaneous. A commonsense explanation might say that the wood comes first, before the whittling. However, this is a logical "coming before"; the properties of the wood are constant and do not involve any time sequence. At any stage of the efficient causal carving, the wood is the determinant of the hard and solid properties of the object. None of Hume's three conditions of causality are required to describe this determinism.

This is not to say that Hume's conditions are not sometimes mixed with material causal determinism. Indeed, the mixing of efficient and material causes is one of the most prominent explanatory frameworks of Western civilization. The properties of the materials are often combined with their efficient causal movement across time. For instance, the determinism of a nail as it moves into the wood is considered to be the efficient causal movement of the hammer in conjunction with the material causal properties of the nail, the hammer, and the wood. Without the dense and rigid material causal qualities of the nail, no amount of efficient causal motion (with the hammer) would move the nail into the wood. Often, however, the significance of material causal qualities is overlooked or considered trivial. The emphasis is instead on the determinism that occurs across time (efficient causation).[10]

Does this mean that behavioral scientists have ignored material causation? Certainly, biological explanations are quite prominent in the behavioral sciences. This is sometimes called *reductionism,* where formal or final causal explanations are "reduced" to biological or material causal explanations. We treat the issue of reductionism in Chapter 5 with greater detail. Here it is sufficient to note that material causal explanations are widespread. In education, for instance, learning difficulties as well as some discipline problems are often viewed as possible neurological deficits. In clinical or counseling psychology, there is hardly a diagnostic category that does not have biological determinism as at least a partial explanation. Many consider even a mild depression to be a biochemical dysfunction of some sort. In cognitive science, as still another example, many memory findings are being explained through neural networks in the brain.

Still, it should be noted that these models and their determinisms are typically a *mixture* of efficient and material causes. The properties of the matter are seen to exert influence over time. The material cause is assumed to have its effects, like an efficient cause, across time. In neurological explanations, for example, the brain is typically not viewed as a static entity consisting of its material properties only. It is seen instead as a *mechanism,* material in sequential linear motion, possessing all the qualities of efficient causation. Blood flows and neurons fire and synaptic gaps are bridged— all across time. The term mechanism is italicized above because this term is typically an indicator of an efficient and material causal mixture. It is rare in the behavioral sciences to find a physiological explanation that is not such a mixture.

Are there purely material causal explanations in behavioral science? This question can be answered affirmatively if we consider the more systemic or organismic understandings of physiological functioning. Although many of these understandings enlist the aid of formal causal determinism, many also attempt to understand the organism in terms of its material properties exclusively. Ludwig von Bertalanffy is perhaps the father of this mode of explanation:

> Mechanism [efficient and material causation] . . . provides us with no grasp of the specific characteristics of organisms, of the organization of organic processes among one another, of organic "wholeness." . . . We must therefore try to establish a new standpoint which—as opposed to mechanism—takes account of organic wholeness, but . . . treats it in a manner which admits of scientific investigation. (quoted in Polkinghorne, 1983, p. 143)

What Bertalanffy seems to advocate is a biology of the organism *as a whole,* without sequence across time. He felt that mechanistic conceptions tend to isolate parts as they move and determine one another, but ignore how the "static" properties of the "material" simultaneously determine its parts. The Russian physiologist Alexander R. Luria, for example, depicts the brain in this manner. Rather than adopting the usual strategy of brain localization, wherein specific portions of the brain are associated with specific physiological functions, such as vision or speech, Luria viewed the brain as operating as a total system, even when carrying out fairly specific functions. Neither Luria nor Bertalanffy rejected change across time. However, both felt that change is a manifestation of the workings of the organic whole as a whole. Efficient causation, by contrast, assumes that changes across time occur one piece at a time.

Final Causality

Final causality also rejects linear determinism across time. Final causality involves the goal, purpose, or end of something. This is the reason that final causal theorists are sometimes referred to as *teleologists*. Teleologists believe that their subjects of inquiry are caused by the *telos,* or purpose, they have. The entity under consideration "behaves for the sake of" a telos, or goal, and is therefore determined by it (Rychlak, 1994). This is often the commonsense understanding of humans—they behave for the sake of their intentions. As long as humans affirm their goals, such as getting a college degree, the goals determine their actions (e.g., attending college classes, reading behavioral science textbooks). If, however, humans change their goals, their actions change along with the change in goals. This applies to short-term goals (e.g., I want a pen) as well as long-term goals (e.g., I want a college degree).

As much as this type of determinism might sound like common sense, final causality or teleology is commonly misunderstood. Most of the misunderstandings stem from the notion that we have to think in terms of Hume's three conditions of causality. The first misunderstanding is that final causality requires antecedence or a sequence of events such that the goal must be set and *then* the actions for the goal will follow later. Although some teleologists seem to speak about goals and actions in this manner, most telic theorists consider the goals and actions to be simultaneous (cf. Rychlak, 1994). This is because intentions and actions are one (a whole). Without an intention, the actions automatically halt. If you suddenly decide not to get your pen, you will not reach for it.

Likewise, if a person is not acting, it is difficult to claim he or she has an intention. This is to say that to have an intention is to act for the sake of it. In other words, a *genuine* intention is one that entails action. A person may not do the action very well or may never finish it, but having a real intention is an act, and requires an act. When we see people who claim to have an intention, but act otherwise, we usually assume they don't really intend to do what they say. Rather, they have a different, more genuine intention. A child may say she intends to help with the dishes, but continues to watch television. We suspect that her genuine intention is to watch television. When intentions are understood this way, one cannot help but act for the sake of an intention. We are determined by them. According to teleologists, goals and actions are simultaneously connected—it is just our nature.

Our tendency to see things sequentially is at the heart of another misunderstanding about final causality—that the goal is in the future causing behavior in the present. This is sometimes referred to as *reverse causality*. Reverse causality is the notion that a cause can follow an effect in time and still produce it. As Bunge (1963) noted, this is very difficult to understand and seems to be prohibited by most formal definitions of causality. If it is in the definition of a cause that it can "produce" the effect, how can it follow the effect? Fortunately, we do not have to answer this question to understand final causal explanations, because teleologists typically do not propound any type of reverse causality. Goals are not viewed as occurring in some future dimension of time that follows the present. Goals are present images of the future, affecting present actions— the present causing the present. Like formal cause theorists, teleologists contend that the goal and the action—cause and effect—are simultane- ous. And as Bunge (1963, p. 189) himself noted, the simultaneity of cause and effect is quite compatible with the formal definitions of causality and determinism.

Another implication of the simultaneity of goal and action is discon- tinuous change—a change in the goal of our behavior can occur instan- taneously. Because the action related to an intention is required only by the intention of that instant, intentions and actions can be changed in the very next instant. No passage of time is necessary. The goal of a college degree—with the accompanying action of reading a textbook—can abruptly be changed to the goal of having fun—with the accompanying action of throwing a frisbee. The goal never has to be completed in any final cause relationship. The final cause merely determines our actions while we main- tain the goal. Theoretically, we can change our intentions and actions at every moment of every day.

Normally, however, we affirm goals across time and act for the sake of whole patterns of action. Often we are not even aware of any "decision" to affirm a goal. We decide on the goal of walking to lunch, and in the decision, the pattern of action is determined. This is a type of teleological habit. Of course, some decisions, such as to obtain a college degree, can determine a goal-oriented behavior pattern lasting several years. Still, even the decision to pursue a degree must be continually, or at least frequently, reaffirmed for the pattern of action to continue. Some of the most stalwart college students occasionally "let go" of their educational goals and pursue other short-term goals, such as throwing a frisbee. These students are likely to return to their long-term goals. However, the fact that they occasionally play with frisbees illustrates the everyday shifting of goals and their determined actions.

Another misunderstanding of final causality is that such intentions are caused by past events. Teleologists hold that intentions and purposes are the causes of the actions that accompany them; they do not result from an efficient causal chain of events that precede them. Nevertheless, the assumed necessity of Hume's antecedence leads many theorists to presuppose that intentions and purposes are themselves caused by events that precede them. For example, many behaviorists postulate that a goal of obtaining a college degree is itself caused by prior conditioning from one's environment. One's parents may have praised or reinforced behaviors and attitudes that resulted in the goals one is *supposedly* "behaving for the sake of."

The term supposedly is italicized because if this description of goal-directed behavior is correct, the goal can no longer be a final cause. In this case, the person is not really behaving for the sake of a goal, as final causation would suggest; the goals and actions of the person are both caused by past experiences. The goal, in this sense, is just a label for accumulated past experiences. In other words, when a goal is itself caused by antecedent experiences, it ceases to be a final cause and becomes instead the result of an efficient cause, and the efficient cause is the real cause of the action. Indeed, as long as antecedence is considered *the* approach to explanation, no final cause can ever be considered to be the true explanation of a phenomenon. Explanation in terms of goals that teleologically determine actions will always be viewed as incomplete explanation. Some antecedent event will always be viewed as taking precedence. If, however, we keep in mind that antecedence is not necessary for explanation, we can begin to entertain nonlinear explanations such as teleology.

Different Types of Teleology

As Rychlak (1981, 1988) describes, three types of teleological explanation have been formulated in the course of our intellectual history. The

first, *deity teleology,* is based on the assumption that entities and events
are determined by the purposes or intentions of a deity. The physicist
Isaac Newton, for example, assumed a deity teleology when he postulated
that God purposely ordered the world so that scientific laws and principles could be discovered. Although Newton presumed that these laws
and principles were themselves efficient causal in nature, their nature was
originally created by the God who acted for the sake of this mechanistic
order (Slife, 1995b). Many behavioral scientists probably make similar
presuppositions, assuming some sort of world order based on religious
beliefs. However, these presuppositions are typically not considered relevant
to today's science. Although this is certainly debatable, science and
religion have historically been seen as antagonistic, and one's theology is
often viewed as irrelevant, if not inimical to one's science.

The second type of teleology is *natural teleology.* This final causal approach
assumes that nature itself is directed in accordance with purposes. Some
formulations of evolution, for example, postulate that nature in its evolutionary movement is "headed toward" the goal of higher development.
Evolution, in this sense, is not pushed by past events as much as it is
pulled by the future. Again, this does not necessarily mean that the cause
follows the effect chronologically, because the purposeful determinants
of natural teleology can be implicit in present evolutionary events and
structures, for example, genetics. Similarly in the behavioral sciences, some
developmentalists have viewed the "evolution" of persons as directed by
a natural teleology. Piaget, for instance, spoke of a "teleonomic" understanding of a person's development (Rychlak, 1981, p. 685). The psychotherapist Carl Rogers (1951) also hypothesized the existence of an
organismic wisdom of the body that naturally "behaved for the sake of"
improvement in one's personality.

The third type of teleology is probably the most common in the
behavioral sciences—*human teleology.* This is the notion that humans can
behave for the sake of their *own* intentions. No assumption of a deity
teleology or a natural teleology is required for this approach, though
neither is necessarily incompatible. Human teleology assumes that people have the capacity to formulate goals and behave for the sake of them.
Many classical personality theorists have made this assumption. Carl Jung,
Alfred Adler, and George Kelly are just a few of the theorists who have
formulated theories that invoke explicitly human teleology. Jung, for example, theorized that humans behave for the sake of conscious and uncon-

scious ideas called complexes. Adler felt that people are largely determined by what has occurred by age 5—but not by efficient causes. Adler believed that humans form their general goals around age 5 and behave for the sake of those goals the remainder of their lives.[11]

Many modern behavioral scientists have endorsed some form of human teleology, particularly those from the so-called third force of behavioral science—humanism. Perhaps surprising, however, many of the best known humanists, such as Carl Rogers and Abraham Maslow, were not explicit about their human teleological leanings. Rogers, for example, clearly had natural teleology in his theorizing, as we noted above. However, Rogers said relatively little about capacities that allow humans to formulate their own goals and behave for the sake of them. More recently, other humanists have been much clearer on this issue. Joseph Rychlak (1994) and George Howard (Howard & Conway, 1986), for example, not only explicitly call themselves human teleologists, but also conduct considerable scientific research on topics related to telic theorizing.

An important aspect of most human teleologies is their association with human agency; many human teleologists assume that humans are agents of their actions, that behaviors are *not* determined by environments. This is because a human teleologist assumes that humans formulate their own intentions and can behave for the sake of them. To formulate goals, humans must be agents. If the environment determines human minds and behaviors by efficient causes—as many behavioral scientists contend—then the environment determines human intentions and goals as well. If this is true, then factors related to the environment, such as conditioning, input, stored memories, stimuli, and so on, are the determiners of goals, and the human being is not. By definition no human teleology would be possible; humans can be assigned goals (e.g., by a boss), but human teleology requires that persons must be able to choose to make these assigned goals their own goals.

FREE WILL AND DETERMINISM

This notion of choosing has been historically important to most final causal theorists. In fact, most teleologists have endorsed some form of *free will* in their explanations (e.g., Howard & Conway, 1986; Rychlak, 1988, 1994; Tageson, 1982). Given the need for human agency in

teleologies, this endorsement is understandable. Teleologists have required some means of separating the intentions from the causal influences
of the past, as well as some means of connecting decision making to goal
orientation. Free will seems to fill both of these requirements quite nicely.
The term *free* connotes its independence from the determinism of past
events; *will* connects persons' decisions to their goals and desires. In this
sense, free will is considered to be important to, if not necessary for, final
causal determinism.

Many behavioral scientists view this linking of free will and causal
determinism as an inherent inconsistency in teleological theories. These
scientists consider free will to be incompatible with, if not diametrically
opposed to, determinism. This is partly because determinism has been
thought to be synonymous with efficient causation. If we view persons
as efficiently caused, then they cannot possess free will. Such persons are
the end products of cause-and-effect chains and must behave consistently
by with those chains. Free will, on the other hand, allows people to "do
otherwise, circumstances remaining the same" (Van Inwagen, 1983)—
that is, persons who are free have the ability to choose a path that is
inconsistent with their past. They can, as *Webster's New Collegiate Dictionary* puts it, "escape causal law" (1981, p. 454). Of course, what this
dictionary terms causal law is *efficient* causal law, but if one must escape
efficient causation to be free, then it should be clear why many people
consider free will and determinism to be incompatible.

Many scientists also consider free will to be unscientific. This is
primarily due to their belief that free will prevents predictability. Predictability is often seen as one of the chief goals of science. Prediction seems
to require efficient causality, earlier events causing later events. If, however, humans have free will, then they could choose or will to do otherwise
than past events would dictate. In that case, a behavioral scientist could
study and examine every event of a person's life and still not be able to
predict the person's future behavior. At any point the person may choose
to act in a way inconsistent with his or her past experiences. For example,
Fred always obeyed his oppressive boss until one day he chooses to tell
him off. Everyone in the office who knows Fred is surprised, because this
is unlike Fred and their 30 years of past experiences with Fred. Nevertheless, free will theorists and many human teleologists hold that this is a
capacity that Fred has always had. He just has not chosen to exercise this
"tell him off" option until now.

Is this an acceptable explanation of Fred's behavior? Many behavioral scientists would say no, because choices are presumably incompatible with determinism and science. However, this negative answer overlooks the fact that this incompatibility involves only efficient causal determinism and efficient causal interpretations of science. As we described above, not only do many teleologists view final causal determinism as compatible with free will, but human teleology seems to require some sort of freedom of will. Moreover, free will is quite compatible with our broader notion of determinism as "that which is responsible for" an effect. A freely willed goal, in this sense, can be responsible for thoughts and behaviors. Indeed, some theorists contend that a person without free will cannot be held *morally* responsible. How can we hold anyone responsible if past programming or family or biology is really responsible for his or her behaviors?

Free will and human teleology have their own form of predictability. Admittedly, this predictability is not based on efficient causes in the sense that past events can predict the present with perfect accuracy. However, if one's will or intention determines one's actions, then any knowledge about this will or intention allows predictability. This predictability is based on a final cause. If Fred had informed us of his intention before he stepped into his boss's office, we would have been able to predict that he was going to tell him off. If we know that someone has moved to a college with the expressed goal (or free will) of pursuing a college degree, we can make several predictions about his or her behavior over the course of many weeks and months. This type of predictability is not the past "pushing" present behaviors and thoughts; according to teleologists, this is the "future" in the present "pulling" them.

Human teleologists also contend that people maintain some consistency in their freely willed choices and goals. For example, most people who pursue the longer-term goal of a college education tend to make shorter-term choices that are consistent with this. There is no mystery in this from the perspective of a teleologist. Why would anyone choose a long-term goal unless he or she intended to make some consistent and predictable effort to achieve it? One aspect of final causal determinism is that intentions and choices often determine other intentions and choices. Sometimes this consistency across time is mistaken for efficient causal consistency, because the past is predictive of the present. However, this consistency is more due to the predictability of one's choices than the causality of past events.

It is true that perfect prediction is not always possible. Fred may get cold feet and decide not to tell off his boss, or a person may decide that a college education is not for him or her and quit school. Still, a type of perfect prediction is achieved with final causation, because one's actions are always consistent with one's goals. If we were able to monitor a person's goals (and changes in the goals) we could theoretically achieve perfect prediction of the accompanying actions. We would see intentions and actions match perfectly every time. However, such perfect prediction does not reflect causality across time. The intention happens simultaneously with the behavior, and this violates our usual (efficient causal) notions of predictability across time. In this sense, then, science itself requires broadening, so that it does not close off other forms of predictability because of mere philosophical bias.

If science were broadened in this manner, many theorists and researchers in the behavioral sciences would be more at home in the behavioral science community. Many, if not the majority of, behavioral scientists use free will language at least part of the time. Terms such as *choice, option, desire, volition, decision making, selection,* and *agency* are found in the theories and models of many behavioral science disciplines. Of course, many third-force theorists, as teleologists, employ these terms quite liberally. However, even some behavioral, cognitive, and psychodynamic theorists, along with like-minded educators, therapists, and business consultants, appear to use these as well. Although some of these behavioral scientists would claim that the meanings of these terms are not based on conventional notions of free will, many cognitive and psychodynamic behavioral scientists seem to have no difficulty adopting some type of free will in their theoretical frameworks (e.g., Bandura, 1986; Kohut, 1978). Even some theorists who consider themselves behaviorists adopt an explanatory language sprinkled with terms like *choice.* These behaviorists take their inspiration from particular readings of the work of B. F. Skinner and are sometimes referred to as radical behaviorists (Lee, 1988). It may be, however, that these neobehaviorists, like other theorists we mention in this section, talk of free will and intentions, but understand the terms in such a way that human agency is not possible.[12]

HUMAN CONTEXT OF AGENCY

Many postmodernists have difficulty adopting explanations for behavior based on the traditional notion of free will. This may seem surprising in view of their explicit rejection of efficient causal frameworks and avowed belief in human agency. Postmodernists, however, are *post*modern in part because they do not accept the dualism of modernism, the dualism of subject and object. Since the time of Descartes, Western thinkers have tended to separate the world into two parts: the inner world of subjectivity and the outer world of objectivity. The inner world supposedly contains our private emotions and thoughts; the outer world supposedly contains the public and real world of objects and environments.

Postmodernists reject this separation of worlds. They believe it must be rejected in order to preserve any meaningful understanding of the world. One's emotions, for instance, cannot be understood apart from the circumstances in which the emotions are embedded. To love without loving something or someone is meaningless. From a postmodern perspective, the subjective aspect of loving—the supposedly private aspect—must be understood in the context of what is considered objective—the loved—for either the subjective or objective to be meaningful. The contextuality of love is not just an interaction of two realms—loving and the loved. They constitute a holistic act. Postmodernists make the case that the two supposed realms must really be only one, and this oneness must itself differ radically from either subjectivity or objectivity. The "loved" cannot first occur (as a separate entity) and *then* be united with someone's "loving" it. This oneness must be a being-in-the-world, the hyphens of this phrase denoting the inseparability of being (as a verb) and world.

The notion of free will, however, is often conceptualized as a subjective capacity that affects objective things through our actions. This dualistic nature is primarily the reason many postmodernists are critical of free will (Williams, 1992). Just as love cannot be understood as an emotion inside the person attached to an object outside, so too free will cannot be understood as an intention inside causing an action outside. In other words, free will cannot be a meaningful or practical thing unless it is seen as an act in the context of circumstances and other actions. A choice to eat vanilla rather than chocolate ice cream cannot be separated from the actuality of the ice cream. A decision to attend one university over another university involves the universities themselves or at least their perceived advantages and disadvantages. Even the list of advantages and disadvantages is embedded in a specific set of circumstances that cannot be considered solely subjective or objective. To be involved enough with the universities to have a list of advantages and disadvantages is after all an action that occurs within a rich context.

Unfortunately, the contextual nature of free will is not just a technicality. Context is not something that can just be "added on" to the conception of a free will. One cannot simply will something freely and *then* translate it into the context in which the willing is done. If one chose between two options *before* considering the context of the options—information about their advantages and disadvantages—this choice could certainly be said to be free. No circumstance or context could be said to have determined or influenced it. However, without these circumstances how meaningful would this choice be? What kind of choice is a choice in a vacuum, before consideration of the information relevant to that choice? Such a choice would necessarily be arbitrary or random, because it could not be based on anything.

If on the other hand we concede that the exercise of free will must be connected in some sense to context and circumstances, what does this do to the "freeness" of will? As we noted in the description of free will above, one of the main attractions of a "free" will is its separation from present circumstances and past experiences. Free will functions to keep people from being determined by those circumstances. If, however, the will cannot be separated from its circumstances, as postmodernists claim, then the original attractiveness and connotation of its freeness would at least be diminished, if not destroyed. No one claims that the circumstances from which we choose are free or under our control, so the degree to which circumstances are related to choices is the degree to which our choices are not free.

What is the answer to this dilemma? A will cannot be free in the sense of total *independence* from its context, because this would imply that our will cannot take into account its own context. This would make the will random or arbitrary. Neither can the will be totally *dependent* on its context, because this would take away the freeness of the will. Context would determine our will and no agency would be possible. What about a mixed approach to free will where our behaviors are partly determined and partly free? This might appear to allow some freedom and some consideration of context. Unfortunately, things cannot function this way. The degree to which this approach is independent is the degree to which it is random, and the degree to which the approach is dependent is the degree to which it is determined. The most that a combination of the two would produce is some form of determined randomness. It is difficult to imagine this approach as a satisfactory answer to the issue of free will.

The postmodernist, then, asks us to forego the illusion of a truly free and autonomous will, at least in the sense of its independence from context. Context and will must be integrally related, if not one whole. This means that constraints on our context (and even our own actions that follow our choices) are constraints on our lived will. Our will must be formulated in terms of a culture and language that meaningfully constrain our choices and desires. The term *constrain,* however, does not necessarily mean *determine* in the way that term is typically used in the behavioral sciences. Indeed, the usual notion of determine is itself a modernist dualism, because the determiner is thought to be separate from the determined (e.g., the environment causing the person). If as some postmodernists would argue, no such separation occurs, then the person is an integral part of the context. This allows for the person to have a *contextual agency.* The person's actions are definitely contributive to the circumstances as a whole, but these actions are not separate from the circumstances and thus not free in the conventional sense.

CONCLUSION

At this point, many ideas related to determinism have been introduced, from holistic patterns to free will. Our goal has been to examine the conventional notion of determinism so that its hidden ideas might be revealed. To that end, we have presented some alternatives to this conventional notion, including optional determinisms as well as free will. Behavioral scientists disagree about the relative merits of these alternatives, and the main purpose for discussing them here is to promote understanding of the assumptions inherent in our usual notions. It is also important to see the philosophical basis of these notions. Often, determinism is presented as though it were an empirical fact or an indisputable axiom. Nothing could be farther from the truth. Not only is determinism a philosophical conception, rather than a fact, but the conventional approach to determinism is highly questionable. Recognition of this should facilitate more discussion about this crucial issue.

Alternative determinisms stem from alternative causalities. The complication is that there are at least four types of cause (and thus determinants) available for explanation. What most behavioral scientists mean by determinism is one type of determinism—efficient causality—that meets the three conditions of causality formulated by David Hume. This means that cause and effect must be highly correlated, occur in a certain chronological order, and be located near to one another. This understanding of causality seemed to set determinism and behavioral science on a firm foundation. Unfortunately, these conditions, as Hume himself realized, are neither necessary nor sufficient for understanding cause and effect. This realization challenges many explanations and practices of the behavioral sciences—most notably the use of the past for explaining the present.

Acknowledging that efficient causality is neither necessary nor sufficient for explaining events also opens the door for alternative notions of causality. Many behavioral scientists employ these alternative conceptions to understand their topics of interest. These other three causes all suggest that events in the present explain the present. Formal causation uses the holistic relations among things, material causation depends on the simultaneous properties of materials, and final causation relies on the present intentions to explain the present. Moreover, without the determinism of the past (and efficient causation), the notion of free will becomes more conceivable and more palatable to many theorists. Final causal theorists in particular have contended that a freely formulated intention (or a will) is necessary to provide adequate grounds for ethics and morality. Without a free will, they argue, how can we hold persons responsible for their actions? Postmodernists raise questions about this argument, but agree that conventional determinism is not the answer.

Notes

1. It is often assumed that knowing the determinants of a malady means that we also know its cure. However, this is not always the case, as with AIDS.

2. Hume's argument is that to know that A causes B, we would need to know that nothing other than A *could* cause B. To know this, we would need to experience or observe B in all possible circumstances, because all knowledge must arise from experience for the

empiricist Hume. Because it is not possible to have every possible experience, it is never possible to conclude that there is no possible cause of B other than A.

3. Of course, the presence of all three conditions does not ensure causality either, as our discussion in the previous section illustrated. A fourth condition is necessary for us to even consider causality—the condition that all other causes have been controlled or disproven. As we noted in Note 2, this is impossible to establish. See Chapter 6 for a more complete discussion.

4. We should acknowledge here that what we present is one reading of Aristotle and his doctrine of causality. It is the one accepted and acknowledged most widely in modern behavioral science. It comes, however, not so much directly from Aristotle as from later interpreters of Aristotle, such as Sir Francis Bacon. On this reading, efficient cause is interpreted roughly as "immediate" or "proximate." During the Enlightenment, this reading led scientists to emphasize temporal sequence and the expending of energy as the defining features of efficient causes. The notion of efficient cause came more and more to resemble what we might call *force*. There is a good argument, however, that this is not what Aristotle himself intended. In his work, the efficient cause is described last, as the one that takes all other elements—material, form, and intention—and combined them effectively into the effect—the house. The example Aristotle gives of the efficient cause is a craftworker or builder. A craftworker is certainly more than energy expended over a period of time.

5. Besides the considerable influence of Hume and his brand of empiricism, another important contributing factor was the dramatic rise of scientific work and the determination on the part of scientists to explain all phenomena of the world in naturalistic terms—in terms of matter, time, and energy. This left little room in science for forms, ends, and purposes as causes of events.

6. The issue here is whether causes (material, efficient, formal, or final) are necessary qualities of explanations or necessary properties of the world itself. Although Aristotle may have begun the discussion of causality with the idea that these causes were necessary properties of good explanations, through history many have come to believe that causes are properties of the real world. This is an important question for people who produce theories to explain human beings.

7. This does not mean that efficient causal explanations are impossible. Some physicists have suggested, for example, that certain particles, sometimes called *tachyons,* fly from one atom to the other at a speed faster than the speed of light. This speed would be necessary to account for the instantaneous relations between the two atoms. Although this speed is considered to be impossible by many physicists, it does preserve the efficient causal notion that something moves across time and space to cause the changes in the counterpart atom.

8. Many structuralists, including radical behaviorists, claim not to be doing causal analysis at all. They see structures of all sorts, including contingent relationships, not to be the causes. We suggest that these theorists have equated causality with efficient causality, and thus do not recognize that their explanations are causal, but based on formal causes.

9. We should note that few systems theorists really adopt thoroughgoing formal causal accounts of systems. More often, these theorists explain systems with efficient causal assumptions. They consider the components of the system to occur across time, with one part of the system causing the next part across time. The implication of this conception is that the system as a whole never exists at any moment in time (see the discussion of temporal reductionism in Chapter 5). The notion of circular causality is an example of an efficient causal systems conception common in systems approaches. Although the system

"bends" back on itself in a feedback loop, it still operates across time in an efficiently caused determinism (see Slife, 1993, chap. 8, for a more thorough discussion).

10. We contend this is a result of our society's emphasis on linear time (see Slife, 1993).

11. Freud's theory also seems to have many human teleological assumptions (cf. Rychlak, 1981).

12. We suspect that this is often the case, but we cannot make the analysis to defend our suspicions here.

❧ 5 ❧

Reductionism

❧ In every science there is general agreement about what sorts of explanations of phenomena are good and sensible, and what sorts are not. These agreements, often called *paradigms* (Kuhn, 1970), allow scientists to relate easily to each other's work and theories, and to establish standards of acceptability for methods and theories. As we have seen, the behavioral sciences include many ideas about the nature of phenomena and explanations for them that, when taken together, could be said to constitute a paradigm for explaining human behavior.[1] In Chapters 3 and 4, we reviewed conventional conceptions of knowing and determinism that are part of this paradigm. In this chapter, we examine another aspect of the paradigm, *reductionism*, specifically as it relates to scientific explanation of behavior.

One of the important aspects of a good explanation, according to the paradigm of the behavioral sciences, is what might be loosely called the "simplicity" of the explanation. It has long been held that the simplest explanations of events are the best. This notion is often traced to the writings of William of Ockham (c. 1290-1349). From his work it has been argued that when there are several explanations for an event, the best one is the one that makes the fewest unsupportable assumptions. This has been interpreted to mean that the best explanations are the ones that do not require a lot of constructs, structures, forces, or other "things" in order to explain what happened and why. It is thought to be especially important that scientists refrain from proposing the existence of things that cannot be fairly directly shown to exist.

This line of reasoning has led many behavioral scientists to insist that *observation* is the only acceptable means of supporting or defending an explanation or theory. Insisting that only observation justifies explanations moves far beyond what Ockham intended. However, *Ockham's razor* (a razor in the sense that it cuts through unnecessary constructs and complications to get at the simplest explanation) has served for centuries as an important criterion for scientists and other scholars for deciding what explanations are best. More recently, a similar idea has been expressed as the Law of Parsimony. C. Lloyd Morgan (1852-1936) is often given credit for introducing this phrase and its interpretation into psychology. Morgan's version of the law says that in explaining the behaviors of animals (or people, for that matter) we should not suggest that they are caused by complex psychological processes when they can be explained by simpler ones. Most often these simpler processes are thought to be physiological or mechanical in nature.

This notion of simplifying human phenomena to nonrational, biological, or mechanical processes has persisted to the present. One of the results of this has been that the behavioral sciences have adopted a style of explaining we will refer to as *reductionism*. At its most basic level, the notion of reductionism is that some complex phenomenon, X, when properly understood will be shown to *really* be (an instance of) a simpler phenomenon, Y. In other words, reductionism is a claim that *X is really Y*. And because Y (the thing or process that explains X) is taken to be simpler than X, reductionism amounts to a claim that X is really *just* Y.

A strategy of reductionism suggests, then, that we should not take a phenomenon we are trying to explain at face value. We should be skeptical of what we see and what it seems to be. This reductionistic mind-set pushes us to look for something underneath what we are trying to explain, something more basic or fundamental. Most often, it is believed, the cause of a phenomenon is not readily apparent—we cannot easily see it.

Thus, one of the primary purposes of experimentation and other empirical methods is to uncover, by a process of inference, hidden concepts or structures behind observable events.[2] We have more to say about this process in Chapter 6. In this chapter, we consider the question of where our tendency to think reductively came from and why it is so appealing to us—why it seems to be such an essential part of the way explanations are given in the behavioral sciences.

THE ORIGINS OF REDUCTIONISM IN THE HISTORY OF WESTERN THOUGHT

We have already suggested that the contemporary tendency to think reductively is often traced to Ockham's razor, the idea that good explanations should be simple and invoke only the minimum number of constructs. This is hardly an adequate history of the idea, however, because the question remains as to why Ockham would think and write this way, and thus, where he got the idea. Ideas, of course, always arise in the context of other ideas. Several streams of thought have come together to influence present-day thinkers to favor and often take for granted reductive explanations. Some of these streams are found in the early writings of the Greek philosophers, the very earliest writings of the Western intellectual tradition. Some were introduced and developed more fully after Ockham's time, during the period of the Enlightenment. We discuss five ideas that have been influential in leading behavioral scientists[3] (and most thinkers in our culture) to think reductively: traditional metaphysics, materialism, mechanism, linear time, and evolutionary theory.

Metaphysics and Reductionism

Nearly all treatments of the history of Western philosophy trace its origins to Thales of Miletus (c. 640-546 B.C.). Because nothing survives of Thales's written work, we depend on what later writers said about him. From those sources, his ideas seem too simple and succinct to qualify as "philosophy" by today's standards. They do, however, illustrate one of the most important and characteristic themes of Greek philosophy. This theme is still very much in evidence in the thinking of our own day—including the behavioral sciences. Thales was concerned with *first principles,* fundamental sources from which everything else derives. He contended that the first principle and origin of all things is *water.* From one perspective this declaration makes a good deal of sense. The earth can be divided fairly neatly into earth and water; one dry, the other wet. Earth can become wet and subsequently change its form and erode. The air is at times infused with water and at other times dry. Water is certainly essential to all life and to the generation of life.

The more important point here, however, is not whether water is in fact the foundation of all things, but that Thales, and the thinkers who followed him, assumed that *something had to be* the foundation. Thales's approach to the explanation of the world is to assume that some principle must serve as the foundation and starting point of all reality. Further, it seemed clear to Thales and later figures that this foundation must be *one thing.* Even though they recognized that the world was extremely varied and changing, consisting of myriad different "things," there nonetheless had to be a single principle or substance, an origin, so to speak, that could in some way unify or account for them all. As this notion developed through Greek thought, it seemed obvious that this fundamental thing had to be *unified* (that is, not itself consisting of different smaller parts that could be considered more fundamental) and *unchanging* (not passing out of existence, nor coming into existence—it always *is*).

Thales held that the one fundamental thing was water; subsequent thinkers suggested other things as candidates for the one underlying reality. Anaximenes (c. 585-528 B.C.), for example, suggested that air was the fundamental substance. Other thinkers taught that the fundamental principle—the one thing—was not any sort of physical material, but something insubstantial and abstract. For them, the principle did not have a physical body. The modern concept of *force* is an example of a causal principle that has no physical body. This is an important quality because as we look around us, everything we see that is physical—having material substance—changes, decays, and even seems to pass from existence. If the fundamental principle or reality is taken to be, of necessity, unchanging and eternal, it must not be physical.[4]

This way of thinking about reality has given rise to metaphysics. The word *metaphysics* can be literally interpreted as "above or beyond" (*meta*) that which is physical. As we have seen, some early Greek thinking explained this (physical) world by assuming there was something more fundamental and nonphysical behind it. However, the term metaphysics, although literally connoting something above or beyond the physical, has come to mean anything that is taken to be fundamental or absolute, and can thus serve as an explanation for the things we encounter in the world. Thus, metaphysical explanations often explain by drawing on the qualities, properties, or powers of unchanging, nonphysical, assumed realities. However, the term metaphysical has also been used more loosely to mean any sort of explanation based on the existence of some ultimate entity or power that itself needs no explanation.

This metaphysical approach to explanation is seen in its most developed and elaborate forms in the work of the classical Greek philosophers Plato (428-348 B.C.) and Aristotle (384-322 B.C.). In Plato's world of forms and Aristotle's characterization of "first philosophy" we see well-developed metaphysical systems of explanation. Due largely to the profound influence of these two figures, this same style of explaining has continued, in one form or another, into the present. It has influenced the development of not only philosophy, but also science and religion. Some might argue that contemporary approaches to explanation in the behavioral sciences share little in common with classical Greek thought. Structuralism, for example, as an intellectual movement developed in part as a reaction to traditional metaphysics. However, by positing the existence of unseen, abstract, and nonphysical structures that operate at a very general level— such as Marxist structures of economic relations, feminist structures of gender relations, or structures governing our cognitive and moral development—structuralism becomes indistinguishable in most respects from traditional metaphysics. Certainly structuralism is reductionistic in exactly the same way.

Cognitive theory, as we have pointed out before, is essentially structuralist in its explanatory approach. Cognitive theorists set out intentionally to be reductive, emphasizing the role of cognitive structures and processes in explaining behavior. Processes and processors that we cannot see determine behaviors that we can observe. These cognitive structures and processes, of course, have no material substance. They are taken to be universal, or nearly so, in the human species. Likewise, they are held to be unchanging. We do not conceive of a time when we did not have short-term memory, nor a time in the future when we will not; nor does it seem reasonable to think that the short-term memories of people generations ago were substantially different from our own. Further, these processes and entities are seen to be the reality behind human cognitive phenomena, and to the extent that we are cognitive creatures, all human behavior. This explanatory strategy is a type of metaphysical reduction.

It is somewhat ironic that behaviorists should have adopted the metaphysical explanatory strategy they did. From the earliest stirrings (e.g., Watson, 1913) of behaviorism, theorists attempted to distance it from, and make it an alternative to, speculative and "metaphysical" psychologies filled with unseen entities like minds, consciousness, and instincts. However, it should be obvious that stimuli, responses, their connections or bonds, as well as reinforcements, are every bit as metaphysical as minds, consciousness, and instincts. Although classical behaviorists sought to confine themselves to explanation only in terms of observables, it must be acknowledged that no stimulus has ever been seen *as* a stimulus. The same is true of responses. We may see a rat press a bar, for example, but the bar press we see is just that—bar pressing. To say that it *is really just* a response is a reductive metaphysical presupposition and not part of the observation. Stimuli, responses, reinforcements, contingencies, and other entities and processes used by behaviorists to explain behavior are all metaphysical constructs.

Furthermore, these entities and processes operate according to abstract principles, or laws, such as the Law of Effect. Although the process of discovering and refining these laws is far from finished (and so, some would prefer to refer to them simply as *regularities*), a number of such laws have been articulated (for a classic text on learning theory, see Hilgard & Bower, 1975). These laws cover a wide range of behaviors and organisms. The laws and principles that guide learning are thought to be atemporal and unchanging—that is, they seem to be fundamental to our nature and they do not come and go. They will not be any less true in 10 years than they are today. These laws are also seen to be universal, at least within the species and situations to which they apply.[5]

Psychodynamic theorists hold that the behaviors we observe in ourselves and others arise from more primitive psychic processes that we do not see, such as *primary process thinking, secondary process thinking, cathexis,* and *catharsis,* among others. These processes, in turn, arise from the innate structure of the psyche itself (the id, the ego, and the superego; and the conscious and the unconscious mind) and its relationship to the body. These structures and their characteristic processes are universal, that is, all people have these same structures. Freud did not intend simply to describe how 19th-century Viennese minds happened to work. The structures are also unchangeable. In spite of what we may accomplish in therapy or successful living, we still have the same structures and processes at work in our behaviors. Any changes or differences are changes in appearances or form, not in the fundamental structures themselves. Furthermore, the processes and structures are nonphysical. They occur only in beings who have physical bodies, but they themselves are not material. The id, for example has no material existence. For Freud and other psychodynamic theorists, the structures and processes of the psyche are the metaphysical reality; behaviors are the superficial appearances or manifestations of the deeper reality. In its proposed structures and processes, psychodynamic theory reflects metaphysical reduction.

As a final observation on metaphysics and its role in reduction, we note that it may seem odd to use the term reduction to refer to a process of explaining something by showing how it is really a part of something bigger, grander, and more eternal than itself—as *reduction* really means "to make smaller." In the sense we are using the term, however, any strategy by which theorists explain something by claiming that it is *really* something else is by definition reductionism. The *something else* in this definition is taken to be less complex and more basic than the thing being reduced. Many types of metaphysical explanations are reductions in this sense.

Materialism and Reductionism

A second line of thought that has had a major influence on the development of reductive thinking is also found in early Greek philosophy, in the work of the materialists Leucippus (c. 490-430 B.C.) and Democritus (460-360 B.C.). These thinkers responded to the question of metaphysics by suggesting that reality consists only of *atoms* (small bits of matter) and *void* (empty space). Atoms are infinite in number and infinitesimally small. They move in any and all directions. Atoms supposedly differ from one another in their shape, in their relations or connections to other atoms, and in their orientation or position.[6]

According to the early materialists, the world we experience is made up of these atoms. The changing nature of our world is due to the atoms of different shapes coming together, coming apart, and changing their orientations. All this activity of the atoms is, of course, unseen and cannot be detected by the senses. For this reason, we need to look below the surface of things to find their explanation—in this case, to things too small to be seen or otherwise detected by the senses. This strategy of explanation is a reduction to the qualities of the material of which things are composed. It is also a type of determinism. The early Greek atomists believed that all that happens is caused by the motion, shape, and interaction of atoms, moving according to a preestablished (rational) necessity. Reductionistic explanations of all sorts, metaphysical as well as materialistic, are most often deterministic (see Chapter 4).

This early Greek materialism is appealing to the modern mind in part because it seems scientific by today's standards, looking as it does to natural (material) rather than supernatural explanations. Materialism also appeals to us because our own scientific theories have suggested there are atoms of matter with particular properties that make up the known world. We display these in the periodic chart of the elements, and we have various theories of the nature of molecules, atoms, and other particles too small to be seen with the naked eye. It is thus not surprising that materialistic reductive explanations have a long history in Western thought, and that they have been common in the behavioral sciences. Indeed, it could be argued that this is the most common type of explanation in contemporary behavioral science. Today it takes the form of explaining people's minds and behaviors in terms of the structure and chemical activity of their nervous systems or the genetic material in their cells. Behaviorists also invoke materialistic explanations in emphasizing that human beings are essentially natural organisms. Our capacities to be conditioned and reinforced are, for behaviorists, rooted deeply in our biological makeup. Even Freud and many humanists could not entirely resist the materialistic tradition. They posited that our instincts and other innate processes exert directing influence over our behaviors.

Mechanism and Reductionism

The reductionistic ideas we have discussed so far (metaphysics and materialism) are among the earliest in the Western tradition, and thus have influenced all the ones that have come later. However, there are other more recent movements in Western philosophy, generally better known to behavioral scientists, that have also contributed to the way we explain things and the reason reductionism is so intellectually attractive.

One of these movements is mechanism. By *mechanism* we mean the tendency to see things and events in the world as being something like a machine, that is, as composed of smaller pieces working smoothly together, the working of the whole being lawfully determined and necessary. Following the period of history known as the Renaissance, Western thinking entered a period known as the Enlightenment (usually designated as the period from the 17th into the 19th century). This period was characterized by a tendency to reject supernatural explanations of events, including religious explanations. It was also characterized by a confidence in the natural order of things, which humans could discover by applying proper rational analysis and scientific methods. This was, of course, the period in which the precepts of modern science were laid down. Moreover, the considerable success of scientists in discovering new knowledge, explaining the previously unexplainable, and generating beneficial technology, fueled scholars' confidence in being able to find answers to all questions in scientific terms.

This was also the period in which many impressive and intricate machines were developed. The machine became the root metaphor, or model, for the natural universe, and by analogy, for much in the human realm as well. Perhaps the most encompassing expression of this mechanistic thinking is Deism. *Deism* is a theological position in which the universe is viewed as a gigantic machine, running in its preestablished order. God "wound it up," so to speak, and does not need to interfere in its present functioning. Everything is unfolding as preordained by the nature and composition of the machine and the laws by which it operates. One of the things that made the mechanistic model of the world so attractive was that machines, being orderly and structured, can be predicted and manipulated. This gave rise to a new confidence in our power to understand and control the events of the world.

Certainly one of the most influential figures during this period was Sir Isaac Newton (1642-1727). Newton not only contributed to the development of scientific methods, but accomplished to a great extent what enlightenment thinkers had wanted to do. He laid down a very few laws that could, with mathematical precision, predict and describe events in the natural world, including the motions of celestial bodies. These laws of motion fulfilled the metaphysical function that the early Greeks had outlined. Everything in nature was seen to be precise and predictable, much like a machine. It was almost irresistible to suppose that the human world might be just as machinelike and predictable.

This mechanistic supposition has been influential in the behavioral sciences from their beginning. The behavioral sciences arose partly out of the attempt to apply a Newtonian sort of natural science to the questions of human behavior (see Slife, 1993). The search for a mechanism that explains behavior is now simply an accepted and expected part of any sustained investigation in the behavioral sciences. We have developed mechanical analogues, or models, for the senses; for perception; for learning and memory; and even for personality and social processes such as attribution, modeling, and psychopathology. Behavioral scientists often reduce activities and behaviors to their underlying mechanisms, with the hope of understanding them better and being able to intervene to effect change (as in therapy, teaching, or attitude change). This is the strategy of mechanistic reductionism.

This strategy is also evident in the more specific theories of the behavioral sciences. Freud and other psychodynamic theorists used hydraulic metaphors to describe the actions of the energy of the mind (libido). This energy can be "dammed up," as in a fixation; it exerts pressure, as in drive or desire; and people are motivated to seek release of the pressure, as in catharsis. Early behaviorist theorists adopted the reflex arc, a very simple mechanism, as the root metaphor for all behavior. Even though more modern radical behaviorists no longer maintain their explicit commitment to the reflex, the mechanistic flavor is retained in their explanations of behavior. In radical behaviorism, behavior is presumably controlled by contingencies that operate independently of people and automatically in ways that appear similar to what we might expect in any mechanism. Cognitive theory, however, is probably the most obviously mechanistic of the theories we have dealt with. As we have mentioned previously, a mechanism, the computer, is the root metaphor for cognitive theorists. Mechanistic explanations abound in the field of artificial intelligence and in comprehensive models of the cognitive system, where images of gates, switches, and filters are plentiful.

Time and Reductionism

Time was extremely important in the thinking of Enlightenment figures, particularly Newton. We discussed in Chapter 4 how the notion of linear time is an unexamined assumption in theories about determinism and causality. What we want to emphasize here is that this view of time has also influenced reductionistic thinking in at least two related ways: the reduction to one dimension of time, and the reduction of a whole process to its parts across time.

Regarding the first of these reductions, if we accept the notion that human events are regulated according to linear time, so that the past causes the present and the future, then we can, and perhaps we must, explain events in the present by showing how they are causally tied to other events that have happened in the past. This is a type of reduction, a *temporal reduction*. It suggests that what we see happening now "is really just" (the sum total of) what has happened before. This explanatory strategy is common in the behavioral sciences. For example, in behaviorist accounts, actions occur because of a history of past instances of conditioning and reinforcement. This kind of temporal reduction is also common in theories of information processing—what is done with the input information at one stage of the process has a strong effect on what information is passed on and how it is processed at a later stage. There are many other examples of this kind of temporal reduction (reduction of the present and future to the past) in the behavioral sciences, some of which we take up later.[7]

Temporal reduction can also refer to the reduction of whole processes to their parts, as each part happens (sequentially) across time. This form of temporal reduction is another implication of Newton's view that time is similar to a line. If we consider time to be linear, then all behaviors and processes must be distributed along this line, one piece or component at a time. This distribution across time means that no process is ever wholly present—only a part of the process is available to us at any one moment. This reduction may seem so obvious that it does not bear mentioning. However, two issues are worth noting that may not be so obvious. The first is that this reduction is the result of a particular view of time, rather than the result of the way in which all processes and behaviors must be understood (Slife, 1993).

The second issue is that this particular view can create problems for the behavioral scientist investigating processes across time. Because our only "window" through which we can observe such processes is the present (according to Newton), our only access to the process is one piece at a time. In this sense, we never have access to the process as a whole. This lack of access means that we cannot know how each piece, which we see as it crosses our window of the present, relates to the whole. Sometimes

the very identity of the piece crossing our window depends on its relation
to other pieces that will not cross our window until sometime later. We
could record or perhaps photograph the pieces in some manner, but we
cannot know how the pieces (as photographs) are related to the whole
without seeing the pieces together simultaneously. And this is impossible if we understand time to be linear. This form of temporal reduction,
then, suggests that wholes must be broken down into parts in order to
identify and understand them. This reduction makes it very difficult to
recognize and understand the holistic and relational qualities of the
parts.[8]

The implications for behavioral science disciplines, such as developmental psychology and education, are important and wide ranging.[9] For
example, developmentalists, in the face of an abundance of knowledge
regarding each stage of development (or each age group), have long
lamented the absence of knowledge regarding how the stages or age groups
are related to one another (e.g., Schaffer, 1988). This situation results
from a temporal reductionism whereby we know a lot about individual
(and reduced) components as they occur piece by piece across time, and
very little about the process as a whole. One would think that developmentalists would at least rejoice about their knowledge of individual age
groups. However, many developmentalists claim that such knowledge is
at best incomplete without a more comprehensive understanding of the
whole of development. Without this whole, the individual parts or age
groups cannot be validly interpreted.

Because the notion of linear time has been so pervasive in our intellectual tradition we might suspect that temporal reduction would be common in the behavioral sciences. We have noted in various places in the book
how psychodynamic theory relies heavily on temporal reduction, with
events early in an individual's life profoundly affecting later life. In cognitive
theory, processing carried on at an earlier stage affects the processing
carried on at later stages. The entire process of cognition—and thus, of
behavior—is sequentialized.[10] Behaviorists privilege the past as well. It
is axiomatic in behaviorist explanations of behavior that stimuli produce
responses, and that stimuli, of necessity, precede the responses in time.
As conditioned responses accumulate and become shaped into complex
behaviors, the effects of previous reinforcements are still manifest in the
behavioral repertoire of an organism. In other words, human behavior is
the result of a chain of previous stimulus-response connections. What has

gone on before, the occurring and connecting of stimuli, responses, and reinforcers—often referred to as reinforcement history—determines what happens in the present and in the future. Temporal reduction is a fundamental part of behaviorist explanatory strategies. This is true even in more modern approaches to behaviorism that substitute the term *environmental contingencies* for *reinforcements*. Once the process of learning begins, it builds up an influential past very quickly.

Evolution and Reductionism

One other intellectual influence has moved contemporary behavioral sciences toward reductionism. It is more recent in origin than the others discussed, and perhaps because of that, it is extremely important. We are speaking here of the theory of evolution, propounded most notably by Charles Darwin (1809-1882). Few ideas or schools of thought have been as influential and far-reaching in their effects on modern thinking as Darwin's theory of evolution and the subsequent work that it has engendered. We want to note here, however, that Darwin's thinking on the subject and the effects of his thought grew quite reasonably out of previous ways of thinking about the world. Even Darwin was subject to the effects of implicit assumptions. It can be shown, therefore, that evolutionary theory grew out of Enlightenment thinking and thus, out of still earlier ideas. What it contributes to our current view of reductionism is thus akin to what we have already described in our treatment of other influences.

Evolutionary theory offers an example of how a reductionistic strategy works in explaining a complex phenomenon such as the biological world. In a sense, Darwin did for the biological world what Newton did for the physical world. He offered an account of the great variability in the biological world in terms of a simple and seemingly precise scientific principle—natural selection. This insight, coupled later with Mendelian genetics, provided a mechanism to account for how species change and adapt, and how the natural world has come to have such variety.

The idea that complex and ongoing behaviors can be explained by the relatively simple mechanism of natural selection has frequently been imported "whole cloth" into the behavioral sciences. It has formed an important aspect of the "nature" side of the nature versus nurture argument. It has been assumed that if various species-specific behaviors in animals can be shown to result from genetic factors, and to have *survival value*, then at least some human behaviors might have similar genetic origins. Sociobiologists, such as E. O. Wilson (1975), have drawn our attention to these possibilities and relationships.

Evolutionary theory has also contributed to reductive thinking in the behavioral sciences in a more subtle way. One of the important contentions of evolutionary theory is that the various species, including humans, have at some point in the very distant past, common origins. Thus, the species are not distinguished by qualitative differences, that is, by virtue of something that makes them inherently different *kinds* of beings. Aristotle, for example, had suggested that humans and animals had different kinds of souls. Current thinking, however, is that species are distinguished by quantitative differences: Some species have moved farther than others along the evolutionary path. Put slightly differently, species can be differentiated on the basis of the evolved structure and function of the brain and the behavioral repertoires that this evolved structure permits. Supposedly, however, there is an underlying continuity to all species. Humans are more "advanced," but otherwise not fundamentally different from the lower species.

The implication of this continuity among the species is that we, as an advanced species, have more in common with the primitive species than perhaps we had once supposed. Given that the process of evolution has been at work in the same mechanical manner among all species, it is reasonable to suppose that other natural processes are also common to all species, including humans. This outlook has led to the development of ethology and comparative psychology. If the processes underlying behavior are assumed to be biological and common to all species, then it makes sense to study these processes in simpler species and less complex situations (e.g., laboratories) to understand the processes in their most basic forms. Understanding of basic forms in lower species can presumably be applied to humans, with whatever modifications in the explanations seem necessary because humans are more complex. Evolutionary theory, then, has lent credence to the notion that human behaviors can be reduced to simple biological mechanisms and to similar behaviors seen more clearly in other species.

In the behavioral sciences, this notion is perhaps most evident in behaviorist theory. The relationship between behaviorist theory and evolutionary theory has always been strong and direct.[11] More recently, behaviorist theorists have attempted to link behaviorism explicitly with Darwinian evolution, suggesting that operant conditioning is the mechanism whereby natural selection takes place (Skinner, 1974). In giving a behavioristic explanation of the behavior of any organism, it is important to consider the organism's evolved capacity to respond—its position on the phylogenetic scale. Organisms cannot be conditioned to learn responses that are not compatible with their innate biological capabilities. Certain organisms have the capacity to be reinforced by certain things because of their relative development.

It is important to note that the principles of behaviorist theory are assumed to generalize across the evolutionary scale—all organisms learn and behave in *essentially* the same way. The processes of learning and conditioning are the same in all species. The particular things that may act as stimuli, responses, and reinforcers vary with the evolutionary development of the organism under study, but the processes are the same. This is the justification for studying subhuman species and then generalizing to human beings.

Science and Reductionism

Before leaving our discussion of the history of reductive thinking we should comment on one important reason this type of thinking has risen to such a position of respect and prominence in the behavioral sciences as well as in Western culture at large. In the minds of some scholars reductionism is *essential* for all scientific explanation. Without the assumption of reductionism, science would not be possible. Part of the reasoning behind this position is that contemporary views of science hold that one of the purposes of science is to formulate general laws and principles that predict a wide range of more specific behaviors. This, of course, is the spirit of traditional metaphysics. Another way of saying this is that science requires that there be fewer explanations than there are phenomena to be explained.

It should be noted, however, that this view of science developed relatively recently in the history of ideas. It developed well after traditional metaphysical principles were laid down, and well after they were already influential. The behavioral sciences are more recent still. We cannot be sure, then, whether we ought to believe in reductionism because good science requires it, or whether our notion of good science requires reductionism because we already accept reductionism. At another level, however, it does seem to make some sense that we need to be able to generalize our explanations of things. Reductionism seems to be an important part of being able to generalize because it suggests that there is a fundamental ground or principle on which all phenomena rest—a single cause at the base of a lot of behaviors. The final reason reductive explanations are taken to be essential for science is because determinism is taken to be essential.

CONCEPTUAL PROBLEMS
ATTENDING REDUCTIONISM

Up to this point in the chapter we have offered a definition of reductionism as it is found in a number of current strategies for explaining human behavior. We have suggested how such strategies might have emerged from the history of ideas. In the next section of the chapter, we look a bit more closely at reductionism in order to make some finer distinctions among types of reductions and to be clearer about the conceptual costs of taking a reductive view of human beings. We frame the discussion in terms of three broad kinds of reductive strategies—the metaphysical reduction, the temporal reduction, and the biological reduction. These categories are broad enough and common enough in the behavioral sciences to provide a good picture of the current state of theorizing. They also arise quite naturally out of the historical sources (metaphysics, materialism, time, mechanism, and evolution) we discussed earlier. Indeed, these historical themes run through them in easily discernible ways.

Traditional metaphysics, as we have shown, is still very much evident in contemporary theorizing. The implications of metaphysical explanations are dealt with in the section on metaphysical reduction. We have also noted that the assumption of linear time is pervasive in the behavioral sciences. Consequently, we also deal briefly with the conceptual implications of temporal reduction. Probably the most popular reductive strategy employed in the behavioral sciences is biological reduction. This strategy has its roots in materialism, mechanism, and evolutionary theory. We address the implications of this strategy in the section on biological reduction.

Implications of Metaphysical Reduction

Earlier in this chapter, we made the point that one of the influences that has led behavioral scientists to adopt reductive strategies is the metaphysical thinking apparent in our Western intellectual tradition, dating from the time of the ancient Greeks. A metaphysical reduction, as we have presented it, explains human behavior by attributing it to general, overarching, universal realities, such as laws or principles.

Such metaphysical explanations have theoretical implications that many theorists do not acknowledge, or at least, do not explore. We deal briefly with two of these. First, metaphysical explanations common in the behavioral sciences make it difficult to retain a sense of uniqueness and individuality. Such explanations, by reducing their behaviors, also reduce human beings to *special cases* of something more general. A person might be seen, for example, as a special case of depression, of an Oedipal complex, of the male or female gender, of the stage of concrete operations, of Stage 4 of moral reasoning, or of inconsistent reinforcement. In the contemporary behavioral sciences, the possibilities are seemingly endless. In this sense, if there are metaphysical principles that make us all who we are, then we are all (in a very real sense) "someone in general." At least, the way the "general" is manifest, or the way the hidden social, developmental, or cognitive structures supposedly work their effects, is what is most important to know and understand about us.[12]

This view of human beings inevitably impacts our understanding of our humanity and our human relationships. For example, as we commonly conceive of it, intimacy with another human being involves knowing him or her directly and individually, rather than knowing general characteristics and qualities he or she may possess, or principles by which he or she operates. To the extent that metaphysical entities and forces are the foundation of our actions and our natures, however, knowing a person well is in fact knowing what metaphysical entities, structures, and forces are operating on the person. If this is true, then in some sense there is no "person" to know at all. Rather, there are qualities, variables, and characteristics being controlled by laws, processes, or structures. In fact, it might be said that to really get to know another person is to know him or her as a bundle of particular variables operating within a lawful system or structure.

The second problem with metaphysical reduction arises because such a reduction almost always results in a deterministic view of human beings. The kinds of laws and principles that behavioral scientists formulate to account for events are assumed (even if they cannot be proven) to be universal, abstract, and fundamental. They constitute the fundamental, unchanging, and orderly reality behind the complex and changing world of real humans and their behaviors. As such, they "just are," and their nature determines the manifestation of human actions and events we see in the world. The issue of determinism and its attendant problems was discussed in Chapter 4. This type of hard determinism, which is implied by metaphysical reduction in which behaviors and events are caused by things that "just are," is arguably incompatible with common conceptions of human agency.[13] If it is incompatible with human agency, this reductionism has important implications for our view of people, what they are capable of, and the meaning of human action.

Metaphysical laws and structures are most often believed to work in a necessary and "lawful" manner—that is, there is no real possibility for things to happen differently from the way the laws and structures require. Simply put, if metaphysical laws and structures are in control of our behaviors, then there is no possibility of doing otherwise than we do. There is no real possibility in human behavior, only necessity. Determinism of this sort makes agency impossible. Extending this line of argument a bit farther, if we are not agents, capable of directing our own actions, then the meaning and sense of morality we commonly attach to our actions is called into question.

The threat to meaningfulness posed by metaphysical reduction can be seen in the effects of structuralist explanations of behavior. For example, Marxist theorists contend that ideas, systems of government, and social practices are all products of the underlying structure of economic relations. Religious practice, in this view, is "really just" the economically powerful exercising control over the economically weak. Some feminist analysts suggest that traditional marriage and family relations are "really just" the institutionalized exploitation of women.

This type of reduction has profound effects on the meanings of our behaviors. For example, a woman, from her own perspective, may understand herself to be participating in her marriage and family out of a sense of love and devotion, a sense of participating in a life-defining relationship with a long and meaningful history. In a reductive feminist analysis, on the other hand, the woman is understood to be trapped in an inherently inequitable system, exploited and victimized by a powerful structure of gender relations. Although she cannot see the structure, it is nonetheless there, and her marriage is "really just" a manifestation of it.

This structuralist analysis also reduces the behavior of the woman in another way. Some people have *raised consciousness* or have otherwise discerned the underlying structures and their effects in our lives. Those who are not aware of the presumed structures and their effects won't understand the "real" meaning of their lives. This failure is often taken to be an example of *false consciousness*. This phrase means that people fail to recognize the structure because the structure itself prevents them from doing so. The structure of male-female relations, for example, is responsible not only for the institution of marriage and its meaning, but also for the failure of men, women, and therapists to recognize and understand (and thus resist) the structure. In effect, the fact that some people recognize the structure and oppose it is taken as evidence of the reality of the structure. However, the fact that most people do not recognize the structure is also taken as evidence of the reality of the structure. This double level of reduction constitutes a powerful assumptive basis and one not easily challenged. This is an important issue for this book. Our purpose is to facilitate examination of assumptive bases such as these. However, the kind of two-tiered reduction common in many structuralist explanations—whether valid or not—effectively shuts down critical discourse.

An alternative line of analysis provides another view of the problem of metaphysical reduction and its effects on meaning. This line would hold that the meaning of a human action arises from the fact that it did not *have to* occur (due to the action of some principle or other); there were other possibilities. In this view, we understand the meaning of an action by contrasting it with other possible actions. We can tell what an actor meant by knowing what else might have been done.[14] For example, if someone were to tell you that he or she "loves" you, you would understand what was meant by knowing what else he or she might have said, what other words might have been used—"like," "respect," "care," "infatuation," and so forth. If the person had no choice of what to say or whether to say anything at all, you would not take it very seriously, nor attach much meaning to it. It would be like the sound your automobile makes when you start it. It just happens.

The same reasoning applies to all our actions. This line of analysis suggests that if there is no choice, no alternative possibility in what we do, then the meaning is lost from our actions. A human action would be no more meaningful than a plant growing or a stone rolling down a hill. These things don't *mean* anything, they just happen. Other human beings might try to attach some meaning to these happenings, but the meaning would be subjectively created and very difficult to sustain when the true story of the behavioral laws and principles is known. In this way, any behavioral science, to the extent that it seeks to explain our behavior by traditional metaphysical laws and structures, threatens the meaningfulness of our actions. Of course, if these scientific explanations are correct, then we had better just accept them and learn to deal with the meaninglessness of our lives. However, if the scientific explanations are simply the result of thinking in a particular reductionistic way and are not necessarily the real story of our actions, then we might very well find other explanations that do not destroy the meaning of those actions. In Chapter 6, we consider whether scientific evidence in fact obligates us to accept a deterministic view of ourselves.

Metaphysically reductive explanations also lead to a loss of responsibility, another indication of the lack of agency and meaning. If there are causal laws and structures that work to determine our behaviors such that we have no agency to direct our own actions, we cannot in fairness hold anyone accountable for his or her actions. Actions just happen as a result of whatever causal laws and structures happen to be operating at the time. If persons cannot be held accountable for their actions, and if there is no genuine possibility that the actions could have been otherwise than they were, then it is not possible to talk about whether the act was "right" or "wrong," "good" or "bad." The act just happened.[15] If our actions are neither right nor wrong, neither good nor bad, then in a very real sense, they do not matter—except in the somewhat limited sense we mentioned above. Although it may seem good to be in a situation of evading responsibility for anything we do, the price we pay for the luxury of not being responsible is the underlying meaninglessness that haunts all our lives and actions when agency is understood to be illusory.

Implications of Temporal Reduction

Temporal reduction, as we have talked about it, is the idea that every action arises from a string of previous actions that occurred earlier in time. Usually time is thought of as being linear, each previous moment existing as a point on the time line, and each moment "containing" an event. Because the time line is "just there," and it never goes away, past events never go away. They remain in our past, exerting some causal influence over what we do now. We can see that this sort of temporal reduction is very much a metaphysical reduction, because time itself is conceived of as an abstract and unchanging reality and very much independent of our own volition. It is taken for granted in our culture that "You cannot change the past." Because we cannot change it, and yet it exerts a strong influence over our present behaviors, the past becomes a strong determiner of our actions. All the conceptual problems we talked about in the previous section that arise as a result of the determinism in metaphysical reductions arise also whenever a temporal reduction is used to explain our behavior.[16]

One of the important and problematic implications of temporal reduction is that the past is essentially in control of the present. In the face of this strong influence out of the past, it becomes difficult to explain how genuine behavior change is possible. It would seem that if everything we do comes about because of past events and their consequences, then we are essentially caught in our pasts and unable to break free. Of course, one possible way of breaking free of the past is to intrude in the ongoing flow of action in the present to slowly produce change by altering the consequences of present behaviors, thereby "building up" a new past. This is the strategy adopted by behaviorists; it is the essence of conditioning. Although this may bring about behavioral change, it does not free a person from the past. It merely substitutes one past for another. Neither does this strategy free the person from the determinism inherent in a temporal reduction. Indeed, behaviorism is an avowedly deterministic explanatory system.

If a change brought about by conditioning is still determined by its past, and if it comes about not by any agentive act of the person, then the question is open whether the change is genuine. Such a change is similar to the change that might occur in your automobile after a tune-up. It runs differently, but did it really change, or is it the same old car with a few new parts? In the case of an automobile, we might be willing to say that new parts make a new automobile. In the case of human beings, it is not so clear. If we succeed in changing behaviors, at what point do we claim to have effected genuine change? In one sense, people *are* the behaviors they perform, so to change the behaviors is to change the person. Change, in this case, would be genuine. But in another sense, if the behaviors are merely determined consequences of previous actions, we begin to wonder whether it makes sense to talk of a *person* at all. The person is simply the medium through which past behaviors affect present ones. This has been the real thrust of reductive explanations throughout the history of the behavioral sciences—to show persons to be something less than persons. This seems the necessary consequence of the sort of reductive strategies we are discussing here.

Some theorists in the behavioral sciences who attempt to explain how change is possible hold that human beings have the capacity to rise above their past and somehow not let it determine their present lives. This may be an attractive approach to consider, but careful analysis shows that it is one thing to hold *that* this sort of transcendence is possible but quite another to show just *how* it is possible.[17] The problem with this approach is twofold. First, once we grant that there is a real past already in place, full of influential events (the essence of the temporal reduction), it seems very difficult to free ourselves from it. We must explain what sort of entity can climb outside the flow of time and be uninfluenced by it. Often in explanations of behavior the self or the mind is invoked precisely to serve this function. If, however, the self manages to rise out of its own past, and free itself from a grounding in the past to take a new view of the present, the next question is where the self is standing while making its evaluations and decisions. In other words, having freed itself from its own past, what grounds does it use to formulate a new perspective on the present? We discussed this problem briefly in dealing with postmodern criticisms of free will in Chapter 4.

A second problem comes from trying to explain change by transcending the past in that this transcendence must always be incomplete. Let us assume, for instance, that there is something in a person's past that she feels is exerting influence over her current behaviors—perhaps a childhood trauma. In order to be free of the influence of the past event, she must somehow rise out of the causal chain of events that supposedly stretches from the trauma to the present to see the whole situation differently and eliminate the power of the past traumatic event. However, we must remember that also contained in this person's past is her knowledge of the language she speaks. It is through this language that she understands her problem in the first place. She does not want to be free of that, or more than likely, she cannot be. Also in the past are her values, her relationships with people important to her, her sense of herself, and the formation of the very project of her life. Certainly she does not want to leave these things behind as she rises out of the past in order to be free of it. As a matter of fact, it is likely that all these factors—her language, her past experiences, her identity, and her relationships—are what motivate her to want to be free of the past trauma in the first place. This presumed ability to transcend the past must therefore be selective. She wants to transcend her trauma, but she does not want to, or cannot, transcend her past entirely. The question is: How can she transcend one without the others?

What we see from this example is that being able to transcend the past is a difficult proposition. Time travel is risky business. Because we cannot transcend the whole of the past, any transcending will be partial. Any psyche sophisticated enough to transcend the past is sophisticated enough to remember having done so. Thus in this memory the past is still alive and not transcended at all. This circularity infects most theoretical reasoning about this issue. Some (chiefly postmodernists) argue that the only solution to these conceptual issues is not to create them in the first place, that is, avoid temporal reduction.

Implications of Biological Reduction

Perhaps the most common and popular form of reductive explanation in contemporary behavioral science is biological reduction. This form of materialistic reduction is the attempt to explain all human action in terms of presumably simpler biological—genetic, chemical, or neural—processes. Inherent in this strategy is the contention that human behavior is "really just" biological activity. This reductive strategy has become increasingly attractive to behavioral scientists as they have struggled to establish the behavioral sciences as sciences. Biological entities and processes lend themselves particularly well to scientific study, and biological terms lend a distinctly scientific air to resulting explanations.

It is for this reason that cognitive theorists, like proponents of many other perspectives in the behavioral sciences, have been eager to embrace biological reductionism. Recent work where the cognitive and brain sciences come together is based on biologically reductive accounts of cognitive processes (see, e.g., Churchland, 1986; Edelman, 1987). In these attempts, cognitive processes are seen to be a direct result of the functioning of the nervous system. At the cutting edge of cognitive theory, human behaviors are seen to be "really just" the results of cognitive processes, and the cognitive processes, in turn, are seen to be "really just" the results of simpler biological processes, as necessitated by the material substances of the nervous system.

Another reason biological reduction has been so popular is that it seems quite obvious that some sort of biological activity is essential for any human behavior to occur. If we were not alive—if our biological processes were not continuing—we might not be able to behave at all (laying aside questions of life after life and related issues). It seems, therefore, quite feasible to establish consistent and "lawful" relationships between biological events and behaviors. Even if such regular relations can be shown to exist, this does not establish that behavioral events are "really just" biological events. There are a number of problems with drawing causal arrows from biological processes to behaviors, claiming the biological processes to be the real story.

If biological events are the real story behind human behaviors, then the behaviors themselves, as well as thoughts, desires, feelings, and purposive acts become *epiphenomenal,* that is, they aren't what they seem to be. They depend entirely on biological processes for their being; they simply reflect our biology. The kind of biological reduction typically sought in the behavioral sciences is an example of what Robinson (1995b) refers to as an "ontological reduction." An ontological reduction is the claim that one phenomenon (in this case the mind or mental processes) does not exist in some sense (i.e., has no ontological status)—that is, there is a reduction in the number of things that are given genuine ontological status (i.e., considered to be real). This desire to reduce the psychological to the physical has a long history in psychology and the other behavioral sciences.

We began this chapter by referring to Lloyd Morgan's canon, also known as the Law of Parsimony. The canon was aimed specifically at psychologists who were attributing cognitive and other human capacities to animals to explain their seemingly meaningful behavior. Lloyd Morgan suggested that we should never explain things in terms of "higher" mental processes if some more primitive biological processes can account for them. In other words, physical processes are taken to be more fundamental than thought and other human attributes. Applied to the notions of human beings, this betrays a clear naturalistic bias and has far-reaching implications for what it means to be a human being and what our actions and relationships mean.

Biological reduction is a type of mechanistic reduction, in essence the idea that what is most true of us is that we are biological mechanisms. One potential consequence of using this type of reduction to explain human behavior is that the meaning of the behavior is called into question. To see how meaning is lost in a biologically reductive framework, consider the example of another mechanism, a clock. On the surface, a clock keeps time. At least that is what we buy clocks for. We might ask, however, how the clock knows what time it is. If it is really keeping time, it should "know" what time it is. As we look a bit more carefully at the clock, opening it up to look at its intricate inner workings, we find that the clock is simply composed of gears, springs, and flywheels. The hands of the clock that we take to be keeping time are actually turned by gears. These gears, in turn, are controlled by other gears that are rotated by the tension of springs and the actions of flywheels. Because we know that gears, springs, and flywheels do not keep time, or even understand how to keep time, as it turns out, no part of the clock is keeping time at all (the behavior of keeping time is epiphenomenal). To say, therefore, that the clock keeps time is handy for conversing about clocks, but misleading. Keeping time is a meaningful activity (it matters to us and it involves an understanding of history, use of language conventions, and some thought), but the activity of gears and springs turning other gears is not. Whatever the clock appears to be doing, when understood at its most fundamental level, there is no meaningful activity going on at all.

If this analogy is applied directly to human behaviors—if they really can be fully explained as the activities of a biological mechanism—there is a real question as to what the behaviors mean. A husband may say, for example, that he loves his wife. He may even feel love in such a way that the experience is "real." A biologically reductive account of his love, however, would suggest that he feels what he feels, thinks what he thinks, and talks about it the way he does because of the particular biological state he is in or the process going on in the meat of his body. A closer examination reveals that neither chromosomes, nor neurons, nor chemicals really love his wife, any more than gears, springs, and flywheels keep time. If the behavior is purely biological, in truth, no part of the husband is doing the loving. Love is, thus, epiphenomenal—it only *appears* to be what it is. Reductionism implies that the love is *not* what it appears, there is no choice involved in the husband's loving, any more than clocks have a choice in keeping time. Without choice, and without the act of loving having a reality of its own, the meaning normally associated with experiences such as love is difficult to maintain. By the same token, the meaning of the loving relationship is called into question. It is an important question whether any human action can retain its meaningfulness if it is simply a reflection of biological structures and processes.

This analysis will not persuade anyone who believes strongly in a biological reduction to quit using biological reductions to explain behavior. An orthodox reductionist generally assumes that actions have no meaning in the first place. Rather, such a reductionist is likely to urge all of us—our culture as well—to accept the fact that our actions do not have the meanings that we have always thought they had. Losing our romantic notions about ourselves and our actions is part of the price we must pay for scientific certainty about ourselves and scientific solutions to our problems. Whether science can really deliver certainty and solution is discussed in the next chapter. Here we examine another issue: whether reducing human behavior to biology in fact results in clearer, simpler, and more compelling explanations.

One thing seems clear enough to be taken as a starting point for analysis. Human behavior as we know it consists of both mental and physical events. Even strict and devoted biological reductionists would not deny the existence of mental events. They simply question whether mental events really are what they seem to be and whether they can stand by themselves as realities. There would be little argument that a physical body without any mental activity going on, such as a corpse, is of little interest to one studying *behavior.* Such physical bodies do not "behave." Similarly, unembodied minds, or mental activities that somehow occur without a physical body (i.e., one with a brain), are in the experience of most of us, rare occurrences and difficult for behavioral scientists to study. The point is that the physical and mental aspects of human beings relate to each other in consistent and orderly ways.

This relationship between mind and body presents a problem for a biological reductionist. To make a biological reduction is to claim that states and processes in the body are fundamental, and that they really account for behavioral and mental phenomena. For example, a reductive account would say that a husband's love for his wife is experienced only because of an occurrence of neurological states or environmental events. We must remember, however, that after the reduction, the mental phenomenon or experience does not simply go away. Even if the love isn't what it seems to be, the husband feels it. He has the experience. In this sense it is real. This means that there must be some process, law, or power that somehow allows physical events in the body to cause mental events in the mind. In other words, if biology is the real cause of what we experience as mental events, then there must be some process by which physical events are transformed into mental ones, some process that bridges the physical and mental, allowing one to cause the other. There must be some process by which neuron firings and chemical flows are transformed into a particular husband's "love."[18] In biologically reductive explanations, this power (or principle or process) is never explained or even named. Reductionistic thinkers seldom recognize that such a "connecting" process exists. However, the nature of biological reduction logically requires that the process exist. Because it is not acknowledged, reductionistic thinkers must take it for granted.

The spirit of reductionism, and what makes it attractive to many behavioral scientists, is that many complex things (behaviors) can be reduced to or explained by one single, supposedly simpler thing (biology). In the case of biological reduction we see that the simplicity is deceptive. The biological reduction appears to claim that one thing (e.g., the presence of a particular chemical in the nervous system) is the reality and explains human behaviors (a host of different responses in a variety of situations, such as test scores, interpersonal relations, reality testing, moods, cognitive abilities, or personal preferences). However, explanation in terms of biological processes always carries the assumption that there is indeed a process by which biological states relate to mental (or behavioral) acts and by which the former cause the latter. So biological reduction never in fact explains in terms of a single underlying reality; there is not one fundamental reality, but two—the biological state within the skin, *and* the principle that allows it to produce mental and behavioral phenomena outside the skin. It might well be asked whether this is a "reduction" at all. Where before we merely had human behavior to explain, our attempt to reduce has resulted in three things to explain: the behavior, the biological processes themselves, and the complex principles or processes whereby they are transformed into mental and behavioral events. These last processes, although virtually never dealt with in the behavioral sciences, are most certainly not simple and straightforward, not at all the sort of things reductionists have sought through the centuries as a simple and unitary foundation for explanation.[19]

Perhaps the best example of this problem with biological reduction is the so-called nature versus nurture issue in the behavioral sciences. At issue is whether human behavior is caused by biological processes (nature) or learning and experience (nurture). Most modern scholars simply note that the best account of human behavior is that *both* nature and nurture affect human behavior. On one level this seems so obvious as to be not only irrefutable but uninteresting, because it doesn't reveal anything to us we didn't already know. On another level, it leaves a very difficult problem. The problem becomes clear when we employ the language that is commonly used in discussing this issue. Behavioral scientists often simply point out that biology and environment *interact* to produce behavior. The nature of this interaction is frequently left unexplained.

In fact, the nature of this interaction is very problematic. If when we talk about the interaction of biology and environment, we simply mean that things that go on in the body influence behavior and things that go on in the environment influence behavior, then this is obvious and few would argue with it. This is not, however, a real *inter*action; we simply have two things acting independently to produce behavior. An interaction implies that there is a *joint* action, and such joint action between body and environment would require a common ground where physical and environmental forces can meet and truly *inter*act. It is not at all obvious where such common ground lies—where events and processes within the skin, composed of chemicals and flesh, can *meet* with events outside the skin, many of which are in the past.

It seems that any genuine interaction between biology and environment relies on the assumption that there is an additional third force in human behavior—some very complex principle, process, or law that allows these other two forces to interact. Because this third factor is very complex and not understood or examined, the explanation of behavior becomes more complex rather than more simple. This is a species of the same problem we pointed out before. A biological reduction reduces complex human behaviors and thoughts to biological processes *and* some complex, ineffable principle or process that allows the biological event to produce a nonbiological one. This is not a biological reduction at all. There is more to explain *after* the reduction than there was before. Thus, when we see the ideas hidden in it, solving the nature versus nurture controversy by invoking an interaction appears not to be a solution at all.

A committed reductionist might still argue that in spite of this problem the behavioral sciences should continue to assume that all behavior has a biological basis and work toward the goal of reducing behavior to biology. An additional problem arises, however, when we ask whether it is possible to *demonstrate scientifically* whether a biological event did in fact produce a behavioral one.[20] In other words, how might a behavioral scientist validate a biological reduction? What would have to be done to demonstrate that a particular biological state or event does in fact give rise to a mental or behavioral event?

To understand this problem we need to think of the project of biological reduction (or any reduction) as a *translation*. The goal is to translate feelings and other behaviors into a simpler language of biological events— that is, reductionists want to do away with the imprecise language of psychology—feelings, cognitions, wants, desires, and so forth—and replace it with a more precise language of biological states and events. If this translation can be shown to be valid, then in a sense we can do away with the imprecise and epiphenomenal language of mental states (psychology) and use only scientific (biological) language. For example, we could replace the imprecise term *love* with its supposedly more precise translation—the biological state that gives rise to it.

By considering a thought experiment we can see what would be necessary to be sure that the biological reduction of some psychological experience were valid. First, we can see that we would have to eliminate all other potential causes of the behavioral event, so that only a particular biological event (or a small set of biological events) could possibly have caused it. As we will suggest in the next chapter, it is impossible to control potential causes in any experimental setting to put them all "out of play." But there is a further problem. Assuming that we could eliminate other potential causes, we would still need some way to produce a particular biological state that would permit us to observe whether the behavior or mental event we are interested in reducing occurs.

Producing simple behaviors like muscle reflexes seems reasonable and straightforward. Producing a mental event, however, is clearly more problematic. To show that a biological event, such as a particular pattern of neural firing in the brain, produces a mental event, such as a feeling of love, we would have to effect the biological event (perhaps by stimulating the brain in a certain manner) and have our research subject report the feeling. If the subject reported feeling love when the neural pattern was produced, and all other causes were eliminated, then we would presumably have evidence that the feeling is nothing more than a biological state. The biological state could now be substituted for the mental term *love* without any loss in meaning.

The problem is that for the subject to report that he is feeling love when the neural pattern is present, he would have to already know what love feels like. Remember the goal of the biological reduction is to replace the psychological language with the more fundamental biological language. However, to validate the biological language, we would need to rely on psychological language and on human beings' knowledge and under-standing of it. In other words, we are trying to validate the biological language so that it can replace the psychological language, but the psycho-logical language must already be in place and understood, and in some sense taken to be valid, in order to validate the biological one. This implies that the psychological language is the more fundamental one. It is concep-tually inconsistent to replace a primary language (one that we need to validate the one we want to use as a substitute) with a substitute language that depends for its validity on the one it is supposed to replace. If the psychological language is more fundamental, it bears asking why anyone would want to replace it in the first place. This problem is not, of course, proof that psychological events *are not* based in biology, but it does suggest that it might never be possible to establish the fact scientifically.

One final problem entailed by the biological reduction deserves men-tion. It is related to a problem we discussed earlier: How is it that biological events can produce psychological events? We pointed out that it is never made explicit in reductionistic theories how bodily events might possibly produce our experience of mental events, or for that matter, how that production would be experimentally validated. An even more fundamen-tal question concerns whether bodily events can produce mental events at all. It is common in the behavioral sciences, as well as in the broader culture, to talk of needs, drives, and preferences as the root causes of behavior, and further, to locate these driving forces in our biology.

This type of theorizing leads to a twofold problem. First, it seems clear that psychological phenomena such as needs or preferences are experi-enced in terms of a specific object or goal—something within a context of possible things that is needed or preferred. In other words, needs and preferences are inherently contextual. They always have a content. We do not "want" in general, we always want *something*. It seems equally clear that biological events do not have meaningful content attached to them. Bio-logical events as chemical reactions, electrochemical potentials, and strings of DNA cannot take account of context, respond to particular contents, and select or direct purposive actions. Biological events are unaware of the world of possibilities—the choices available—outside the skin or in the mind. To simply assert that they are aware or do select particular contents is to appeal to the complex and always undefined process we discussed earlier. It assumes that biological reduction happens in order to explain *how* it happens.

The second aspect of this problem is that it seems unlikely that physical bodies *want* or *prefer* at all. For example, we might consider something that clearly seems to be a biological drive—hunger. However, what we know about hunger is that when the body is not regularly supplied with food, certain biological processes (stomach contractions, muscle weakness, etc.) occur. Although these processes may be experienced by us as unpleasant, it cannot be concluded that the body wants food. The body is likely to do things we find unpleasant if we do not eat, but it might be all the same to the body to do those things—although *we* may experience as unpleasant the body's responses to a lack of food, it may not make sense to suggest that the body itself experiences its own responses as unpleasant. Because it has to do something, it might as well contract the stomach, and so forth. These bodily functions may result in other bodily functions, but they seem unlikely to result in wants or preferences. Only we, as real human beings, *want* food. It seems implausible that bodies *want* at all. Wanting seems to be inherently contextual. It seems all at once to be mental, emotional, physical, historical, and particular. It seems conceptually impossible to capture such a phenomenon and decide that it is "really just" physical.

AN ALTERNATIVE APPROACH
TO THE PROBLEM OF REDUCTION

The previous section of the chapter illustrated the conceptual problems encountered by explanations of behavior that adopt the traditional metaphysical, temporal, or biological reductive strategies that are so common in contemporary behavioral science. If we are to view these problems as problems, and not as inherent difficulties of working in the behavioral sciences, then alternative strategies must be available to us. Indeed, we need such alternatives if we are going to be able to see the common reductive strategies as merely possible explanatory strategies rather than as necessary in any or all explanations. Postmodern theory provides the beginnings of an alternate approach.

Most theorists who identify themselves with postmodern approaches to the behavioral sciences have been explicitly and radically critical of the traditional theories, and this criticism has often been directly aimed at what they perceive to be the reductive tendencies in the theories. Postmodern analysts of the common strategies of reduction emphasize two points. First, all reductionist strategies that we have reviewed—those currently available in the mainstream behavioral sciences—entail essentially the same problems. The agency, meaning, and morality of human life are threatened.[21] Second, given this threat, there is reason to explore an alternative way of explaining human behavior that might not entail these same problems. In other words, the problem is not finding the "correct" explanation—the one that reduces everything to the "correct" entity or principle, but finding a *way of explaining* that does not reduce in the way these other approaches reduce.

The question of whether it might be possible to have a behavioral science, or a theory of human behavior, that is not reductionistic at all is an interesting one, and one with no easy answer. For many postmodernists, reductionism is inevitable in any explanation of human phenomena.[22] To illustrate, let us consider an example. Assume that Jane has stopped to rest in a large and beautiful park. She is near the top of a fairly tall hill. Before her is a panorama of sights and sounds. There is a stream flowing not far from the bottom of the hill. Across the stream a group of teenagers is playing softball. Birds are flying overhead as well as singing in nearby trees. Cars are crossing the bridge downstream a bit to her left. Someone is fishing in the stream. There is a playground near the stream where several small children are playing. Jane spots a swing set where a little boy is swinging. Suddenly, another group of children change their minds about what to play, running in front of the swing. There is a collision, and the boy falls out of the swing. As Jane rushes to help, the boy's mother arrives, and Jane recounts what happened.

Jane's account will likely include descriptions of the children's behavior, attributions about what was going on in their minds when they changed directions, and descriptions of how the boy was hurt. The account will likely not include the fact that one of the softball players hit a home run, that certain chemicals were in the boy's brain, that a car was crossing the bridge, that the river was flowing, or that the angler caught a fish. In other words, Jane's account will be a selective (and thus reductive) summary of what happened—an abstraction. It will not include everything.

One might argue that Jane's account is not a "full" account, because she was not aware of *everything* that was going on. However, she might very well have been aware of many of the things we mentioned. Certainly she could be aware of some of them. In any account there are a substantial number of things that although available to the one giving the account, are left out. In leaving them out, we necessarily reduce a phenomenon to something simpler and smaller in scope. One might also argue that Jane left things out of her account that could not possibly have affected the event she was most interested in. Although we might have to grant this on a practical level (leaving aside a very interesting philosophical argument about the possibility that virtually all events are meaningfully connected; see, e.g., Bohm, 1980), on another level, this is precisely the point. As soon as Jane begins to make sense of something, she inevitably includes some things and leaves others out, deciding what the phenomenon is, and making a reduced account of it. This is the process of *abstraction*.

This example fits our definition of reductionism because Jane is essentially saying that the accident involving the child is "really just" the children doing something, the swing doing something, or the boy doing something. The accident is *not* the home run being hit, the fish being caught, or the car crossing the bridge. In this sense, every account of an event or a thing is a reduction. Postmodern theory suggests that in precisely this way, every theory is a reduction of events or phenomena. Theories are written precisely to abstract events or things, and offer explanations that account for them. Theories do not or should not include extraneous constructs; they cannot include everything. They give us an explanatory language that tells us what is important and what is not. And they inevitably leave out a great deal.

According to many postmodern approaches, this is true not only of theories, but of all stories, accounts, or descriptions of events. In fact, it is true of all language use. Whatever we say is a reduction because no matter what we say about anything, we cannot say everything that could be said. Every account is thus a partial account. This may seem so obvious as to be uninteresting. It is an important point, however, in light of our previous discussion of ways of knowing in Chapter 3. In postmodern theories, what is true of an act of describing is true of an act of knowing. Knowing is always an interpretive construction. It is participatory, not objective.

It arises out of what is there to be known, but is not *caused* by it. In an important and essential way, the explanation or knowledge of something is not removed from what is being known, yet is also not the product of what is being known. Thus, although all explanations "reduce," it is possible to have explanations that do not reduce *to some thing* (structure or physical entity). This is a very different sense of the term reduction than we have discussed previously.

It is also an important point in understanding the postmodern perspective on reduction. If some sort of reduction is inevitable in all language use, and thus, in all theorizing, then perhaps our major concern is not *whether* theories in the behavioral sciences are reductive, but *how* they are reductive. It matters how theorists perform the reduction. It is also vital to understand what is taken to be the fundamental reality in each theory. If some aspects of a situation, such as the boy swinging, are considered important and included in the explanation, whereas others are considered unimportant and omitted from the explanation, an important question is why? Why are certain aspects important? Careful consideration of the answer to this question shows us what is assumed in a theory to be true of human beings without question and what the implications (theoretical costs and benefits) of such assumptions are. In a sense, the answering of this question for metaphysical, material, and temporal reductionists has been our task in this chapter so far.

Recasting the problem of reduction in these terms opens the door to an account of human behavior (compatible with some types of postmodern or hermeneutic perspectives) that is quite different from the more prominent theories in the behavioral sciences. This different account starts with a realization, illustrated in our example above, that everything human beings do, because it involves language, understanding, and knowing, is interpretive. Also, this lived experience is richly contextual, situated in a history and network of social relations and interpretations. Further, as we noted in the example above, it is inevitable that this kind of interpretive activity is reductive, because all language is. Perhaps, some postmodernists argue, this very inevitability makes it a good starting point for explaining ourselves and our actions. In other words, the alternative kind of explanation we consider here takes the interpretive lived experience of human beings, *acts* of knowing, being, and expressing, to be fundamental. Although these acts will never be fully captured and contained in any explanation (reduction is inevitable), *they are not reducible to anything else more fundamental.* These acts do not need to be explained by appealing to any structure or entity other than the acts themselves. Traditional reductive explanations propose various entities to which the acts are supposedly reduced: an underlying but unseen structure for metaphysics, an underlying but physical entity for materialism, and a nonpresent but primary time dimension for temporal reductionism.

Postmodern theorists do suggest that because all explanation has to start somewhere, every explanation has to assume a grounding for itself. Some type of "metaphysics" is always going to be necessary in a theory or other account of behavior. The question is not whether we have a metaphysical starting point in our theory, but rather, what that starting point is. In this sense, both reduction and metaphysics seem to be inevitable. The problems with metaphysically reductive explanations of behavior, as found in contemporary behavioral science, result not from the metaphysical or reductive nature of the explanations, but from the type of entity or principle that is taken to be the metaphysical reality and the type of reduction carried out.

The starting point or fundamental reality that postmodernists offer as an alternative is not a principle, law, or structure; neither is it a mechanism or material substrate. It is the interpretive act itself. Postmodernists consider the grounding for explanations to be the interpretive act of a human agent in a social context. Although this grounding is still reductive, it is presumed to avoid the conceptual problems that beset other explanations in the behavioral sciences. It also offers the possibility of accounting for human beings that does not sacrifice meaning (and thus humanity) to preconceived ideas of what explanations must look like.

The question remains whether this alternative to traditional reductionism rules out biological influences. From a postmodern perspective, human beings are physically embodied, and the biological processes that are part of the experience of being human are important and ought to be understood. It is common in postmodern approaches to refer to the relationship between persons and bodies as *embodiment*.[23] The idea of embodiment is simply that although humans are always found with physical bodies and experience the world *with* and *through* their bodies, it is not the case that human activity arises *from* the body the way that traditional causal theories would describe. As we have also outlined above, there is considerable question whether compelling empirical or logical evidence for biological reduction could be found. Certainly, we have no everyday, lived experience of biological reductionism.

This suggests that in *some* ways, persons cannot be understood as separate from their material bodies. At least we seldom encounter people in an unembodied state. However, the way in which the body is important is a matter of some discussion. Biological reduction suggests that the body is important because it is the (direct mechanistic) cause of our actions. Postmodern notions of embodiment suggest that the body is important because we experience the world and interpret it in a way that must include the reality the body imposes on us. Our bodies are important because they act as an important part of the assumptive basis for our lives. For example, because we have material bodies, we know what to expect of other things that also have material bodies. Bodies are important because some experiences, such as physical pain, hunger, and exhaustion, and the meanings of these experiences, seem to be possible only because we have bodies. Also, bodies locate us in time and space, and thus help form our understanding of time and space, rather than time and space forming our understanding of our bodies. In the postmodern perspective we are describing here, bodies are part of the world of experience of which we must be aware and take account, instead of being the cause of behavior. We must take account of the body and what it makes available to us if we are to interpret well and live effectively. Because of our embodiment, we must take the body seriously, but we are not caused by it. It is, instead, one of the assumptions on which our behaviors are based. This alternative starting point for explanation gives rise to a view of human beings as active interpretive agents for whom meaningful involvement in the world is the irreducible and defining reality of humanity itself.

CONCLUSION

In the Western intellectual tradition there has been a preference for simpler over more complex explanations for phenomena. Simplicity has been conceptualized in terms of the number of assumptions made or the number of constructs invoked (fewer is better), as well as in terms of biological and mechanical, as opposed to rational processes. This preference is expressed in contemporary behavioral sciences as reductionism.

The essence of reductionistic explanation is to claim that some phenomenon (X) is "really just" something else (Y). This something else that accounts for the phenomenon X is considered to be more basic and fundamental than the phenomenon itself, and thus explains it.

Contemporary strategies of reductive explanation have grown out of various intellectual sources, including traditional metaphysical thinking, materialism, and Enlightenment ideas characterized by mechanism, the notion of linear time, and theories of evolution. Each of these lines of thought has given rise to reductive thinking in the behavioral sciences. Explaining human phenomena in terms of metaphysical, temporal, materialistic, mechanical, or biological reduction has been an appealing strategy because it offers the illusion of simplicity. However, because of its implicit assumptions, it brings with it certain problematic implications for the meaning of human life and human beings themselves.

Careful examination of these reductive approaches to the behavioral sciences raises questions about whether they are compelling and can be shown to be valid. At the same time, they have important implications about our human nature. A review of the dominant theories in the behavioral sciences suggests that they employ, in one form or another, all the reductive strategies described in the chapter. Postmodern theorists take a radically different perspective on the issue of reductionism, suggesting that some form of reduction is unavoidable, but that the ultimate grounding for reductive explanation is human lived experience. Postmodernists do not attempt to privilege some physical or nonphysical structure underlying lived experience, nor do they rely on changeless and unified principles. Rather, they take experience as it is lived—at face value, so to speak—with all the changing and disunified context in which it is inextricably embedded.

Notes

1. We recognize that many behavioral scientists and philosophers disagree that any of the behavioral sciences, let alone the aggregate of them, has a paradigm in the sense that Kuhn uses the term. Part of the problem lies in differences of opinion about what does or does not constitute such a paradigm, and even about what Kuhn may have meant. Developing an adequate argument in support of our contention is beyond the scope of this book. Rather, we prefer to use the term *paradigm* in a very general and global sense—as we choose to read Kuhn—suggesting simply that there must be a common assumptive basis underlying scientific, or any other scholarly work, and that various aspects of this

common assumptive basis can be seen across theories and disciplines in the behavioral sciences.

2. It is somewhat ironic that in the behavioral sciences, a dedication to the importance of studying only observables and to observation as the most solid foundation for explanation exists side by side with a tendency to look to hidden and unobservable causes and constructs as explanations. We do not have time to explore this issue, or the irony, but it seems, nonetheless, to be true of the behavioral sciences. Empirical methods are involved in the issue, because they are employed in the attempt to make the unobservable observable. Operationalization is the process by which this is accomplished. Here we can only invite the reader to accept this seeming contradiction and hope that the exploration of the topics in this chapter and the next will clarify the issues.

3. The tendency to think reductively is not unique to the behavioral sciences. We believe reductionism has become deeply ingrained in our Western culture and is thus an unacknowledged assumption for lay persons as well as behavioral scientists. The extended cultural critique necessary to establish this point is beyond the scope of this book.

4. The term often used by scholars to refer to this abstract fundamental principle is *Being*. In contrast to *Being*, the changing particulars of the world are referred to as *Becoming*.

5. The examples we have given here to suggest that behaviorist theory is descendant from classical metaphysics are all taken from traditional behaviorism—what some refer to as *methodological behaviorism* (Lee, 1988). Proponents of newer brands of behaviorism— known as *radical behaviorism*—have attempted to distance themselves from their forebears, preferring to render explanations in terms of functional relationships and contingencies. For example, radical behaviorists refuse to speculate on the cause of reinforcement—on how it works—preferring to simply observe and record that behavioral increases are coordinated with certain occurrences. Such occurrences are evidence of what are called contingencies—functional relationships between behaviors and environmental events. This step away from the kinds of explanations offered in more traditional behaviorism is a step in the direction of abstraction. This high level of abstraction in which contingencies exist and operate is a metaphysical realm. New and radical strains of behaviorism are fundamentally metaphysical, and thus, perhaps, not so radical at all.

6. See Wheelwright (1960) for a fuller discussion and for citations from Aristotle and others that clarify atomism.

7. This type of temporal reductionism can also include explanations that reduce the process under study to the present or future temporal dimensions. Although reduction to the past is by far the most common tack in behavioral science explanation, explanations that focus *exclusively* on the present or future qualify as temporal reductions as well.

8. As an example of this, Slife (in press) shows how the linearization of information fails to capture its holistic and relational properties, obviating the meaning supposedly contained in the information.

9. Slife, in a 1993 book on the topic of time, describes the effects of both forms of reductionism on several subdisciplines of psychology, including developmental psychology. Although Schaffer (1988) does not refer to temporal reduction explicitly, his article does articulate, in part, the problems that developmental psychology encounters as a result of Newton's view of time. We refer the reader to p. 91 in particular.

10. The possibility of so-called parallel processes has been a question of considerable interest to cognitive theorists from the beginnings of the cognitive movement. We lack the space here to review the history of the efforts to uncover and explicate such processes, but we believe it is still fair to say that the preponderance of research is carried out on

sequential processes, and that sequential processes are at the heart of most mainstream cognitive models.

11. See, for example, the discussion in Leahey (1992) on the origins of behaviorism.

12. Some kinds of metaphysical explanations do not necessarily have this theoretical consequence. We are only arguing that most of the ones that are common in the behavioral sciences do.

13. Some theorists posit the existence of metaphysical givens and do so in defense of human agency. Rychlak (1994) offers a conceptualization of mind, suggesting that although the mind is innate, and logically a priori to human experience, it has the capacity to transcend the given and generate genuine alternatives to thought and behavior.

14. See Williams (1987, 1992) for a fuller argument as to why possibility and agency are necessary for meaning.

15. We might meaningfully say that it is bad *that* the act happened. However, to say it is bad *that* an act occurred is not the same thing as saying that *the act itself* is bad. Even to claim that it is bad that an event occurred, we would need to refer to some criterion for making such a judgment. Most who make this argument base their judgment on preference or some sense of the pragmatic consequences of the act. These assessments of the consequences of an act say nothing of the morality of the act itself. For example, many people would agree that is is bad *that* an act, such as drinking alcohol, results in domestic violence, but they would not condemn the act of drinking itself as bad.

16. The reader is referred to Slife (1993) for an expanded treatment of time and its role in psychological explanation. He shows how pervasive the assumption of linear time has been in the behavioral sciences, owing primarily to Newton's influence. He discusses the conceptual problems entailed in believing in linear time and in relying on it in our explanations of human events. He also offers alternative explanatory approaches that do not rely on linear time and develops them to an extent that we are unable to in this chapter.

17. The reader is referred to Williams (1995) for a more complete argument to the effect that this sort of transcendence is not possible. However, this does not mean that people are indeed trapped in the flow of past events. Rather, the problem is shown to result from the acceptance of time as linear time and the traditional notion of causality. It is also argued that when time and transcendence are properly understood, it becomes unnecessary to break away from the past because there is nothing like the sort of past that would need to be broken away from. Rather, the past exists only as kept alive in present activity. What is required for change then is simply "having the world" differently, a creative, interpretive act. The full analysis, available in these sources, is not reproduced in this discussion.

18. This process of transformation must occur at times that by and large make sense to the husband—when it seems reasonable to feel love—and almost never when it makes no sense. Thus, the process must be extremely sensitive to history, context, and appropriateness.

19. One other complicating issue results from the fact that even if an experience such as love can be shown to result from a biological state, the experience is nonetheless real—it does not just go away. If it is shown experimentally that John's experience of love for his wife can be produced by a chemical state, he still experiences love. It will also be the case that his experience of love can be produced by a letter from his wife—a nonbiological event. We have a difficult case, then, in which the same experience results from two very different things, one biological and the other not. This is hardly a reduction. A reductionist might argue that the letter only produces the experience of love by producing a biological state, which in turn produces the experience of love. This is a reduction, clearly enough, but not a biological reduction. The letter seems to be the prior cause, and thus, the most fundamental thing.

20. This question raises an additional one of whether scientists can ever validate any of their theories and hypotheses, which we will postpone until the next chapter. Here we will deal with a slightly different issue.

21. That we raise this issue in terms of a postmodern analysis should not be taken to mean that only the postmodernists recognize the problem or describe it in this way. It should not even be taken to mean that the postmodern rendition of the problem is the best one. Many from the perspective of classical rationalism, some religious perspectives, or non-Western traditions, just to name a few, would immediately recognize these problems and have a number of responses to them. We deal with the issue as we do in the attempt to articulate a possible response to it from a (one particular) postmodern perspective.

22. If it truly is inevitable, we suspect, or at least hope, that it is harmless and will not entrap us in serious conceptual problems. Whether, or how, this might be the case remains to be seen.

23. The best-known and most influential work done on the problem of embodiment is that of Maurice Merleau-Ponty (see especially, 1962). Our treatment of embodiment is taken from his work but does not in the space available do it justice. We hope it will serve as an introduction for interested readers.

✺ 6 ✺

Science and Human Behavior

✺ The history of the behavioral sciences is marked by a struggle to separate these sciences from philosophy and establish them as a distinct set of scholarly disciplines. This struggle has led to a continuing concern about their scientific status. In fact, the behavioral sciences are distinguished from philosophy precisely because they rely on scientific methods and the application of science to questions of human behavior, whereas in philosophy rational analysis is applied. Because of the success of natural scientists in understanding the natural world and solving practical problems, it seems reasonable to suggest that the same success might be achieved in the realm of human behavior. Somewhere in the communal mind-set of behavioral scientists lies the expectation that careful scientific study of human beings will yield solutions to our most perplexing human problems. Our culture as a whole seems to share this expectation, continuing to respect scientific findings and turning to the behavioral sciences for answers to life's problems.

In this chapter, we examine the nature of science to see why people in our culture have come to trust it for answers to our important human problems and whether the behavioral sciences

can, or indeed *should,* be scientific. The assumption that human
beings can and ought to be studied using natural science
methods has important implications for how we understand
human beings.

THE NATURE OF SCIENCE

To be confident about whether the behavioral sciences are or should
be sciences, we need to answer the question: What is science? On first
examination, this may seem a trivial question with an easy and straightforward answer, but on closer examination we see that the answer is not
as simple as it seems. Science and scientific findings have had a pronounced
impact on philosophy since the time of the early Enlightenment and through
the work of early scientists such as Galileo and Newton. It is also true,
however, that our understanding of science has changed as various philosophical views have become popular and replaced earlier views over the
past several centuries.

It might seem strange to suggest that changes in philosophical thinking
have produced changes in our understanding of science, especially as
science is often contrasted with philosophy. Philosophy is seen as being
speculative and fraught with uncertainty, whereas science is seen as being
objective and exact. We do not have space here to trace the history of science
to show how philosophy has affected it, but later in the chapter we review
some of the issues that have been important in this history. For now, it is
important simply to note that science itself is based on a set of ideas—
assumptions about what the world is like and how it should be studied.

The word *science* comes from a Latin word meaning "knowledge." In
Greek philosophy, knowledge was contrasted with mere opinion. According to this ancient view, knowledge—if it is to count as true knowledge—
is knowledge of what is real or true. We cannot have knowledge about what
is not real or true. That which is not real or true is mere opinion. In this
way science got connected to the question of truth, and this connection
remains very much a part of our beliefs about science even today. In the
minds of many, science encompasses what we *know* to be true, in contrast
with what we only think to be true. In our modern age, we attach some
importance to the idea that we have, in science, a method of distinguishing what is true and real from what is not. This idea lies at the very heart

of our understanding of science and our confidence in it. Knowledge gained through science can be trusted.

In contemporary scholarly discourse, the term science is used to refer both to a type of knowledge that is trustworthy and to a method of arriving at that type of knowledge. Both of these meanings are important for our discussion. However, in the behavioral sciences, discussions of science are most often focused on the issue of method. As we noted above, the behavioral sciences have developed largely from the attempt to bring scientific methods to bear on the study of human beings.

It is common in our culture to refer to the *scientific method* as if it were a single thing about which all people agree. It should be pointed out, however, that there is no such thing as *the* scientific method. There are as many scientific methods as there are scientists doing research. There are, however, some commonalities among scientists in the sort of methods they use, so it is possible to study their methods and talk about what qualifies as science. And the idea of proper scientific method has changed over time.

The early Greeks are generally considered to be the first scientists. In the Western tradition we trace most of our sciences to them—as we do the Western intellectual tradition itself. As noted above, science was knowledge for these early Greeks, and knowledge was gained through careful observation and skilled exercise of rationality. Clear analytical thinking and careful discourse were very much a part of science. The Greek word meaning "discourse" (among other things) was *logos* and this word is the root of our modern suffix *-ology*, which we often use to designate a discipline as a science, as in biology, psychology, and so forth.

Many of our modern sciences owe much to Aristotle, who developed formal logic as a tool for doing science, that is, for generating knowledge that could be trusted. Science in the time of Aristotle was much closer to philosophy than we generally think of it today. Much of the work in science was aimed at classifying things of the world and placing them in categories that related to other categories of things in a rational and meaningful way. A major project in biology, for example, was the classification of living things.

In later centuries, scholars became skeptical about whether reason and logic alone could produce useful and trustworthy knowledge. It was felt that reason and logic were too likely to be influenced by traditions, habitual ways of thinking, and authority. Reason and logic were unable to correct themselves when they did go wrong. Sir Francis Bacon, a slightly older contemporary of Isaac Newton, was one of the first to make this criticism explicit in his writing about what he called *idols*. Idols, for Bacon, are worshipped and endowed with authority although they are false and do not deserve to be seen as authoritative. Among the idols Bacon wrote about are authority, habit, imprecise use of language, and other things that keep us from more useful and trustworthy truths. Bacon suggested that careful observation of the world would allow us to discern the secrets of nature. The test of whether we have, indeed, discerned the secrets is whether we can exercise power and control over nature to bring about practical ends. This dual emphasis on careful observation in the pursuit of truth and (practical) control over the natural world is at the heart of our modern notion of science.

Since the Enlightenment, science has been thought of as a method for testing ideas and opinions through observation. Observation takes place through the medium of sensory experience. This emphasis on observation of the world as a way of attaining true knowledge is the essence of *empiricism* (see Chapter 3). Scientists thus came to be empirical in their methods, meaning that they came to trust observation over what can be established by "merely" rational thought. We should note, however, that the early Enlightenment scientists such as Bacon, Galileo, and Newton did not abandon reason altogether. They still recognized that it is important for science to "make sense," and they also realized that careful rational analysis was an essential part of all scientific work. They did, however, suggest that at some point scientific ideas should be subjected to an empirical test, and that the empirical test was crucial to an idea's being accepted as true.

OUR MODERN VIEW OF SCIENCE

In our post-Enlightenment culture we continue to trust science and rely on it to produce trustworthy knowledge. The question should be asked, however, what it is about science that recommends it to us so strongly. In answering this question, we formulate the qualities and characteristics of science that give it its great credibility. We have already mentioned one of the important characteristics of science: Science emerged as a trusted source of knowledge, in part, because it *relies on observation and* not *just rationality*. For a number of reasons, we have come to trust our senses more than we trust our thoughts and ideas.

It should be pointed out, however, that just relying on sensory observation is not enough to establish science as a good source of knowledge. All people make sensory observations all the time. What sets science apart from what ordinary people routinely do is the *way* the observations are made. One of the hallmarks of scientific observation is that it is made under *objective* conditions. This is usually understood to mean that what scientists observe is not influenced by "outside" factors such as the values, expectations, and desires of the scientist, or by Bacon's idols such as traditions, authority, or habitual ways of thinking. Objective observation means that the scientist, as observer, stands on some "privileged" ground to make the observations. When made from these grounds, the observations have scientific credibility.

Another important aspect of scientific observation is that it is made under *controlled* conditions. Through the process of experimentation, scientists control the conditions under which they make their observations. Good scientific practice entails the scientist's *predicting* what he or she will observe under certain specified conditions. If the prediction is found to hold true, the theory or hypothesis that led the scientist to make the prediction is validated. Knowing what conditions to control and how to control them is often seen to be the crucial test of scientific knowledge. We therefore trust scientific knowledge because it gives us the ability to control and predict events in experimental settings. Being able to control and predict in experimental settings gives some expectation that we will be able to control and predict in real-world settings as well. This confidence in the process of control and prediction is at the heart of the desire for the behavioral sciences to truly be sciences.

This movement from the experimental setting to the real world is made possible by *technology*. When scientific knowledge is successfully applied to the solution of a real-world problem, we have technological advance. Some scientists maintain that science should, at least sometimes, be pursued for the sake of knowledge itself without any necessary hope or promise that it will "pay off" in technological advance. This position supports a sort of "pure" science, or "pure" research, in contrast to "applied" work. Even if we grant a place for scientific work for the sake of knowledge alone, it is difficult to deny that technology is one of the major reasons science is given so much credibility. The fact that the natural sciences have been so successful over the past few centuries in producing unprecedented technological advances contributes greatly to this credibility. Indeed, the ability to produce technology that solves problems has come to be an acid test for any discipline or activity that is claimed to be scientific. It is thus easy to see why researchers in the behavioral sciences have wanted their disciplines to be sciences. First, there is considerable prestige attached to the sciences because of the impressive technological success they have enjoyed. Second, behavioral scientists hold out the hope that a technology for dealing with the problems of human behavior might be developed with much the same beneficial results as in the natural sciences.

There are other characteristics of scientific work that contribute to its credibility. Scientific work is conducted in *public,* in the sense that the results are open to public scrutiny. The knowledge gained through scientific methods is thus available to all who can read and understand the research, or perform the scientific experiment for themselves. Scientific knowledge also increases in credibility when the results of scientific investigation are *repeatable.* We believe that if something is true it should be susceptible to being demonstrated for all to see and repeat.[1]

One other characteristic of science deserves mention. Science has always been closely associated with mathematics. To a great extent *science has mathematics* as its language. The idea that nature "speaks" the language of mathematics is a very old one, going back at least to Pythagoras (6th century B.C.). If nature speaks a mathematical language, then scientists should try to understand it. Compared to the language in which people normally communicate, the mathematical language is perceived as being more precise and less open to error and interpretation. The truths of mathematics seem sure and certain when compared to the ideas of philosophy and other forms of theoretical speculation. It seems intuitively obvious, for example, that $(2 + 3) = (3 + 2)$. We find it very difficult to argue that this is not so. Because science is often conducted in mathematical language, and because it explains many phenomena in the world mathematically, the precision and certainty of mathematics has generalized to science.

This mathematical precision is probably best represented in the machines we build. Mechanical systems of all sorts can be described accurately and precisely by mathematical operations. Indeed, mathematics has made it possible to build such machines. This relationship between mathematical precision and mechanism is part of the reason scientific explanations are often mechanistic and deterministic. Mathematics lends itself to these types of explanations. It seems reasonable for behavioral scientists to want that same precision and power in their explanations and predictions of human behavior.

All the characteristics and qualities we have mentioned here contribute to the perceived legitimacy of science. Because of the way science is done, the knowledge produced with it is seen to be more trustworthy than knowledge attained in other ways. Scientists seem to be able to prove things true or false, establish with some authority the causes of events, and provide an understanding of phenomena that is objective and uncontaminated by traditions and subjective speculations. The question remains, however, whether the behavioral sciences should be included among the truly scientific disciplines.

ARE THE BEHAVIORAL SCIENCES SCIENTIFIC?

Whether the behavioral sciences should be regarded as scientific depends on what we take science to be. On the basis of the preceding discussion about the characteristics and qualities that lend science its credibility, we are in a position to talk about what science is in a way that might help us see how the behavioral sciences are situated in the larger scientific enterprise. There are two conceptualizations of science that are relevant in considering the status of the behavioral sciences. According to the first conceptualization, science consists of a body of knowledge that explains the nature of the world (or that aspect of the world that is the subject matter of the particular science in question, e.g., psychology, biology, family science). From this perspective, a *scientific* body of knowledge is recognizable by two main characteristics. First, scientific explanations for the most part involve rejecting supernatural explanations of phenomena in favor of naturalistic explanations. Scientific explanations are usually given in terms of matter or other naturalistic constructs. Second, scientific knowledge is generally framed in terms of laws and principles that are assumed to determine the events of the world. These laws are taken to be the real causes of the events, and because of their lawful regularity, it is possible, at least in theory, to control and predict the events.

By these characteristics of science, the majority of the behavioral sciences would probably not qualify as sciences in the minds of many. Although behavioral scientists have largely rejected supernatural explanations and tried to explain human behavior in strictly naturalistic terms, the attempt has not been wholly successful. Also, the behavioral sciences have for the most part been unable to formulate universal laws that fully account for human behavior. Behavioral scientists have assumed a deterministic posture toward human behavior, but they have not been able to demonstrate the kind of control and prediction that have been achieved in the natural sciences. This is generally assumed to be the result of there being so many variables that cannot be controlled when dealing with human beings that reliable predictions are impossible. These problematic variables make human behavior so complex that it is likely never to be as neatly controlled and predictable as other natural events. For this reason, the behavioral sciences are often referred to as *soft* sciences. If this portrayal of human life as complex and consisting of many subtle and uncontrollable variables is correct, it seems likely that the behavioral sciences will never be scientific in the same way as the natural sciences.

The second common way of speaking about the nature of science is to say that science is primarily a *method* of studying phenomena. This method involves careful empirical observation, control and prediction in the experimental setting, and most often, measurement and mathematization of the phenomena being studied. By this definition, any discipline in which the scientific method is used qualifies as a science. From this point of view, the behavioral sciences probably qualify as sciences because recognizably scientific methods are employed in them. Of course, the degree to which behavioral scientists are able to apply those methods is a matter of some debate. It seems difficult to measure many important aspects of human beings, because we lack the instruments to do so and because it is often not apparent what scales or units of measure are appropriate. For example, what are the proper units for measuring anger? Furthermore, human beings in many settings actively resist strict control and prediction.

As we mentioned earlier in the chapter, one of the hallmarks of science is that it produces technology. The natural sciences have an impressive record of technological advance. In this respect, the behavioral sciences are again at a disadvantage. Although the behavioral sciences have undoubtedly resulted in beneficial strategies for therapy, education, and business, the effectiveness of those "technologies," especially in comparison with technologies of the natural sciences, such as medicine and engineering, has been questioned. By comparison, the behavioral sciences seem to contribute few technological wonders in the modern age. It should be noted, however, that the literature in nearly all the behavioral sciences contains considerable commitment to finding solutions to human problems.

In summary, then, the behavioral sciences probably do not qualify under the first of these two conceptualizations of science. However, as we will see later, the natural sciences may not qualify either. Under the second conceptualization, the behavioral sciences probably qualify as sciences, but we are left with two important questions. First, is adherence to a method adequate ground for a discipline's status as a science? From this ground, on the one hand, many students of paranormal phenomena, such as ESP, have undertaken to study these phenomena scientifically, and thus the field of parapsychology should qualify as a science. However, many scientists would be reluctant to allow parapsychologists under the umbrella of science. On the other hand, physicists working on the frontiers of quantum mechanics often do not do recognizably scientific experiments. Albert Einstein, for example, never conducted an experiment involving observation of phenomena in a laboratory. In fact, many of the things he theorized about could not be observed at the time he theorized about them. We seem quite willing, however, to refer to Einstein as a scientist.

Even if we are content to conclude that the behavioral sciences are indeed sciences because of their adherence to scientific methods, a second question remains: Are such classically scientific methods the best methods for studying human behavior? Remember that scientific methods are based on certain assumptions about the nature of truth and the world. If these assumptions are not true of the human world and of human phenomena, then the scientific methods based on these assumptions may not be appropriate for studying people. We return to this question later in the chapter, but for now, considering this question leads us to see that we need to be more explicit about the assumptions that underlie our contemporary conceptualization of science.

THE ASSUMPTIONS OF SCIENCE

It should be clear by now that it is not altogether easy to decide just what science is. It is important to note this, because science is generally accepted as the best means to settle issues and find explanations of things. It is problematic to expect science to settle issues if we cannot be entirely settled about what science is. One of the first issues that needs to be considered is whether science is, as many people in our culture have believed, a clearly defined method that always works to uncover truth. Many people believe that science is self-correcting when it goes wrong. Many also expect that science should be virtually the same in all disciplines that researchers want to call sciences. They assume that science is objective and free from the changing disciplinary influences of tradition, values, and social forces. Many recent observers of science have challenged these views. They propose that science is an activity, a way of approaching a problem, but certainly not the only way. Science is thus something human beings do, rather than a monolithic system that runs itself apart from other human activities and concerns.

In assessing the nature of science, it will be helpful to discuss two general conceptions that have been used as frameworks for talking about science: *positivism* and *Weltanschauung*. Positivism should be distinguished from *realism*. The difference between realism and positivism is closely related to the difference between empiricism and rationalism, as discussed in Chapter 3. Realism is the older view. Proponents of this position hold that the methods of science allow the scientist direct access to the reality of the world. In other words, if scientists properly apply the methods of science, they can directly observe the world as it is. Scientific explanations, in this view, describe the world as it really exists. This is a very strong position to take, because the nature of reality and our capacity as humans to discover that nature have been in question since the beginnings of the Western intellectual tradition. That people take such a strong position in relation to science is testimony to the esteem in which science is held, as compared to philosophy and other more speculative ways of studying the world.

Positivism is, in some sense, a more moderate position.[2] Its proponents do not hold that scientists study things the way they really are. Rather, the purpose of science is to help scientists formulate a coherent view, or model, of the world. From this position, scientists gain confidence about certain regularities on the basis of experiments, then they formulate laws and constructs that they use to explain those regularities. For example, we might consider scientific work dealing with gravity. Realists would suggest that gravity is a reality and that we see it at work as we observe gravitational phenomena. Positivists, on the other hand, would claim that gravity is a useful construct for explaining why things move and fall as they do. They would not necessarily claim to be observing gravity, or even that gravity exists as described. They would claim only that the concept of gravity helps us explain the world in a coherent fashion.

Two things are important to note as we compare these two positions. First, it seems very difficult for positivists not to take the next conceptual step and begin to believe that the constructs formulated to explain the regularities of the world (e.g., gravity) are in some sense real. There is rarely any constraining influence within science itself to prevent this. Especially when scientific advance leads to real technological advance, it is difficult to keep reminding ourselves, "This is only a construct." We are tempted instead to think, "If it works, it must be real." What this means is that positivist positions often shade into realist positions, especially among scientists who care more about their work than about philosophical questions.

The second point to be noted is that both realists and positivists put great emphasis on observation. The subject matter of science is what is observable, and what is observed is the court of final appeal for establishing the truth or validity of any conception of the world. Proponents of the two positions emphasize the observable for slightly different reasons. Realists emphasize what is observable because they are interested in dealing with what is real, and what is real ought to have some observable manifestation. For positivists, it is important to deal with the observable because all constructs used to explain the world ought to be tied directly and rather tightly to what can be observed. There is no value in claiming that a construct is important or useful in explaining the world if it cannot be shown that there is some observable phenomenon for the construct to explain. For example, why talk about gravity at all if there is not some observable phenomenon, such as things falling down, that gravity is supposed to explain? For our purposes, it is important to note that both the realist and positivist consider the subject matter of science to be what is observable. Both approaches are thus wedded ultimately to empiricism as their epistemology (see Chapter 3).

As the behavioral sciences developed as sciences in the latter part of the 19th and early 20th centuries, the dominant view of science was positivism. During this period a particular brand of positivism, *logical positivism,* was very influential in Europe as well as the United States. Later on, the work of Carl Hempel (1965) came to be very influential. The view of science that he set down has come to be the one that for the most part, behavioral scientists still recognize as the foundation of their scientific approach. We will not go into detail about Hempel's philosophy of science; however, certain aspects of his approach should be mentioned.[3] Hempel held that the purpose of science was the formulation of general or universal *covering laws*. These are laws that explain a wide range of phenomena over a wide range of conditions. Part of the formulation of the laws was the specification of *limiting conditions* under which the laws apply. Experimentation in which control is exercised over the observational conditions is the best way to specify and refine the limiting conditions.

As this project is undertaken in the behavioral sciences, the purpose is to uncover fundamental causal laws of human behavior that apply very broadly, if not universally. As these laws are "discovered,"[4] through careful experimental study, we can specify the conditions under which they will apply, and isolate and identify the variables that affect whether the law applies. Once the laws are sufficiently known and refined that all the relevant variables and conditions can be taken into account, we are able to use the laws to our advantage. Through manipulation of the relevant variables, we can control and predict behavior in the real world as well as in the laboratory.

This positivist approach by Hempel has been challenged in recent years by a number of philosophers of science. Perhaps the best-known alternative position concerns the second general framework for discussing science, that of Thomas Kuhn (1970).[5] This framework is sometimes referred to as the *Weltanschauung* approach (e.g., Leahey, 1992), using the German word that can be translated as "worldview." This way of understanding science suggests that it is not as objective and free from cultural influences as realists and positivists have thought. The view of the world that each scientist has and shares with other scientists (and nonscientists) influences the way science is done. This worldview (in Kuhn's terms, a *paradigm*) leads scientists to think about their science in the way they do, even though they usually do not recognize their view as a worldview. The way they formulate their questions, the methods they believe to be appropriate, and the sorts of explanations they hold to be acceptable are all influenced by the worldview in which they live, as shared by a "culture" of scientists and the larger culture.

This Weltanschauung view of science is a direct challenge to positivism. If scientists cannot escape their own paradigms, culture, and history, then they cannot claim to be about the business of discovering anything universal. All scientific knowledge will emerge from, and thus apply only within, the culturally derived paradigm that led scientists to think about the problem in that way in the first place. This argument is important, because it calls into question not only the possibility of doing what positivists suggest science ought to be doing—getting at universal laws—but also all the characteristics and qualities that have traditionally been attributed to science (objectivity, determinism, certainty, etc.). This issue might well cause behavioral scientists to carefully consider their commitment to science, at least as it has developed in the behavioral sciences.

In the behavioral sciences, however, study of the philosophy of science has not typically been emphasized as an integral part of the curricula. As a result, behavioral scientists have largely adopted science as they perceived it to be, without sustained reflection about whether what they perceived about science was true or appropriate for their subject matter. Sigmund Koch (1959), for example, observed that psychology developed during the period of history (the late 19th century) when logical positivism was the dominant force in the natural sciences, and so researchers in psychology and other behavioral sciences adopted that view. Over time, however, natural scientists became dissatisfied with logical positivism and abandoned it. The behavioral scientists, on the other hand, were not so inclined. Koch (1959) also observed that in psychology, unlike the natural sciences, researchers settled on methods before they developed their questions—that is, they did not decide psychology was a science because they were faced with questions that seemed to require a scientific method to answer. Rather, psychologists seem to have first made the decision to use scientific methods and then framed their disciplinary questions according to what could be studied using that method. It seems clear that many other behavioral sciences can be similarly characterized.

Even a cursory survey of texts and other scholarly work suggests that behavioral scientists have adopted science in a fairly eclectic form, without careful consideration of its virtues, limits, or philosophical implications. Critical discussions of these issues are rare in both text and classroom. Behavioral scientists have been mostly positivistic, but with leanings and propensities toward realism. They have acknowledged the work of Kuhn, but this has not seriously detracted from a basic commitment to the formulation of general laws of human behavior. What seems to have been constant throughout the formative years of the behavioral sciences is a commitment to *method* as the essence of science and the distinguishing feature that would make the behavioral sciences real sciences. Thus, behavioral scientists have approached their subject matter—human beings —convinced of the importance of objectivity and scientific certainty, and intent on uncovering general or universal causal laws, formulating deterministic and mechanistic explanations of behavior, and trying to develop technological solutions to human problems.

It is important to consider whether human beings are really the sort of entities best described by mechanism, determinism, and efficient causality. If they are, then the traditional methods of science may be the most appropriate methods to employ. If they are not, then the cost of traditional scientific methods may be the use of a mechanical explanation without any real grounds for or awareness of this use. It is important to emphasize that the question of whether human beings are indeed natural objects amenable to study by traditional scientific methods is not itself a question that can be solved by scientific method. Scientific method itself is based on certain assumptions about the nature of the thing it studies. We have more to say about this point later. For now we simply suggest that we ought to examine traditional science, its assumptions and implications.

EXAMINATION OF SCIENCE AND THE POSSIBILITY OF BEHAVIORAL SCIENCE

The Truth/Method Question

One of the main reasons science is so attractive is that it seems to hold the promise of truth. At least science appears to be a more trustworthy way of testing the truth of our ideas than others ways that have been developed. However, this perception of science is based on an assumption. The assumption is that truth will be found by applying some method to answer the question at hand. In other words, one of the foundations for our faith in science is the idea that truth results from the proper application of some method. The trick to finding truth, then, is to find the proper method and apply it correctly. Science is often taken to be that method.

One of the reasons this idea appeals to us is that it suggests that truth is available to anyone who follows the proper procedures. If this is so, science can serve as a defense against truth claims based on power, authority, tradition, or intellectual abilities. In this sense, science is a very egalitarian institution; anyone with training can use it. Moreover, behavioral scientists have prided themselves on their egalitarian approach to human problems, often challenging traditions and authority of all kinds.

There is, however, a conceptual problem that must be confronted before we accept the idea that truth results from the proper application of method. This problem comes from the fact that all methods for accruing knowledge in the scholarly disciplines, including science, were developed by human beings as they confronted the problems and questions in their world. We might consider the development of tools as a useful analogy. It seems reasonable to suggest—and a good deal of history supports the notion—that human beings developed tools in order to accomplish particular purposes. They designed the tools they needed to accomplish what they wanted to do, given their understanding of the world. For example, hammers are designed the way they are because of our understanding of hammering tasks. We make hammers the way we do because of what we want to do with them and because of our understanding of what we have to work with. We develop the tools we need to build the sort of house we want, rather than build only the sort of house that can be built with the tools available.

A similar point can be made in the development of science. Scientific method was developed the way it was because it seemed like a good way to go about understanding and explaining—getting at the truth of the world. Science was conceived and made the way it was because the people who developed it assumed that truth and the nature of the world were such that science, as they conceived it, would be a good way to get at truth and the world. In other words, *prior* to the formulation of any method of study, such as science, people already have an idea of what truth is (what the world is like). Method is then designed as the best way to get at that truth.

The hermeneutic philosopher Hans Georg Gadamer (1982) argues a similar point. Prior to the application, or even the development of any method, there is always an operative understanding of truth. It is this (pre)understanding of truth that makes it possible to frame any method at all. Without this understanding we could not formulate any method because we would not know what the method should be like—or that we even need a method. This means that understandings of truth produce methods, rather than methods producing truth. If this is the case, then we cannot be confident that properly and carefully applying scientific methods to the study of human behavior will get us to the truth. Rather, scientific method can only give us a picture of human behavior that reflects the assumptions about human behavior that we held in earlier centuries as we developed scientific methods.

One obvious conclusion to be drawn from this is that many important questions about human behavior can only be solved by careful theoretical work, not by the application of method. Methods, including the scientific method, are only devices we use to convince ourselves and others that our ideas are in some sense sound. They do not establish the truth of the matter. They only help us establish whether our observations are consistent with what we already take to be the truth of the matter.

A related conclusion is that all methods, including scientific methods, can only find the sorts of things they are "tuned" for. To illustrate, consider that a piece of scientific equipment (such as a thermometer) can only measure what it was made to measure (temperature); it is not capable of sensing other qualities (such as air pressure). Likewise scientific methods in the behavioral sciences are only good for certain functions. If what is being looked for is not what is most true and important about a subject matter, then the results deriving from the methods will not reflect what is most true and important. In the behavioral sciences, if our methods are not "tuned" for human beings, then the method can miss what is true and important about human beings. In this way, methods can act as blinders as much as they can reveal something important to us.

The Persuasive Power of Scientific Studies

In evaluating the commitment of the behavioral sciences to traditional scientific methods, it is important to understand how science has come to command such respect. The obvious answer is that science is persuasive. We are persuaded through scientific experiments that their results are trustworthy and accurate. The next question, of course, is why it is that scientific experiments are persuasive. When we look at the issue carefully, it seems clear that scientific experiments are persuasive because they follow the form and structure of a logical argument. The persuasive power of science, in this sense, is simply the persuasive power of logic.

The relation between science and logic can be traced to Aristotle, who invented formal logic as a way of doing science. It seemed to him (and does to most 20th-century thinkers as well) that following logical procedures is our best guarantee against unwarranted conclusions and errors in thinking. The form of logical argument that Aristotle developed was the *syllogism*. A syllogism consists of three statements that together make up an argument. The first statement is the *major premise*. This statement is a very general (categorical) statement that must be accepted as primary and true if the rest of the argument is going to be valid. An example of a major premise is the statement, "All men are mortal." The second statement of a syllogism is the *minor premise,* which is a more particular statement (also categorical) about some element contained in the major premise. A minor premise related to our major premise is, "Socrates is a man." The third statement in the argument is the *conclusion*. The conclusion is the logical consequence of the relation between the major and minor premises (and the category relations they express). In this case, our conclusion is, "Therefore, Socrates is mortal."

Putting the argument together we have:

Major Premise: All men are mortal.
Minor Premise: Socrates is a man.
Conclusion: Therefore, Socrates is mortal.

The question arises, however: Why are we persuaded by these statements to arrive at the conclusion that Socrates is mortal? An immediate response is that we are persuaded that the conclusion is true because it is *logical.* That answer leaves us with another question: Why are we persuaded by *logic?* To point out that a conclusion is logical is simply to beg the question. At this point, some behavioral scientists might be inclined to suggest that logic is some sort of universal category or structure to which the things of the mind and the world must conform. They might add that the human mind is capable of "seeing" logic and thus conforming to it in knowledge and understanding. This is an important part of many rationalist positions, as articulated in Chapter 3.

However, there is another explanation for the persuasiveness of logical arguments. This explanation holds that logical arguments are based on rules of language that people who use the language understand and agree to abide by. This agreement is rarely something we, as language users, are explicitly aware of. The rules of language are most often understood without explicit awareness. They are just part of knowing how to use language to make sense of things. For example, in the syllogism above, we are compelled to conclude that Socrates is mortal because we all know and accept the meaning of the words in the major and minor premises. We agree on what the word *all* means, and what the word *is* means, and how nouns like *men* and *mortal* and *Socrates* function in the language to specify categories of things. In other words, we agree that *if* all men are mortal, and *if* Socrates is a man, *then* Socrates is mortal, because that's what the sentences of the major and minor premises mean to all people who speak the language in which the syllogism is expressed. Most reasonable people have implicitly agreed to abide by these rules of language (and thus the rules of logic).

The point is that logic is persuasive because of the language rules, not because of the universal logical structure of things to which all our knowledge must conform.[6] There is some support for the language position in the fact that formal logic has not developed in all cultures in the way that it has in Western cultures. Certainly, people in other cultures do not have the same confidence in logic that we have. Also, they do not seem to think the way we do in the way they formulate questions and answers.

This point about the persuasive power of logic is important for our discussion of science, because a scientific experiment is essentially a logical argument. An experiment is set up much like a logical argument of the form "If _____ , then _____." Essentially, the researcher says, "*If* I measure these certain variables in this way, and *if* I control for those other variables in that way, and *if* I make observations under these specified conditions, *then* I will observe that particular result." Further, the scientific community—all those who read the research and understand it—evaluates experimentation according to a similar logical form. There is an implicit agreement between the community and the researcher that says in essence, "*If* you measure those variables in those acceptable ways, and *if* you control for those other variables, and *if* you make your observations under those specified conditions, *then* we will accept your results as valid and true." All the conditions of measurement, control, and observation specified in the "if" parts of the argument (the antecedent) are those conditions that a "good" experiment ought to include. This logical form, then, is the reason that an experiment is persuasive to the community. It follows the logical argument very carefully, and it contains within it all the elements of the argument that people familiar with the subject might sensibly think are influential to the outcome.

For our analysis of science here, the important thing to note is that a scientific experiment is not persuasive because it possesses some hidden power to reach the truth despite all obstacles. Instead, it is persuasive because it constitutes a logical argument that rational people intuitively recognize and generally find persuasive. Remember that the persuasive power of logic is based simply on agreements about how language is and should be used. We can also see that science is not really an alternative to reason, or rational analysis, as some have suggested. It is a type of rational analysis. What scientists do in the laboratory and what theorists do is essentially the same thing—logical analysis. That empirical scientists deal in observations may seem like an advantage, and indeed, observation is often persuasive. Still, its persuasive power ultimately rests on the rational, logical analysis that frames our expectancies and our understanding of what we observe. Without a rational organization or analysis, observations completely lose their authority and cogency.

The final point to keep in mind, then, is that science is essentially a "language game" (Wittgenstein, 1953). By this we do not mean to imply that it is a game in the trivial sense of the term. Language games, in the sense we (and Wittgenstein) intend, are very serious. They are the means whereby we make sense of the world, decide what is real and good, and understand ourselves. Our point here is that science may not deserve the status of the *only* method for understanding and explaining the world. This may be especially true in the behavioral sciences, in which there are no unchallengeable technological accomplishments. Unlike natural scientists, behavioral scientists cannot appeal to this technology as evidence that scientific method deserves the status of the only method.

The Possibility of Verification

Many people assume that by using empirical methods scientists prove their theories or hypotheses to be true. As we have just shown, the power of scientists to persuade is based on their using the logical form, "If _____ , then _____." We now look more closely at whether it might be possible to prove something using this logical form. We can convert the syllogism we used above into the if-then form:

If Socrates is a man, then he is mortal.

Note that we still have to assume that the major premise (that all men are mortal) is true or the argument cannot proceed. The part of the statement following "if" is referred to as the *antecedent,* and the part following "then" is the *consequent.* To proceed with the argument and reach the logical conclusion, the next step is to *affirm,* or demonstrate in some way, that the antecedent is true. In other words, we need to demonstrate that, indeed:

Socrates is a man.

If this is demonstrated and accepted, then we can conclude that the consequent follows, and in fact:

He is mortal.

One of the classic logical fallacies that is exposed in all introductory logic courses is called *affirming the consequent.* This happens when instead of affirming that the antecedent of the argument is true and concluding that the consequent follows, we affirm that the consequent is true and conclude that the antecedent must therefore be true as well. For example:

If Socrates is a man, then he is mortal.
Socrates is mortal. (Affirming the consequent)
Therefore he is a man. (Concluding the antecedent is true)

This is obviously not a good argument, because showing that Socrates is mortal does not necessarily show he is a man. He could be a dog or a bush or any other mortal thing.

When we look at an empirical experiment as this sort of logical argument, an important problem arises. Classically, the experiment is framed like this:

If the hypothesis is true, then X will be observed.

That the hypothesis is true is the antecedent, and the observation of X (some empirical result) is the consequent. When the study is actually conducted, the result is that:

X is observed. (Affirming the consequent)

and we might try to conclude:

Therefore, the hypothesis is true.

This procedure is a classic example of affirming the consequent of an if-then argument. What it means is that the very way empirical studies are set up can always and only demonstrate the consequent. Thus, it is impossible—by the rules of logic implicit in the experiment itself—to prove any hypothesis true.

That experimentation cannot prove anything true has been known for a long time.[7] Nevertheless, the full implications have not been completely examined in the curriculum of the behavioral sciences. One of those implications is that there are, in principle, an unlimited number of possible explanations for any experimental result. Our knowledge that Socrates is a mortal (through affirming the consequent in our previous example) allows us to interpret this mortality in unlimited ways; Socrates could be a bush, a man, a dog, and so forth. Likewise, the data of an experiment can be interpreted in many different ways, no one of which can be shown necessarily to be true by empirical scientific test. This means, of course, that in addition to data not *proving* a hypothesis, data cannot "tell" or "indicate" to the researcher which of the many interpretations is correct. The common notion that data "tell" scientists things or "give information" is misleading or true only in a very restricted sense. Many behavioral scientists recognize these problems, but the problems are seldom taught in textbooks and classes on research methods, and they seldom enter into discussions of the limitations of science as a method. Furthermore, the situation is not well understood by lay people, who continue to give much credibility to scientific study because of the popular notion that scientific data can prove things or indicate truth.

The Possibility of Falsification

Among philosophers of science the problem of affirming the consequent has been recognized for some time. This recognition, in part, led some (e.g., Popper, 1959) to suggest that although scientists cannot validate their theories or hypotheses, a very real power lies in the fact that they can *falsify* them. In other words, even if we can't prove true things to be true using science, we can prove false things false. Then, by implication, if we rule out all the false theories and hypotheses, we arrive at the truth by process of elimination. This strategy of falsifying hypotheses is valid according to the rules of logic, involving a form of argument known as *negating* (or *denying*) *the consequent*. It takes the following form:

> If the hypothesis is true, then X will be observed.
> X was not observed. (Negating the consequent)
> Therefore, the hypothesis is not true. (The antecedent is false)

Although the logic of falsification is valid, there remains a serious difficulty when it comes to actually falsifying a theory or hypothesis in practice. For example, we might frame a theoretical argument this way:

> If symbolic interactionism is true, then people's self-perceptions will be affected by others' evaluations of them.

Assume next that we were to study one particular subject and find no evidence for a change in self-perception, even after she heard evaluations by others. According to the logic of falsification, we should publish our results because they falsify the theory of symbolic interactionism. The falsifying logic would flow like this:

> This person is unaffected by others' evaluations. (Negating the consequent)
> Therefore, symbolic interactionism is not true. (The antecedent is false)

The problem, of course, is that scholars (mostly symbolic interactionists) have several explanations for our results: We just used a peculiar person, the evaluation was not proper or strong enough, we need more than one person and a larger number of evaluations, or we did the study wrong (in any number of ways). In other words, the strategy of falsification will not work unless we are sure that our test or experiment is the *crucial test* of the theory or hypothesis. No experiment will be a crucial test unless all possible variables (or limiting conditions) have been controlled or taken into account. There must be no other possible explanation for the failure of the experiment except the falsity of the hypothesis. This degree of control is, of course, impossible—practically and in principle. There are, in principle, an infinite number of things to be controlled in order to falsify any theory or hypothesis.[8] Not all of them can be controlled, if only because there is no control over the particular point on the space-time continuum where any study is conducted—that is, each study is conducted at a particular place and time. Consequently, the effects of that *particular* context can never be controlled experimentally.

One conclusion to draw from this analysis is that the methods of empirical science cannot falsify theories or hypotheses. This point also has been well recognized among philosophers of science (e.g., Lakatos, 1970), but again its implications are not well developed in the literature and training of behavioral scientists. Some who do understand the impossibility of falsification suggest that although no one study suffices to falsify a theory or hypothesis, if we keep conducting studies over time, we can achieve an overall falsification. This strategy does seem to be useful for replicating our experiments, controlling for different influences each time. However, the argument against falsification is an argument *in principle*—the problem is not that we cannot do enough experiments fast enough or well enough to falsify, it is that in principle we cannot exercise sufficient control to falsify a theory or hypothesis. Because each study adds a new and unique combination of variables, measurements, and controls to the discussion, conducting more studies increases the complexity of the context of falsification, making falsification less, rather than more, likely. Whatever scientific methods may be good for, they cannot be used to *verify* theories, in the sense of affirming the consequent, or *falsify* theories, in the sense of negating the consequent. In other words, we cannot through scientific methods discover whether theories and hypotheses are true or false.

The Problem of Establishing Causality

The impossibility of establishing a crucial test (as shown above) casts some doubt on whether scientists can be confident about establishing cause-and-effect relationships among variables (as also discussed in Chapter 4 on Hume). It is widely assumed that one of the hallmarks of science, including behavioral science, is that it uniquely uncovers causal relationships in the world. As a result, behavioral scientists commonly distinguish between *experimental designs* and *correlational designs* as research strategies. The distinction is almost always introduced by noting that correlational designs do not allow scientists to establish causal relationships, but experimental designs do. What really distinguishes correlational from experimental research strategies is the amount of control the experimenter exercises over variables that might influence the variable under study. In a correlational design, it is common to exercise very little control. The researcher simply observes how two variables seem to be related. Let us consider a simple research question as an example. Suppose we are interested in the relationship between hunger and motivation. We might get together a group of people and observe how long they had gone without eating (hunger) and how motivated they are (with some test of motivation or some measure of performance on some task).

In experimental research, one variable is designated the *independent variable*—the one we expect to produce some observed effect. In our example this would be hunger. The other variable is designated the *dependent variable*—the one we observe to see the effects of the independent variable. In our example this would be motivation. To be confident that what we observed in the dependent variable (how motivated our people were) was *caused by* the independent variable (how hungry they were), we would have to control absolutely everything else that might possibly have an effect on the dependent variable (their level of motivation) *except* the independent variable (how hungry they were). It seems unreasonable to suppose that we could know about, and eliminate from the lives of our subjects, everything that might possibly motivate them. As we discussed above, this degree of control is not only unreasonable, but in principle, impossible. For this reason, it is in principle impossible for an experiment to establish or verify that a cause-and-effect relationship exists between any two variables in a study, as Hume noted long ago.

A researcher might well admit that it is *conceptually* impossible to prove by means of scientific experiments that one variable causes another, but still point out that every time the independent variable is present a particular effect is observed in the dependent variable. In other words, this researcher might argue that if we can make something happen, we are getting at the cause of it.[9] However, to claim that we know what caused an experimental result based simply on the fact that it happens whenever the independent variable is present, commits the logical fallacy of affirming the consequent again:

If X is the cause of Y, then whenever X is present, Y occurs.
Whenever X is present, Y occurs.
Therefore, X is the cause of Y.

Again, just because the independent variable and dependent variable always seem to occur together (i.e., are correlated) does not mean that some other, as yet unidentified, variable could not always be present as the real cause.

The Problem of Operationalization

A hallmark of traditional scientific method is observation. To perform a scientific test, we must be able to observe the phenomenon we are trying to study. This is not always an easy or straightforward thing to do, even in the natural sciences. For example, a clearly scientific construct like gravity is never observed directly. We can observe what we take to be the effects of gravity, but not gravity itself.[10] When the construct under scientific scrutiny is one that cannot be observed directly (e.g., gravity), the scientist must observe something else that he or she can assume represents the construct or results from the construct (e.g., the fact that an object falls). This process of letting something we can observe represent something we cannot observe is called *operationalizing*. When we let the falling of an object represent gravity, our observation of the object's falling is called an *operational definition*. An operational definition is a translation of some theoretical construct into observable or measurable terms.[11]

Many things behavioral scientists study cannot be observed directly. In fact, most of what is important and human about us is unobservable. In the previous section, we used the example of a simple study looking at the relationship between hunger and motivation. Neither hunger nor motivation can be directly observed. We suggested that we might be able to get some measurement (observation) of how long it had been since our subjects had eaten. Thus "hours of food deprivation" was our operational definition of hunger. For motivation, we suggested we might be able to observe or measure how well our subjects performed some task, or we might ask them to fill out a questionnaire about their level of motivation. These would both be operational definitions of motivation. However, we have no direct access either to motivation or to hunger.

The process of operationalizing always keeps the scientist one step removed from what he or she really wants to study. If we were to do our simple study on hunger and motivation, we would presumably know something about the relationship between hours of food deprivation and responses to a questionnaire, but we would not *necessarily* know anything about the relationship between hunger and motivation—which is really what we wanted to know about. The reason for this is that knowing how long it has been since a person ate is not necessarily knowing how hungry the person is. Hours of food deprivation is *not* hunger. By the same token, the way a person answers a questionnaire is *not* motivation. Just how well the operational definitions represent the constructs under study is always open to question, and it is the most basic factor affecting the quality of the knowledge that can be gained by scientific investigation.[12]

In the natural sciences, researchers are not too concerned about the problem of operationalization. If we were to challenge a physicist on this point, he or she may very well admit to not *really* getting at constructs like "gravity," "force," or "mass." However, he or she might be quick to point out that bridges stay up and airplanes fly all the same. The point is that, again, a presumably impressive technology validates natural sciences. Also, most nonscientists are not equipped with alternative explanations of why planes fly and bridges stay up. If technology is the major purpose of scientific investigation, these questions about operationalizing and the accuracy of construct representation matter little.

In the behavioral sciences, however, the situation is somewhat different. First, of course, the behavioral sciences do not have an impressive technology, at least in comparison with the natural sciences. Second, there is an extra difficulty in trying to capture human phenomena with operational definitions. We might ask, for example, what operational definition is going to adequately represent "love," "altruism," or "agency." Third, even though most of us do not have an alternative explanation for why objects fall, most of us can and do have alternative explanations for why people behave as they do. (Recall the many explanations of a friend's rude behavior at the beginning of this book.) Although few people are in a position to provide insight into the nature and workings of gravity, most are arguably in a position to give valuable insight into the nature and workings of human beings. Behavior is something with which they have a good deal of experience. Insight from the people who are actually behaving should be seriously considered.

Before closing our discussion of operationalization we might ask whether the purpose of science really is technological application. This is a particularly important question for the behavioral sciences. Technology in the natural sciences amounts to power over the entities studied as a result of manipulation. In the behavioral sciences, however, it is open to debate whether people can in fact be manipulated by behavioral technology. There is wisdom in taking great care about how and why we would ever pursue such a project. There is also a good argument that the first and most important goal of science is not manipulation or control, but understanding. If this is true, then the problem of operationalization—the fact that we are always one step removed from what we want to study—is of great concern for the behavioral sciences.

The Problem of Objectivity

Although observation is a hallmark of scientific method, it must be the case that the observation is performed objectively. Objectivity, as we discussed above, is an essential part of scientists' claim to credibility. By objectivity we mean that scientists make observations in such a way that they do not distort or misread what they observe as a result of tradition, values, emotions, or other subjective influences. Objectivity calls for the scientist to achieve some grounds from which to observe that are independent of, or shielded from, all subjective influences. These "grounds," of course, are not spatial, a place where a particular scientist might literally stand. Rather, the grounds are conceptual, a mind-set in which the scientist can avoid subjectivity. Because subjective influences—values, emotions— are essential to the very identity of the scientist as a person, and because our history, culture, and so forth are often held implicitly rather than explicitly, it seems unlikely that we would ever achieve this kind objective grounds from which to observe anything, including experimental results. This is one of the major implications of Thomas Kuhn's (1970) work, as discussed earlier.

Someone might argue that it is possible for a scientist to achieve some sort of objectivity in the laboratory—perhaps by using a machine instead of a person to register the observations. However, once the data of the experiment are gathered by the machine, the scientist still needs to examine the data and make sense of what the machine recorded. At this point, the objectivity of the scientist again becomes an issue. More subtly, the subjective understandings, assumptions, and expectations of scientists come into play because they must decide how to make the machine make the observations, what it will be sensitive to, and how it will recognize what to record. Furthermore, scientists decide what to study, how to understand what is being studied, how to measure it, what to control for, and what not to control. The very definitions and framing of a research question are shot through with traditions, history, expectations, values, and other subjective factors. It seems unlikely that at any stage the research process is objective.

We should note, however, that it is questionable whether this kind of objectivity is necessary for the work of science to continue. Science, if we mean simply what scientists do, can be (and is being) done without this sort of objectivity. All that is required is that scientists be open to alternative explanations, be honest, and reserve judgment about what is "actually" going on. Hypotheses can still be submitted to empirical test. There is no reason to assume that technological advance will be slowed. It is only when we expect science to be capable of making truth claims that objectivity seems to be so important.

What is important for the purposes of this book is that the characteristics of science, as they are often held up for the behavioral sciences to emulate, are fully exposed for thoughtful examination. Natural science methods may not be capable of serving the validational function that many behavioral scientists desire. The best that science can offer may be *one* way of viewing human behavior, without any special warrant for claiming that it is the only or even the best way. If this is the case, then whether the behavioral sciences can or should be sciences, and just what it might mean to claim that they are sciences, remain open to question.

ALTERNATIVE VIEWS OF THE NATURE AND ROLE OF SCIENCE IN THE BEHAVIORAL SCIENCES

In this chapter, we have illustrated some of the conceptual questions regarding the nature of science and scientific knowledge. There are grounds for questioning the claim that any method, such as science, is capable of revealing truth. All the issues discussed here provide reasons for reexamining our view of the nature of science and its role in understanding and explaining human behavior.

If science cannot enable us to definitively settle theoretical questions and establish truth with certainty, the question arises, What can we accomplish with science as a method for studying human behavior? In exploring this question, an insight articulated in some postmodern theoretical positions might be helpful: Science might best be understood as a language with which or through which people try to understand the world. All languages have rules that determine what are acceptable sentences and how utterances are to be understood. Similarly, scientific rules tell us which experiments are acceptable and how one interprets the results. It is also the case, however, that like any language, the language of science is full of ambiguity. Scientists' procedures and explanations are influenced by their culture, history, and subjective factors. Just as no one would claim that English is the only, or even the best, language through which to understand the world, no such claim need be made for science.

This view suggests that every language opens the world to us[13] and helps us understand it in a particular way, from a particular perspective. The same is true of science. However, as every language opens the world to us in some ways, it closes it down in other ways. Just as everything cannot be said in a single language, everything cannot be understood and explained through a single method—science. In fact, many in the postmodern tradition have noted that the language of science, when applied to the study of human beings, is a relatively impoverished language. Using traditional scientific investigations, we force ourselves to study human beings from a distance. We measure them instead of talking to them; we ask them to fill out questionnaires from which we extract numbers as our data. Postmodern theorists remind us that the language of numbers is not the native language in which we experience or understand the world. Nowhere is this evidenced more clearly than when scientists interpret their findings to the community. Scientists quickly leave the language of numbers in order to communicate with colleagues.

Given all of this, some benefits still may accrue from applying traditional scientific methods to the study of human behavior. First, it might be possible to learn something new and unexpected by forcing ourselves and our subjects to think about the world in a strange language—one we are not as familiar with—such as the language of numbers. We may notice something we might otherwise overlook. This has certainly happened in the natural sciences—mathematics has helped guide new discoveries. Although this view does not eliminate all the problems that may come from studying people with empirical scientific methods, benefits could ensue.

Second, whatever else we may say about traditional scientific methods, we need to acknowledge that they force behavioral scientists to be public, careful, and systematic in their work. Traditional methods force us to check whether our theories and hypotheses can be shown to have any demonstrable consequences or effects in the world we live in. Even if the methods of demonstrating such an effect are flawed and not capable of verifying or falsifying, they do enable us to see whether we can relate our thoughts and theories to what we can observe among real people.

As a means of demonstrating, then, the methods of traditional empirical science may be useful. But it must be kept in mind that every demonstration is only one demonstration among many demonstrations that might be made. No one demonstration, or even a set of demonstrations, can verify, falsify, or establish the "truth of the matter" or "the way things are." Demonstrations are, moreover, seductive. If we can demonstrate something we believe, we tend to think there must be something true about the way we are thinking.[14] Someone who defends or advocates science on pragmatic grounds—based on claims that "it works"—must constantly defend against this tendency to confuse what can be demonstrated with what is true, real, or important. The fact that an experiment comes out as predicted is not evidence that it does so for any of the reasons arising from the use of any particular theory.

Empirical science also has a part to play in understanding the human world. There are some genuinely empirical questions in the human world. Such genuinely empirical questions can profitably be investigated by the methods of empirical science. A genuinely empirical question would be one that pertains entirely to things that can be observed, measured, or counted with insignificant distortion or interpretation. For example, if we want to know the average height of adult females in a given place, the sensible thing would be to measure them. If we want to know how much a particular brain cell fires while a person is doing some sort of cognitive task, it would be a good idea to put an electrode near the neuron, get the person to perform the task, and record the firing pattern. Finally, if our interest is whether people tend to buy one brand of breakfast cereal over another, it makes sense to watch them and count how many of each they buy.

We should note, however, that the foregoing examples are, in some sense, fairly mundane questions. There is little theoretical or philosophical meaning attached to a genuinely empirical question. It is debatable whether the important questions of a human being can be satisfactorily framed in a genuinely empirical language. We doubt that they can. To investigate such questions in the behavioral sciences we believe it is necessary to think again about the role of methods in general and the role of scientific methods in particular.

If we are to understand science, we must deal with a fundamental issue—the relation between truth and method. The tradition out of which the behavioral sciences developed includes the assumption that truth can be found through the application of method. The analysis we have made in this chapter, and much work in contemporary philosophy, suggests the reverse—that prior to any method is an assumptive understanding of what is true. Taking this latter position implies that behavioral scientists have no alternative but to be constantly and perpetually involved in the difficult analytical work of theorizing, investigating the preunderstanding from which all methods arise.[15] Science will never put "philosophical" questions to rest, because science rests on philosophical assumptions. In short, scholars in all disciplines, including the behavioral sciences, must take on the question of truth directly. On such questions, empirical science must speak through theory.

On questions of method, and the scientific status of the behavioral sciences, the theories we have analyzed throughout the book represent various positions. Eclectic and structuralist researchers have varied so much in their strategies and commitments to science that little can be said regarding the matter. Psychodynamic theorists have traditionally not been too concerned with doing scientific research, or even with the question of whether it is a good method to employ. Psychodynamic theory was built largely on individual case studies and rational and historical analysis. Among other behavioral scientists, psychodynamic theory is often criticized and marginalized for its lack of scientific rigor.

Humanistic theory has largely shared the same fate, for the same reasons. The most rigorous attempts to bring traditional scientific methods to bear on these perspectives have come from therapists and educators interested in scientifically assessing the effectiveness of strategies derived from the perspectives. Such attempts have met with mixed reviews. Of the traditional perspectives available in the behavioral sciences, behavioristic and cognitive theories have been the most actively and explicitly scientific. That behavioral scientists in general seem to share this zeal for traditional science is testimony to how influential these perspectives have been.

Alternative Views of the Role
of Method in Behavioral Science

In recent years, alternative views of the role of method in the behavioral sciences have emerged. Some take issue with more traditional views of what science is and whether a *science* of human behavior is possible. We review three such perspectives. Proponents of the position exemplified in the work of Joseph Rychlak (1988, 1994) recognize most of the limitations of traditional scientific method as discussed in this chapter. Nevertheless, they recommend that behavioral scientists not abandon traditional empirical methods. Rychlak considers such methods to be essential if there is to be any behavioral science.

The importance of empirical validation is that in essence it requires the behavioral scientist to "put up or shut up." Theories should be submitted to rigorous tests. One type of test of a theory is analytical, based on reason and argument. The theory must be demonstrated to be internally consistent and coherent, and it must be able to explain or subsume an acceptably wide range of phenomena. However, in addition to this "coherence" test, a theory should be able to stand up to a test of empirical validation. Even though such tests always require operationalization, and thus never really test the theory itself, it is important for the theorist to demonstrate that the constructs of the theory can be represented in ways that relate to actual, observable behavior. Often, designing and executing this type of test demands considerable creativity on the part of the scientist.

According to this position, it is essential that theories and methods are independent of each other. This means that the methods of science can be used to test theories of all types, not only mechanistic and deterministic ones, but theories in which free will is advocated as well. It also means that all types of theories, even ones that advocate agency and thus do not look "scientific," should be considered credible so long as they can pass scientific muster according to traditional methods.

A second alternative position on the question of methods (e.g., Gergen, 1982; Giorgi, 1985; van Manen, 1990) derives mainly from postmodern thought. Proponents of this position argue that theories and methods can never be independent of each other. If we take the theoretical position that human beings are not simply natural objects, not fundamentally like mechanisms, and not determined by laws and forces the way natural objects are, then it is inappropriate to use the methods developed to study natural objects. Use of methods developed for natural objects will result in imposing this naturalistic theoretical outlook on human beings. Some who hold this perspective argue that adequate study of human beings requires a "human science"—natural objects can be studied by the methods of natural science, but human beings require human science methods.[16] In this view, human scientists accept lived experience (or ready-to-hand engagement, discussed in Chapter 3) as the origin for understanding as well as the object to be understood. Methods of study must be faithful to and grounded in lived experiences. Methods developed for detached (or present-at-hand) study of natural objects will be inadequate.

Many human science methods are grouped under the rubric *qualitative methods*.[17] The thrust of qualitative research methods is to reject the philosophical assumptions of traditional methods. Researchers avoid measurement and quantification, allowing subjects to describe their own behaviors and experiences in the language native to their experience. The analysis of the data is likewise carried out in conversational language rather than with statistics. The qualitative researcher is essentially involved in a project of careful questioning, describing, and interpreting. Many people who subscribe to human science methods argue that qualitative methods are superior to quantitative methods and ought to be the method of choice for all the behavioral sciences.

Because most advocates of qualitative research acknowledge that theories and methods are intimately tied to each other, there is a tendency among behavioral scientists to evolve their own particular methods, faithful to the assumptions and goals of their particular theory. Thus, there seem to be almost as many qualitative methods as there are theories, making it difficult to categorize qualitative methods. One possible organization of the methods groups them into three categories: ethnography, phenomenology, and studies of artifacts.[18]

Ethnography is arguably the best known of the qualitative research traditions. Its roots are in anthropology, where it has become the predominant method of study. It has also become a significant part of research programs in nearly all the behavioral sciences. The distinguishing characteristic of ethnography is an emphasis on careful and detailed observation.[19] This observation is usually carried out by a researcher actively participating in the group or setting that is being studied. The primary objective is a detailed, participative understanding of the group or setting.

Phenomenology has as a primary interest the study of the meaning of concrete human experiences. Its roots are a bit more difficult to trace, but certainly the work of Edmund Husserl and others in the phenomenological tradition in philosophy has been important.[20] To get at the meaning of experiences, phenomenological researchers rely heavily on interviews and other verbal or written accounts of experiences. The researchers then carefully analyze these accounts in order to understand not only the individual, private meaning of the experiences, but also what is general and illuminating in understanding the meaning of human experience in a wider context of people and situations.

The third category of qualitative methods is much smaller than the other two. We have coined the term *studies of artifacts* to describe attempts to study physical objects produced by people and groups. Archeology and physical anthropology are good examples of well-established fields engaged in similar studies. Some behavioral scientists have developed methods to study cartoons, advertisements, built environments (homes, other buildings, and villages), and many other artifacts. The idea is that the artifacts—objects—that people produce and use can tell us much about their lives, what they believe, what they value, and what they understand.[21]

Qualitative research methods are becoming increasingly accepted as a legitimate alternative to traditional empirical methods. They now form an important part of the literature of many behavioral science disciplines, including education (Goetz & LeCompte, 1984), family science (Gilgun, Daly, & Handel, 1992), health care (Crabtree & Miller, 1992), psychology (van Zuuren, Wertz, & Mook, 1987), and organizational (and other kinds of) evaluation (Patton, 1990). The unique understanding these methods provide, and the fact that they are perceived to be more compatible with increasingly popular postmodern theoretical approaches, suggest that they will come to be an increasingly important tool for scholarship in the behavioral sciences.

A third position on the issue of method can be derived from a particular reading of some postmodern perspectives. Its proponents call for methodological pluralism (Faulconer & Williams, 1985, 1990; Polkinghorne, 1983).[22] They hold that the question of method is not the crucially important one for the behavioral sciences. Because all methods are languages through which we attempt to make sense of the world, we ought to make our choice of methods based on the nature of the problem we are investigating. Considerations include how we frame the problem and the relevant strengths and weaknesses of possible methods. This position makes it all the more important that behavioral scientists are aware of their theoretical assumptions, for their assumptions influence their view of the world and their decision about what method of study seems most appropriate.[23]

All languages (and methods) open a world of understanding in some way, but leave it closed in other ways. None can open all understandings. Therefore, no method we might devise can claim preeminence. From this perspective, the issue of method is less important than how we formulate the questions to which any method may be applied. What is most important for the behavioral sciences, therefore, can only be accomplished by careful, sustained, and sophisticated theoretical work. It is to the end of fostering sophisticated theoretical work that this book has been dedicated.

CONCLUSION

Traditional science has long held a position of respect and prominence in intellectual circles and the broader culture. This position is based on the promise that science is a more trustworthy means of discovering the truth about the world than other methods. The justification for this position is deeply rooted in the history of ideas. Science is seen to have the attributes necessary for testing our ideas about the world in a way that affords some certainty. This is due to the fact that science is based on objective observation, its observations are repeatable and public, it approaches the world mathematically, and its hypotheses and predictions are tested under conditions of control. Also important in understanding the status of science is scientists' record of producing impressive technology, and thus achieving control over the world of nature.

The question of whether the behavioral sciences are really sciences depends on what we understand science to be. If science is taken to be a precise body of knowledge with well-established laws and perfect predictability, the behavioral sciences probably do not qualify. If, however, science is taken to be a method of study common to scientific practice, then the behavioral sciences are probably legitimately scientific.

Although many have held that science is different from and more sure than philosophy, recent work in the philosophy of science makes it clear that science itself is based on theories and assumptions. And because it is based on ideas, it cannot includes tests of its own assumptive basis. Alternative views of science have emerged that suggest that science is a social practice based on paradigms that govern the legitimacy of questions, methods, and explanations. If this is true, then it seems justified to investigate science more closely to see what can and cannot be done with it.

There are lines of argument that suggest that science cannot, as has often been assumed, verify or falsify its own theories and hypotheses. Neither can it support cause-and-effect statements with certainty. Rather, it is argued, science can be understood as a logical argument, resting on language games, and thus a form of rational analysis. Given this view, many in the postmodern tradition have suggested that as science does not uncover truth, but rather requires a preexisting view of truth to proceed, the question of truth is more important than any question of method. Although traditional methods may be important as a means of gaining confidence in ideas, ultimately the work of the behavioral sciences is done at the conceptual, theoretical level.

Notes

1. One of Hume's conditions of causality, constant conjunction, is largely responsible for the importance of repeatability (see Chapter 4). This requirement has been translated into the methods of science because two (or more) events must be observed to be constantly conjoined in order to be a candidate for causal relation.

2. We are using the term *positivism* in a very general sense. Many readers will be most familiar with logical positivism as an important movement of the late 19th and early 20th centuries. Most of what we say about positivism in the broad sense we intend also applies to logical positivism, some with more direct relevance to more recent manifestations of positivism. For purposes of the discussion in this book, we do not believe finer distinctions are necessary.

3. The interested reader is referred to other sources such as Hempel (1965), of course, and discussions in secondary sources, including Bohman (1991) and Robinson (1985, 1995a).

4. It is, of course, a matter of some debate whether the laws behavioral scientists seek are discovered or simply formulated. Putting quotation marks around the word discovered is not an adequate response to that question, but a longer discussion would take us on a detour that we judge not to be helpful at this point. It is hoped that the discussion in the remainder of the chapter sheds some light on this issue.

5. The interested reader is also referred to the writings of Lakatos (1970) and the somewhat more radical works of Feyerabend (1975, 1987).

6. Some scholars, mostly rationalists, argue that there is a difference between the content of a syllogism and the process of conceiving the syllogism or being convinced by it. The former requires language, but they argue, the latter is language independent. We

think there is a strong argument that even the process of logical argument is inseparable from the language content and structure in which the process is carried out. However, this argument is beyond the scope of the present discussion.

7. In psychology, one of the first attempts to introduce this argument into the literature was made by Donald K. Adams (1937). The reader is also referred to a fuller treatment of this issue by Joseph F. Rychlak (1981).

8. This may be an overstatement. There may be, in the real world, only a relatively small number of things that have an effect on any particular phenomenon. The problem is that there is no way to know whether this is true, or what the influential things are before the experiment. So, although it may not be the case that there truly are an infinite number of things affecting a phenomenon, it makes some sense to say that a potentially infinite number of things may be influential. The decision as to how many there are, and thus which ones need to be controlled to make a crucial test, cannot be answered by empirical science. We could turn to philosophy, but then it is not a scientific question. Or we could proceed to eliminate things one at a time—but we are faced with a potentially infinite number of experiments.

9. This is essentially an appeal to *pragmatics*. If it works, it must be true. We have more to say about such a pragmatic approach to science later in the chapter, but here we are concerned with pointing out theoretical and philosophical questions about science and whether the behavioral sciences are or should be scientific in the traditional sense. Whether something like science is pragmatically useful does not necessarily have much bearing on the theoretical or philosophical evaluation of what science is or what it can and cannot do. We hope that once we are clear about the conceptual limitations and theoretical issues that are part of science we might understand better what it really means when we see an experiment "work" in the laboratory. What we want to avoid is jumping to premature and naive conclusions about causality, even when our experiments seem to "work."

10. The same is true for other properties of matter (weight, mass, etc.) as well as properties of behavioral science entities such as stimuli, responses, and so forth, as we noted in Chapters 2 and 5.

11. The term *operational definition* is meant to imply also that *operations* are important. When we are representing a construct by something that can be observed, most often it is necessary to perform some operation to make the observation possible. For example, if one were to represent gravity as the force exerted on one body by another, it would be necessary to perform some operation on the bodies so that it would be possible to measure the force. They would have to be put into a situation where the force could operate and measurement could be made.

12. What is at issue here is validity. Many behavioral scientists recognize that the validity of our measures is the most important factor affecting the quality of scientific research.

13. This expression reminds us of the experience of someone born blind or deaf, incapable of language communication. To learn language and have a means of expressing ideas and interacting with others is like an opening of the world. Language provides a frame within which things can be related and understood differently than they were before.

14. It is undoubtedly the case that there *is something* true about what we are thinking if we can make a prediction and accrue empirical support for it. The problem is that what it is that might be true, and just what it means, cannot be revealed in empirical findings.

15. Of course, any way this is done constitutes a sort of method. Scholarly investigation is thus always circular in the sense that understanding informs methods and methods help to inform understanding. This is one manifestation of what is often referred to as the *hermeneutic circle.*

16. The distinction between human sciences and natural sciences has been very influential in continental philosophy since at least the 19th century. Much is entailed in the distinction that we do not have time to develop. We refer the interested reader to Giorgi (1970) and Polkinghorne (1983).

17. The term *qualitative methods* is extremely broad. It refers to a number of methods that reflect a significant range of philosophical orientations as well as methodological approaches. Some of those who advocate the use of qualitative methods would not be considered postmodern or would not consider themselves to be. However, much literature in various postmodern perspectives advocates the use of qualitative methods. The reader is referred to the recent *Handbook of Qualitative Research* (Denzin & Lincoln, 1994) for a very good treatment of this diverse and growing field.

18. This is our own categorization, offered only for the purpose of giving the reader some way of organizing the field and perceiving the flavor of the important characteristics of qualitative research.

19. The type of observation that results from ethnographic methods is not intended to meet the standards of objectivity usually associated with traditional scientific methods. It is simply granted that observation is affected by theories, biases, and perspectives of the researcher. Ethnographers attempt, however, to be aware of these influences, acknowledge them, and take a critical stance toward them as part of the research method itself.

20. Some scholars, such as Amadeo Giorgi (1985) use the term *phenomenological* in a strict sense, applying it only to studies faithful to the work, insights, and methods of Husserl. Others use the term more broadly to apply to all attempts to study meaning and experience. We use the term in this broader sense.

21. Outside the fields of archeology and physical anthropology, there is much less literature on this area of qualitative research than on ethnology or phenomenology. The interested reader is referred to a small volume by Ball and Smith (1992) as a beginning source.

22. This methodological pluralism is not to be equated with theoretical eclecticism as described in Chapter 2. We contend that behavioral scientists need coherent theories, and they need constantly to be concerned about the adequacy, coherence, and even the truth of their theories. Eclecticism almost always involves a repudiation of this concern. However, behavioral scientists should employ whatever methods seem to offer the best possibility of learning something important in any given setting. An analogy might help clarify. To build, repair, or service electronic devices, one needs a single, adequate, coherent, and even true theory of electronics. However, one also ought to take advantage of tools built to perform particular relevant functions when one is actually engaged in building or repairing a device.

23. We note here that the behavioral scientists routinely use the term *methodology* to refer to the particular method used in a research study. However, the etymology of the term suggests that methodology is discourse *about* methods—the study, and evaluation of methods and what they can do. In methodology, methods are the objects of study, not the tools for study. Proponents of the third position we have articulated, methodological pluralism, suggest that methodology—in this latter sense—should be the primary concern, and choices of methods will derive from careful methodology.

❧ 7 ❧

Conclusion

❧ Throughout this book, many conventional ideas in the behavioral sciences have been challenged. Although none of these well-accepted ideas has been declared wrong or bad, their privileged status as the best or most correct ideas has been questioned. Many readers have been taught *the* scientific method or *the* learning theory as if there were only one basic method or one fundamental theory of learning. These notions are challenged here. We have reviewed criticisms of conventional views and described viable alternatives to conventional methods and theories. Examining these criticisms and alternatives is necessary for the development of theoretical skills. Learning to critique a theory allows us to identify and question our own theories about human behavior, and positing alternative theories facilitates our exploration of other potentially effective ways of thinking.

Initially, however, these criticisms of theories and alternatives to conventional ideas can be a bit disconcerting to students of the behavioral sciences, and here we mean students broadly speaking.[1] Challenges to the usual ways of thinking leave many students feeling bewildered, because they have been taught in

205

other classes the conceptions that appear to be in question here. The comfortable theoretical "rug" seems to have been pulled out from under them, without an obvious alternate rug being proposed to take its place. Moreover, there are many alternative conceptions. Readers of this book may feel confronted by an array of novel ways of thinking and new information that may be difficult to grasp or organize. This final chapter is intended to help readers with these issues.

This chapter is designed to assist readers in three ways. First, we anticipate some common responses to our questioning of behavioral science's foundations: eclecticism, nihilism, and denial. Although these reactions are understandable, they may be ways of avoiding the difficult conceptual issues that beset the behavioral sciences. Second, we show one way the various ideas presented in the previous chapters can be summarized. This could help readers organize the material and begin to grasp it as a whole. Third, we offer our own view of the contemporary trends in behavioral science concerning both current directions and where behavioral science ought to be heading. Of course, our view is not unbiased. Still, it may serve as a springboard for readers to continue their own thinking about theories in the behavioral sciences.

COMMON RESPONSES

Actually, some experience of discomfort or insecurity while analyzing the theories of the behavioral sciences is probably a positive sign. This discomfort may mean that the reader takes the ideas of the behavioral sciences seriously. Too often, students of the behavioral sciences are, as Bertrand Russell once put it, "allergic to thinking." For students with this allergy, challenges to the status of conventional ideas are just more words to memorize for the test. These students may be frustrated that the foundations of the behavioral sciences are not clearly laid out for them to simply memorize. However, they are unlikely to experience the kind of growth in analytical skills that comes from truly seeking to understand the behavioral sciences and then finding their understanding challenged, as in the preceding chapters. Seeking to refute or make sense of such challenges may lead to eclecticism, nihilism, and denial.

Eclecticism

In Chapter 2, we discussed the growing trend among psychologists to avoid adherence to specific schools of thought and endorse some combination of theories. Adopting eclecticism here is similar, except that here we are dealing with assumptions rather than schools of thought. Because conventional assumptions can be criticized and many alternatives can seem viable, the tendency is to wonder whether working through the critical issues is truly helpful or merely another specialty of the behavioral sciences reserved for those who enjoy that kind of thing. This doubt can lead one to believe that all assumptions must have something to offer, and thus, to be truly open-minded, one must be open to all assumptions or combinations of assumptions.[2] In this view, all the ideas in the world can be mixed in a large vat and the mixture can still be acceptably true.

Eclecticism rarely functions in this manner, however. In Chapter 2, we note many of the problems inherent in eclecticism as a theoretical stance in the behavioral sciences. First, an eclectic has not avoided assumptions through broad-mindedness, because eclecticism is itself an assumption about how assumptions ought to be handled. As such, it is subject to the same types of criticisms as any other assumption. Second, the incompatibility of many assumptions is obvious. Some readers may desire some combination of free will and efficient causal determinism in their theorizing, but the ways in which these assumptions are typically defined make any mixing of the two incoherent. One can *re*define these assumptions, but then one is not really dealing with the assumptions as they are. This redefinition itself needs to be subjected to criticism and contrasted with other possible definitions.

Is it possible for readers to formulate their own theories from the assumptions of the behavioral sciences? The answer is yes, though it must be remembered that this newly formulated theory is itself a single theory, not a simple combination of ideas. Although the original inspiration for a reader's theory may stem from several divergent ideas, bringing these divergent ideas under one conceptual umbrella (as "my theory") is likely to change their identities from their original use or definition. Freud, for example, drew from many divergent sources—physiology, physics, philosophy—in formulating his theory of psychoanalysis, but few would consider his theory to be eclectic. This is because he unified his divergent ideas into a single coherent whole and thus altered the ideas from their original use. The point is that a new theoretical whole, even if it is made up of the parts of old ideas, gives a new and different meaning to the parts. The parts (ideas) of theories mean something different depending on what other parts (ideas) they have to fit together with. This procedure may yield a new theory, but it does not yield a simple eclectic composite.

Nihilism

A second response to the discomfort felt when the foundations of the behavioral sciences are challenged is nihilism. The word *nihilism* in this context means that readers sometimes throw up their hands in frustration and give up on the behavioral science enterprise. Because most or all of the ideas and assumptions of behavioral science can be criticized, these readers assume that a solid foundation for the behavioral sciences is not possible. Many readers, for example, have presumed that science provides a solid foundation for the behavioral sciences. In other words, the behavioral sciences may have problems, but many readers have assumed (and have been taught) a rigorous adherence to the tenets of science will ultimately solve these problems.

This book illustrates the difficulty presented by an uncritical faith in science. Science itself has many critics with many valid criticisms (see Chapter 6). Indeed, the notion that science is an objective source of truths is shown to be one among many notions of science that may not be appropriate for the behavioral sciences. A nihilist concludes from this that no foundation for the behavioral sciences is possible, and thus behavioral science itself is not possible. Because science in this particular sense is doubtable, the behavioral sciences are lost on a sea of doubtable ideas. Readers with this reaction may move away from studies of the behavioral sciences entirely, opting perhaps for the presumably "harder" sciences with more solid and valid foundations.

This response to the challenges outlined here would be regrettable. Nihilism would be regrettable first of all because many of the criticisms of behavioral scientific methods are equally applicable to the harder sciences—no discipline, including the natural sciences, escapes questions about its foundational ideas. Indeed, because of the continual need to search for foundations and respond to critical questions, some disciplines, such as physics, include fields (e.g., theoretical physics) in which the job in part is to constantly examine and reexamine the assumptions underlying the discipline. This book, then, is an attempt to give the reader a taste of a similar role in the behavioral sciences—what could be called a *theoretical behavioral scientist*. The bottom line, however, is that a thoughtful reader of any discipline will turn up similar controversies and uncertainties.

Of course, the postmodernist (see Chapter 2) would probably question the need for a solid foundation to begin with. Could this need actually be counterproductive in the behavioral sciences? Could unquestionably solid assumptive foundations lead to questionable practices? As we have noted, many question the determinism of biological structures or metaphysical principles because this foundation leaves people without responsibility for their actions. Is it possible that the behavioral sciences are better off without an indubitable foundation? Readers should attempt to answer this question for themselves before they react nihilistically. After all, to give up on the behavioral science enterprise is to give up on the scholarly project of understanding people and their social relationships. Surely, this is an unproductive attitude to take. Further, it is doubtful that any person can truly take this attitude. Whether formally or informally, all of us are constantly attempting to understand other people and our relationships with them.

Denial

A third reaction to discomfort is denial. When conventional understandings of the behavioral sciences are challenged, readers sometimes want to deny the validity of these challenges. Whether in criticisms or in alternative formulations, the challenges are simply written off, or dismissed. Consider materialistic reductionism, for example (see Chapter 5). Many readers assume (and have been taught) that the ultimate explanation of any set of behavioral events is a biological explanation. Therefore, schizophrenia must ultimately be biologically determined; learning disabilities must ultimately have a biological explanation; group dynamics must ultimately be reducible to the biochemistry of the group members. In other words, the truth of the matter (no pun intended) has already been discerned. And challenges to the truth are false by definition.

Of course, challenges to assumptions may indeed be misguided or wrong. Clearly, the validity of any such challenge is questionable. However, denial can lead to a rejection of criticisms and alternatives without giving them *any* consideration. This practice has obvious problems in a learning environment. How can one learn if all new ideas are rejected out of hand? Interestingly, it is sometimes the learning environment itself that promotes this rejection. Similar to any institution or organization, learning environments include many people with a stake in the status quo. Professors and students can easily have such a stake, and in many cases, should have such a stake. Unfortunately, this stake in the status quo often tempts professors and students to dismiss criticisms of the mainstream without giving them due consideration. It is vital, then, that students be sure they understand a new idea *before* they pass judgment on it. This is difficult (and perhaps impossible in some ultimate sense), but the attempt is important to true learning.

Perhaps the greatest obstacle to giving due consideration to new or critical ideas is *familiarity*. Sometimes ideas that are familiar or better known are automatically given higher status than ideas that are unfamiliar or less well known. This higher status may be bestowed on familiar ideas in spite of clear evidence to the contrary. Someone may stick with old notions and conventional ideas simply because they are old and conventional. "Conventional ideas must be around for some reason," they seem to say. This attitude is well known in psychotherapy. Therapists routinely see behaviors in their clients that are clearly self-defeating—even in the judgment of the clients themselves—yet the old and customary ways of doing things are continued. Why? One common explanation is, "Familiar is better." The old way may be wrong for me and the new way may be better, but the new way is scary and uncertain. The new way entails unknown consequences and may require abilities I do not possess. Students who learn new theories may have similar feelings. However, with both clients and students (and each of us is always a student) learning is impossible without overcoming the "familiar is better" attitude.

Developing a Coping Strategy

The problems with these three responses to the challenges of the behavioral sciences should now be evident. In the language of psychoanalysis, all three are *defense mechanisms,* but none are *coping strategies*. Each of the responses is an attempt to deal with the conceptual problems of the behavioral sciences by denying in some sense that the problems exist. This is a common purpose of a defense mechanism. It allays our anxiety or discomfort to some degree, but it does not resolve the problems at their source. Eclecticism is a denial of the problems in the behavioral sciences through an attempt to embrace all assumptions (to some degree or other). Nihilism is a denial of the problems of the behavioral sciences through an attempt to embrace none of the assumptions. And those who use denial to deal with the criticisms of the mainstream are, of course, straightforwardly denying the problems exist.

A coping strategy, on the other hand, involves facing the problems, identifying their sources, and finding ways of addressing them as they stand. Actually, the determination not to succumb to one of the three responses above is a first step in coping with the theoretical issues of the behavioral sciences. It is our hope that identifying these defense mechanisms will facilitate your avoiding them, and hence further your facing the challenges that beset the behavioral sciences. Part of facing these challenges is not denying the existence of differing, often mutually incompatible, assumptions in the behavioral sciences. These differences preclude our meaningfully embracing all or even most of the competing assumptions.

Facing the problems also means taking a stand on assumptions. One cannot "do" anything in the behavioral sciences without adopting one or more of the assumptions available. One can, of course, do *nothing* in the behavioral sciences and abandon the formal discipline (or major) altogether. However, one can never abandon the behavioral sciences in the informal sense of relating to others. We have more to say about an appropriate direction for the discipline later. Suffice it to say here that responses that involve denying or hiding problems work no better in this intellectual context than they do in any other context: The problems remain, itching at us, and we cannot help but scratch them, often in unproductive ways.

ORGANIZING THE ASSUMPTIONS

A more productive way to react to the myriad of competing assumptions of the behavioral sciences is in fact our second step in developing a coping strategy. This second step requires a good understanding of the source of the bewilderment. Often this means beginning to organize and make sense of the various approaches to the behavioral sciences. As mentioned earlier, the sheer number and variety of ideas presented in the behavioral sciences often prevent readers from knowing what the problems of the behavioral sciences are. Unfortunately, the usual chapter organization of behavioral science texts leaves many important and useful connections among competing ideas unstated. Consequently, we illustrate here how the various assumptions can be connected, even across chapters. We do not attempt to describe all the relationships among the many ideas described in the previous chapters; that task is unwieldy and probably not that helpful. Still, our experience is that some connecting can help readers greatly in organizing the material and beginning to grasp it as a whole.

There are a significant number of metatheoretical schemes available for this task. The term *metatheoretical* refers to a theory that is "above" or more general than other theories. A metatheory, then, can be a theory or a set of categories that specifies some of the relationships among theories and assumptions. We choose the categories *necessity* and *possibility* here because of their relevance to the behavioral sciences and because they are readily understandable to most readers. They are not the only or even necessarily the best way of tying together the various ideas and assumptions of the behavioral sciences, but they offer a brief and relatively jargon-free means of comparing many of the diverse theories of the previous chapters. These comparisons are admittedly simplified in many cases. Still, we believe that the instructional benefits of such a metatheoretical scheme outweigh its intellectual costs, as long as the simplification is recognized as a temporary strategy with limited value.

Necessity

We begin by pointing out that in most of the behavioral sciences necessity has been embraced in one form or other. By *necessity*, we mean the belief that events of interest to the behavioral sciences (human behaviors) *must* (of necessity) happen the way they do. This sense of the term may remind many readers of other closely related conceptions discussed primarily in Chapter 3—determinism and causality. All of the four causes (or four determinisms) entail some form of necessity. Efficient causality is, of course, the most obvious example. Efficient causality assumes that events are the necessary end product of chains of causation from the past—that is, the result of this causal chain cannot be otherwise than it is. It is a necessary result and thus perfectly predictable with the right knowledge of the preceding conditions of the chain.

Perhaps less known is the necessity that is entailed by the other three causations. Material causation means that the resulting effect is necessitated by the material involved. Given the properties of the matter, the effect of a material cause cannot be otherwise. Formal causation, likewise, produces a necessary effect. The structure or design of an entity leads to a particular gestalt or wholeness that the entity cannot escape. Final causation, too, entails necessity. Regardless of the type of teleology, or final causal account, necessity is involved at two levels. First, the entity under consideration must be purposeful. In the case of human teleology, the teleologist holds that humans are inherently goal-oriented. Second, the entity's "actions" are totally constrained by the goals or purposes affirmed. Again, with human teleology, all behaviors and thoughts flow from or to the goal being affirmed at the time.

The types of reductionism described in Chapter 5 also involve necessity. In a sense, reductionism in general is an attempt to reduce everything to a necessary principle or phenomenon. Temporal reductionism is a good example. This form of reductionism reduces the three dimensions of time—past, present, and future—to one dimension, the past. It is therefore akin to efficient causality, which also depends on the past for its causal power. Mechanistic reductionism is also integrally related to efficient causation. Explaining behavior with a machine metaphor inevitably involves a reduction to chains of causation across time and the primacy of the past as in all efficient causal explanations.

Materialistic reduction is similarly related to material causation, though the former often involves efficient causation as well. When, for example, the human is thought to be nothing more than a biological organism (an instance of materialistic reductionism), the principles of explanation normally include properties of the matter and efficient causal chains across time. On the other hand, nonphysical types of reductionism—metaphysical reductionism—are often related to the less physical forms of causation and determinism. Formal and final causation, though often associated with a physical entity, do not require a physical presence to make their effect felt. A formal cause is a kind of pure structure (e.g., the architect's plan for a building), whereas a final cause may be the purpose of a nonphysical deity. Those theorists invoking a formal or final cause principle to explain events generally perform a type of metaphysical reduction in which the formal or final cause *necessitates* the occurrence of the events "explained."

With determinism and reductionism so closely related to necessity, it is probably easy to see how science itself has been so closely allied with necessity. Much of what we consider to be science is technology used to predict or control aspects of the physical world—animal, vegetable, and mineral. Most notions of predictability and control involve necessity. If events of the world *must* (of necessity) happen the way they do, then the world is potentially predictable and completely controllable with the instruments and methods of the scientist. The only task for the scientist is to discover how this necessary world operates. This discovery process has become a search for natural laws. Laws, of course, imply necessity. Unlike the laws of a political organization, one has no choice about whether one obeys scientific laws. As discussed in Chapters 4 and 5, one form or another of determinism and reductionism is used in the behavioral sciences. Although critics have disliked the implications of the idea of a perfectly predictable human being, the clear virtue of this view is that it makes the behavioral sciences truly scientific in the positivistic sense.

Of course, this positivistic view of science depends on empiricism for its epistemological base. Positivists contend that we can only know what is ultimately observable, but *this* contention is based on the assumption that we *can* know what is observable. This is where empiricism is required. Empiricism establishes the basis for assuming that we can know what is "out there" objectively in the world via our sensory experiences. Without empiricism, positivistic science has no justification. Rationalists, for instance, would claim that we are often hoodwinked by our experiences— even our scientific experiences—and thus we should not depend on the data of experimentation. As we described in Chapter 6, however, modern science has successfully incorporated parts of both epistemologies to cover all the bases. The modern scientist not only gathers the data via sensory experiences but also organizes it with the logical reasoning of the rationalist.

It is important to recognize here that even this combination of the two epistemologies entails necessity. According to empiricism, the human mind must follow the dictates of sensory experiences. If the human mind could do other than what our sensory experiences dictate, then the mind and its knowledge would be the result of something other than sensory experiences, and empiricism would be incomplete, if not wrong. Rationalism is in a similar state. Rationality must follow what is sometimes called *logical necessity*. In other words, logic has its own necessity, its own governing principles that require a certain result given certain antecedents. If Bill is a man, and all men are mortal, then Bill must (of necessity) be a mortal. Remember that it is this necessity that originally inspired rationalists by providing a firm and necessary grounding for knowledge. In this rationalist sense, the conclusion of all reasoning or theorizing (e.g., Bill is a mortal) is already determined and necessary.

At this point, the widespread use of necessity in the behavioral sciences should be evident. Because it is involved in virtually all forms of determinism, reductionism, epistemology, and many forms of science, it is involved in nearly all the ideas of the behavioral sciences. With its empiricistic, efficient causal, positivistic, and mechanistic bases, behaviorism clearly requires necessity. Although cognitive psychology is often differentiated from behaviorism, its assumptions include virtually all the assumptions of behaviorism. Cognitive psychology, thus, requires necessity. Psychoanalysis differs qualitatively in the assumptions it employs, including some final and formal types of determinism as well as some metaphysical and rationalistic assumptions. However, these assumptions offer no exclusion from necessity. And surely, the combination of these schools of thought—eclecticism—cannot exclude necessity, because any combination of schools would have to maintain in some way the assumptions of the original schools.

Mainstream humanism is more difficult to characterize, because in many ways the proponents of the humanistic school of thought have sought to escape necessity. Indeed, this rejection of necessity has been the one thing that seemed to unite humanists (cf. Koch, 1959). Famous humanists, such as Carl Rogers and Abraham Maslow, historically have been critical of all types of explanations that invoke necessity, including the determinism of the environment, the reduction of the human to a mechanistic entity, and the restriction of knowledge to observable events or sensory experiences. As a result, humanists have sought alternative assumptions with which to justify and support their theories and beliefs. Unfortunately, the alternatives they found were other forms of determinism or other forms of reductionism. As noted in Chapter 2, Rogers's elegant theorizing has many final causal, materialistic, and rationalistic themes underpinning it (see also Rychlak, 1981). The humanists' efforts to escape necessity are perhaps valiant, but most do not succeed.

This attempt to escape necessity raises an important question: Is it possible for there to be a theory in the behavioral sciences that is not dependent on necessity in some way or other? The widespread use of necessity would seem to argue for a negative answer to this question. From epistemology to reductionism to determinism, all the foundations of science and schools of thought seem to be characterized by necessity. All the events studied by the behavioral sciences—at least as viewed from the perspective of the mainstream schools—must happen as they do. Readers will recognize, however, that we have not discussed one "school" described in Chapter 2—postmodernism—and we have also implied that there may be humanistic and perhaps even psychodynamic theorists outside the mainstream who have moved to other assumptions. This brings us to the category of possibility.

Possibility

Possibility is a category of assumptions with no "must" in it; the events observed by the behavioral sciences do not have to happen as they do. There is at least the potential for events to occur that were not necessitated by previous events. There is the opportunity for events to occur that cannot be explained by universal laws or sensory experiences or logical reasoning. Some events happen without being necessarily determined, either across time (efficient causation) or within time (material, formal, and final causation). Some events happen that are not the result of mechanistic or physical or nonphysical necessity. Some events could have had several possible manifestations and therefore several explanations. The event could have been *other than* (rather than *must have been*) how it was.

The notion of *free will* is an obvious example of an idea that is compatible with possibility. Indeed, free will is often defined in a manner similar to our definition of possibility—the ability of a person to act "other than" he or she did. In other words, the person had a choice, a means of thinking about the action or doing the action in a nonnecessitated way. Proponents of necessity specifically must deny this ability. Therefore, scientists who affirm a person's free will are scientists who seek to affirm the notion of possibility. A note of caution is important here, however. The term *free will* has a variety of meanings in the behavioral sciences. Many theorists, such as the cognitivists, talk about choices and decisions, but have not included in their models or theories any means by which a free choice or decision is possible. In fact, for most of these theorists, a free will would destroy or disrupt the model or theory they espouse.

Of all the schools of thought, the humanists and psychodynamicists are most open to possibility. As discussed, however, the most influential factions in these schools affirm necessity. However, many humanists (e.g., Howard & Conway, 1986; Rychlak, 1988, 1994; Tageson, 1982) and psychodynamicists (Jung, 1960; Kohut, 1978) have affirmed a type of possibility—via constructs such as free will—in their theorizing. How is this possible? As the humanist Joseph Rychlak has shown, this is primarily possible if the theories rely on final causation. This may sound like a contradiction in theoretical terms. However, Rychlak has shown that even though one must necessarily be determined by one's goals and purposes (final causation), one may nevertheless have the free will ability to formulate those goals and purposes. Rychlak and psychoanalysts such as Jung refer to this ability as the *dialectic*, the ability to think oppositionally. This ability allows all sorts of goals to be considered, so that one has a choice about how one determines oneself. With a dialectic capacity, final causation becomes a type of self-determinism and thus a variation on free will.

Many postmodernists also affirm the possibility in events. As described in several previous chapters, these theorists reject most variations of metaphysical reductionism and determinism. Postmodernists clearly affirm the opportunities implicit in any action or context. However, these theorists do not identify this possibility with a free will that someone supposedly possesses. Free will sometimes connotes a subjective ability to be free of the world, free of the context of one's behaving (Slife, 1994a, 1994b). Postmodernists, on the other hand, view all abilities and actions as grounded and constrained by their contexts. Nothing for them is free of context, including our choices and decisions. Postmodernists would even contend that our choices are bound to our past—that no choosing or decision making goes on without influences from our past (Williams, 1992).

This would appear to make possibility impossible. Indeed, this approach must seem similar to the temporal reductionism of a behaviorist or cognitivist. But here is precisely where most postmodern thinkers part company with theorists who believe in necessity. Most postmodernists are not temporal reductionists. To describe how postmodernists escape temporal reductionism would take us well beyond the scope of this section. Suffice it to say that many postmodernists affirm a view of time that is closer to temporal holism than temporal reductionism (e.g., Heidegger, 1962). All dimensions of time are simultaneously involved, and no one dimension of time is given a privileged status (cf. Slife, 1993, 1994a, 1994b, for more information).

The crucial point is that a postmodern view of time allows for the present (and future) to be constrained by the past and yet also admit possibility. The present is constrained by the past because no present is ever free of past context. For someone to make a meaningful choice in the present, the person must have some knowledge of the choice—the options available, their consequences, and so forth. This knowledge of the choice stems from the past. Indeed, without some past, the person would not even know that a choice was to be made. However, the present is not determined (necessitated) by the past, because the past itself is not determined or necessary. The past, according to many postmodernists, is "alive" and changeable, dependent on the possibilities of present and future contexts. Rather than lawful necessity being the rule of our nature, change and temporality provide better understandings. These notions also fit with the postmodern distaste for types of certainty and determinism that disallow possibility (see Chapter 2).

Although free will theorists and postmodernists are the most ardent defenders of possibility, possibility exists in many other interesting places in the behavioral sciences. Perhaps most intriguingly, many applied behavioral scientists use possibility in their practical techniques. Many psychotherapists, for example, seem to sneak possibility in the backdoor of the consulting room. We say "backdoor," because most of these therapies are supposedly based on theories of normal and abnormal behavior that are themselves grounded in necessity. In other words, there is no theoretical justification for the therapist's inclusion of possibility in the therapy session. Possibility is nevertheless present in the conceptions and techniques of the therapist. Cognitive behavioral therapists, for instance, are steeped in theories of necessity (cognitivism, behaviorism), yet many of the techniques that they espouse have clear implications of possibility—the techniques assume that the patient has the power to do *other than* what he or she has done in the past (see Slife, 1993, in press).

The reason for this inconsistency between theory and application is not clear. A free will theorist or postmodern thinker would undoubtedly want to say that the cognitive behaviorist (or anyone whose practices are grounded in theories that espouse necessity) is recognizing the possibility of the client, *despite* their theorizing. This, of course, is another way of saying that theories of necessity are wrong. However, we do not feel that the brand of necessity found in the behavioral sciences is this easily defeated, nor should it be. At this point, we merely wish to note that not all ideas of possibility in the behavioral sciences are clearly espoused or defended as part of a theory. Some forms of possibility in the behavioral sciences are hidden in the techniques and lore of the applied subdisciplines.

In conclusion, the categories of necessity and possibility allow us to organize nearly all the ideas of the behavioral sciences into roughly two categories. Necessity is clearly the dominant intellectual force, because it encompasses the vast majority of the reigning ideas and theories of the behavioral sciences. Indeed, one is tempted to describe necessity (as we have here) as the primary assumption in the behavioral sciences. Possibility has not been widely accepted in the behavioral sciences. Possibility is found in the work of some humanists and psychoanalysts, but these theorists are most likely to be outside the mainstream, at least if they espouse possibility explicitly. The postmodern view of time is one reason for this. Possibility requires such radically new assumptions about such conventionally understood concepts as time that its advocates would have to fight a host of battles, not the least of which is the assumption that "Familiar is better."

We move now to the third step in our "coping strategy." Recall that we urged readers to steer clear of eclecticism, nihilism, and denial. Doing so enables readers to face the conceptual issues of the behavioral sciences, and then as a second step, begin to make sense of these issues. This section on necessity and possibility is one way of beginning to take this second step. Our third step is intended to help the reader to deal actively with the theoretical issues outlined, establishing for the reader some sense of direction in *addressing* these issues. We hesitate to say here *resolving* these issues, because we do not feel that a resolution of all the issues is necessary. Indeed, we would question whether a resolution of all the issues is possible. We feel instead that some guidance for addressing these issues is required, without quashing reader exploration and discovery along the way.

BEHAVIORAL SCIENCES: PRESENT AND FUTURE

Here is our interpretation of where the behavioral sciences currently are and where we feel the behavioral sciences ought to go. Similar to the friend's account of the city in which she lives (see Chapter 3), our view of the behavioral sciences is biased and vague on some points. However theory laden or biased an interpretation may be, our experience is that advancing *some* perspective is often a helpful starting point for more fruitful thought and discussion. In this spirit, we offer our perspective here.

From our point of view, the behavioral sciences have settled into something like Kuhn's (1970) "normal science." As discussed in chapter 6, normal science occurs when a discipline has adopted a unifying assumption or *paradigm*. Although most commentators have held that the behavioral sciences are not unified, we feel that there are many related assumptions that are viable candidates for the status of unifying assumption. Certainly, the category of *necessity* (as just reviewed) is one such candidate. Necessity clearly serves as a unifier for most of the prominent ideas and theories of the behavioral sciences. One of the authors has made a case for *linear time*—an assumption related to necessity—as being a paradigmatic assumption in one of the behavioral sciences (Slife, 1993).

Once an assumption takes on this paradigmatic role, researchers accepting that assumption go about solving only the superficial problems raised by the assumption in their discipline. Nearly everyone in the discipline assumes that the main, or "deep," questions have already been answered. The only remaining work is a kind of mopping-up operation wherein all the implications or *puzzles* (to use Kuhn's 1970 term) that arise from the assumption are fully investigated and applied to practical problems. In other words, there is no examination of assumptions and virtually no criticism of widely held ideas. Perhaps most pertinent to this book, there is no reason for extensive theoretical criticism. All of the most important theoretical questions (e.g., necessity versus possibility) have supposedly been answered.

One manifestation of normal science in the behavioral sciences is a tendency toward model building rather than theorizing. A model helps us visualize how something might work and what variables should be taken into account. Behavioral scientists seem to be content building these models and testing them empirically. On the basis of such testing, a model is modified or rejected, and correct models will supposedly be selected on a trial-and-error basis. Unfortunately, however, model testing does not question the assumptions on which the model was built. Models rarely expand our most basic understandings of the phenomena being modeled. There is no model, for example, that sheds light on the question of whether empiricism or rationalism best explains human thought and knowledge. There is no model that helps us know whether humans are better explained with temporal or metaphysical reductionism.

Another manifestation of normal science in the behavioral sciences is the increasing emphasis on the application of knowledge to human problems (e.g., education, therapy). However, there are at least two difficulties with this emphasis. First, when we assume that a main goal of the discipline is the solution of practical problems, we naturally become impatient. There are real problems out there, after all, and we need solutions as quickly as possible. Although this attitude is understandable—perhaps even laudable—it often results in a disdain for critical thinking and theory. In the rush to practical application, there is considerable temptation to claim a level of understanding and a precision in our knowledge that cannot be supported. This claim can result in techniques and practical strategies that are ineffective, or worse, counterproductive, with relatively few practitioners recognizing that better theorizing leads to better practice.

Along with an impatient charge to help people, there is often a comparable haste to find answers to seemingly practical questions that are themselves not well considered. In the field of education, for instance, some have asked the seemingly reasonable question: How does one apply learning theory to the educational process? This question is problematic because this usually assumes that there is only one theory of learning, a theory that is basically empiricist in nature. What about a rationalistic approach to learning (see Chapter 4)? Have there been experiments conducted that have conclusively shown that one epistemology or learning theory has triumphed over another? We see no evidence of this in the literature of the behavioral sciences. Most often, only empiricist approaches to learning have been tested, with no comparison to rationalist approaches or hermeneutic modes of engagement even attempted.

Before behavioral scientists launch research operations, applying theory to practical problems, we may need to ask more fundamental questions: What does it mean to learn? How is learning experienced and expressed? What does it mean to be educated? What is the nature of the relationship between the human being and the world? Is an empiricist relationship (as in most learning and memory models) the best approach to explaining this relationship? These questions are not the sort that are easily addressed with empirical methods.

One of the implications of this situation is that applied and empirical work must always *follow* good theoretical work. We would admit that empirical work could give us something new to think carefully and critically about, but even this admission is risky given that empirical "facts" are never purely factual nor purely empirical. They are always interpreted in the light of what the observer is looking for and how the observer frames what he or she sees. We assert that *science must always start with ideas*, ideas that at the very least are taken to be the givens of the matter. Otherwise, there would be nothing to study. Once the investigative process is started, of course, observation and theory feed each other. However, because observations themselves are theoretical interpretations, theory must *always* come first (logically, if not chronologically).

This means that *theoretical skills* are required: clear and careful thinking that brings many possible frames of reference to bear on whatever information and data we have. Theoretical skills means reading broadly and situating the issues historically, so that we know where questions fundamental to theories come from, why they have been asked the way they have, and why we might be tempted to think about them in the way that seems so "natural" to us. Theoretical skills ought to take their place alongside research and statistical skills as necessary competencies for any behavioral scientist.

Further, there is never a time that we can cease to be concerned with theory. The history of the natural sciences has taught us that lesson. The people of every epoch tend to think that they have gone about as far as they can in their knowledge. They feel assured that their understandings must reflect reality. For instance, many physicists were patting one another on the back at the turn of this century. With the help of Newton's mechanics, they felt that all the laws of nature had been discovered and examined. Then came Einstein and the quantum physicists. Their new ideas did not just expand on those of Newton; their new ideas challenged and ultimately replaced those of Newton (except in the more technological disciplines, such as engineering). This most recent historical case—Newton and Einstein—reminded physicists that their ideas and knowledge claims are always relative to their paradigmatic assumptions.

We have no reason to suspect that the behavioral sciences have discovered an immutable and irreplaceable paradigm. Indeed, the relative youth of the behavioral sciences should make anyone in these disciplines careful about knowledge claims. Surprisingly, however, the reverse is often the case. Persons in the less mature disciplines often make the most exaggerated (and groundless) claims. Perhaps where there is so little history there is also little history of problems.

Natural scientists have sometimes been excused (or excused themselves) from taking a lively interest in theoretical issues, holding up their impressive technology as a justification for and vindication of their work. Many have considered their technology (e.g., medicine, engineering) as evidence that they require little theoretical correction. Of course, whether this is true—particularly whether this technology is an unmitigated blessing—is itself another debatable question we cannot answer here. It *is* clear, however, that these questions are themselves theoretical questions. To answer them at any level requires some careful and sophisticated thinking. The answers depend on assumptions we hold about life, about what is good, and about what we should be doing and learning.

More to the point, however, is the fact that the behavioral sciences have no impressive technology. This is not to discount the beneficial work that has occurred and is ongoing, but it is difficult to consider this work of sufficient import to justify not being deeply involved in theoretical work. We cannot point to great strides in learning and teaching, certainly not as measured in school performance. We cannot claim an impressive technology for dealing with psychopathology, nor for testing and evaluation. The most technologically advanced subdisciplines, such as neuroscience, have usually borrowed their technology from the natural sciences. In other words, we have adapted technology for observing phenomena of interest, but in the behavioral sciences per se we have not developed an impressive enough technology to warrant dismissal of the more deeply embedded philosophical problems.

What seems to have happened in the behavioral sciences is that we have become content with the theoretical perspectives already available. In psychology, for example, it is common to discuss four fundamental perspectives on virtually any topic: psychodynamic, behavioral, humanistic, and cognitive. Little attention is given to their adequacy or the advisability of looking at a particular topic through the lenses these perspectives provide. It is almost as if psychologists are grateful that *only* four perspectives were discovered, so that they can get down to the business of verification and application. Students of the behavioral sciences should ask themselves: Who are the three greatest living theorists in my field today? By this question, we mean people who have made fundamental breakthroughs in their disciplines or formulated new perspectives on how we understand human beings.

Our experience is that most psychology students are hard-pressed to name many theorists at the level of Freud, Rogers, and Skinner. More often, the names that come to mind are of people known for a particular model or for expanding the scope of an existing theory. This, we feel, is an unacceptable situation in any discipline for which its proponents aspire to claim scientific status. Someone might argue, of course, that it takes time for genuine and legitimate alternatives to develop. However, we see few encouraging trends in the development of theory. The most recent so-called revolutionary development—the cognitive revolution—is not a revolution in any theoretical sense. As noted throughout this book, cognitivism partakes of the same assumptions as behaviorism. If there was a revolution when cognitivism developed, it was methodological, not theoretical. There were no ideas that were not already implicit in the empiricistic epistemology of behaviorism.

This brings us to the topic of where we feel the behavioral sciences *should* be headed. Up to this point, we have shown that the behavioral sciences are currently mired in a normal science that ignores fundamental questions. We have suggested that this ignorance is counterproductive, particularly when practical applications are involved. We have argued that theoretical questions are always at the heart of every discipline, in its focus, methods, and results. By now, our notion of what is needed in the behavioral sciences may be obvious to the reader: We need careful, considered thinking about the philosophical and theoretical issues. We need new ideas to provide contrast with the old ideas. Without such contrasts, a true evaluation of the old ideas is impossible.

Of course, newness in itself is not necessarily a virtue. Recall the problems we mentioned above regarding the youthfulness of the behavioral sciences. New ideas are only good ideas when they are better than old ideas or when they challenge the old to the extent that the old are reappraised and reappreciated. This is one of the virtues of recent developments, such as postmodernism, in our view. Through postmodernists' emphasis on possibility and temporal holism—new ideas for many behavioral scientists—we can become aware of the dominance in our field of the old ideas of necessity and temporal reductionism.

A call for new theorizing, however, raises an interesting question. Perhaps the problem is less one of "new" thinking than one of reconsidering "old" thinking. It can be validly argued, in our view, that we do not need new ideas for the behavioral sciences. Perhaps all the important issues have already been raised. There are enough ideas in Plato, Aristotle, Aquinas, Descartes, and Kant to keep us busy for the next several decades, if not centuries.[3] In this sense, the problem is not new theorizing but more careful, clear, and sophisticated theorizing, drawing from our already rich intellectual tradition. (It can be argued that there is no such thing as a new idea anyway.) What is needed, then, to respond to the conceptual problems of the behavioral sciences is already there in the history of ideas.

In either case—drawing from the well of our intellectual tradition or formulating fundamentally new conceptions of the behavioral sciences— the need for theoretical skills is clear. Teaching such skills entails sensitizing students to the history of ideas. This means, in particular, acquainting them with how this history is vitally present. Theoretically skillful students need to know our historical legacy, both in terms of the ideas that we have inherited and the ideas that are all but lost. Theoretical skills also demand critical analysis of content and process, ideas and methods, premises and logic. This is not to say that such skills would only be used to *deconstruct*, or tear down, the reigning ideas. Theoretical skills would also provide proficiency in constructing and guiding new ideas and developing systems of thought. What ideas are worthy of consideration, test, or application? Do historians of previous considerations, tests, and applications have anything to say, so that we do not "reinvent the wheel"? Given that a particular theory has a particular assumption, what can we say about that theory? Will its characteristics and properties allow the desired result?

The skills that would productively engage these questions need to be taught as part of every behavioral science curriculum. In our view, such skills should be given a status and an emphasis that is comparable to statistics; research methods; and at the graduate level, clinical skills. Courses in the history and theories of a discipline are rarely sufficient. It is the exceptional history course that delves into the philosophical ideas surrounding historical thinkers. It is the exceptional theory course that explicates the hidden assumptions of the great thinkers of our disciplines. Too often discussions of philosophical ideas and hidden assumptions are conducted at the professional or graduate levels. These discussions, especially those in print, are rarely accessible to undergraduates. The assumption is that undergraduates are too unsophisticated to handle highly theoretical issues. These students must learn the "basics" of the discipline before such issues can be thoughtfully entertained.

We question this educational assumption. Often it is the basics that contain all the hidden philosophy of the discipline. Because of this, students are often converted to a particular view of the world before they know that different worldviews exist. This discourages active learning and conceptual ownership of the available ideas. Students end up treating the basics as items to memorize or jargon to master, and the truly interesting issues are lost, along with much of the students' interest in pursuing them. We advocate more discussion of theory earlier, *far* earlier than is currently the case. Our experience is that such discussion provides a needed backdrop and context for the basics. Students also become more active in their learning. With adequate skills to understand and analyze theories, the panoply of historic options, along with the successes and failures of similar ideas, are within their conceptual grasp.

Notes

1. Although the majority of readers will undoubtedly be students in the narrower and more formal sense of taking behavioral science classes, we consider this chapter to be relevant to the more general student of the behavioral sciences as well.

2. In this book, we ask for another type of openness, a willingness to question all assumptions, evaluate the theories, and press the implications to their logical conclusions. We are inviting entrance into a never-ending discussion, as it were.

3. Of course, we must be aware of the implicit assumptions of historical ideas and those who interpret them. The feminist literature, for example, has called our attention to the fact that most of what we consider our intellectual history consists of the thinking of dead white European males.

Glossary

A

A priori factors. As expressed by Immanuel Kant, those mental factors that are prior to experience.

Abstraction. The process by which, in making description, some aspects of a thing are noted and others are omitted. The term is also used to refer to a very general principle, a nonphysical entity.

Affirming the consequent. The logical fallacy that occurs when instead of demonstrating that the antecedent (i.e., the *if* portion of the *if-then* statement) of the argument is true and concluding that the consequence (i.e., the *then* portion of the *if-then* statement) follows, we claim that because the consequent is true, the antecedent must be true as well.

AUTHORS' NOTE: This glossary will not satisfy many readers because it is not precise. Our attempt is to provide a quick reference to important terms used in the book that will help readers see the main idea or issue under discussion. Scholars with backgrounds in theory and philosophy will likely find the definitions mundane. We have decided to accept the consequences of these informal definitions in the interest of helping readers with less formal training and more general interests. We hope the body of the text and the chapter notes will partially respond to the interests of the more critical reader.

Antecedence. One of David Hume's necessary conditions for establishing causality (the others are contiguity, constant conjunction, and necessary conjunction), requiring that the cause must precede the effect for a causal relation to be inferred.

Assumption. The historical roots of a theory and the ideas about the world necessary for the theory to be true.

Autonomous. The state or condition in which action occurs in a self-governing way, free from external determining factors.

Axiom. A statement held as a truth without being derived from another more fundamental truth.

B

Behavioral sciences. Those scientific disciplines engaged in the study and explanation of a broad range of human behaviors.

C

Classical conditioning. The process by which an organism learns to respond to a new stimulus because of its being associated with another stimulus that previously produced the response.

Conditioning. A process by which organisms come to behave in certain ways under certain circumstances. It is a way of talking about learning without making reference to the mind or the will or mental processes.

Constant conjunction. One of David Hume's necessary conditions for establishing causality (the others are antecedence, contiguity, and necessary conjunction), requiring that two events must always be associated with one another for a causal relation to be inferred. That is, if A causes B, then every time A occurs, B occurs.

Contiguity. One of David Hume's necessary conditions for establishing causality (the others are antecedence, constant conjunction, and necessary conjunction), requiring that events must be in contact with each other in space or time for a causal relation to be inferred.

Continuum. A series of events, phenomena, and so on, in which no discernible separations among parts can be detected.

Control. The process of holding all circumstances or aspects of an environment constant, so that the phenomenon of interest can be observed without influence from extraneous sources.

Convention. Belief, assumption, and so on that is upheld through tradition and consensual agreement.

Correlational design. A research design that theoretically does not allow the scientist to establish causal relations among variables, because of the absence of careful control of possibly influential variables.

Covering law. A law that explains a wide range of phenomena over a wide range of conditions.

Crucial test. An experiment in which all possible variables or limiting conditions have been controlled or taken into account, so that there is no other possible explanation for the failure of the experiment except the falsity of the hypothesis.

D

Deism. A theological position in which the universe is viewed as a machine, running in an order preestablished by God.

Deity teleology. An account in which it is held that God or Deity acts for the sake of intended goals, purposes, and so on, and that this purposive action is manifest in the events of the world.

Dependent variable. The variable we observe and in which we expect to see the effect of the treatment or independent variable.

Descartes, René. A 17th-century philosopher considered to be the founder of modern rationalism.

Determinant. A cause.

Dualism. An account in which the phenomenon to be explained is considered in terms of two fundamental aspects (e.g., the human is composed of both mind and body).

E

Eclecticism. A theoretical stance in which it is claimed that there is not one true theory governing human behavior—that all theories may be true, or at least, have some truth in them.

Efficient causation. Aristotle's notion of cause, which is usually interpreted as requiring movement, or the sequence of events, over time. Whether this is what Aristotle intended is a matter of some debate.

Empiricism. An epistemology in which it is assumed that learning, memory, and ideas are primarily derived from one's sensory experiences.

Enlightenment. A period of European history (around the 18th century) characterized by an emphasis on learning, rationality, and science.

Epiphenomenal. The idea that things are not as they appear, but rather manifestations of something else. The result of reductionism is to make certain things epiphenomenal.

Epistemology. In philosophy, epistemology concerns the nature, origins, and limits of knowledge.

Ethnocentrism. A prejudice in which one's ethnic group is considered to be the norm against which all other groups and practices are judged.

Experimental design. A research design in which theoretically the scientist can establish causal relations among variables because other potentially influential variables are controlled.

F

Falsificationism. The belief that the real power of science lies in its ability to falsify theories or hypotheses, as opposed to verifying them.

Final causation. Aristotle's notion of cause, which depends on the goal or purpose for which anything may exist or any activity may be carried out.

Formal causation. Aristotle's notion of cause, which depends on the form, essence, or pattern that a thing may take and allows for individual parts to combine into larger wholes.

Free will. An account of human behavior in which goals or purposes are not rigidly determined by biology or the environment; rather, humans can always choose otherwise, all circumstances remaining the same.

G

Gestalt. A German term that refers to the relationship of various parts of a pattern to the whole and implies that the whole is greater than the sum of its parts.

H

Heidegger, Martin. A 20th-century philosopher who introduced, among other things, the notion of hermeneutical modes of engagement: present-at-hand and ready-to-hand. Heidegger is arguably the most influential figure in postmodern philosophy.

Hermeneutics. A method originally used by biblical scholars in their interpretation of biblical texts, which has also been extended in some of the behavioral science disciplines to study meaningful human phenomena on the basis of practical understanding. Hermeneuticists suggest that understanding human actions is similar to understanding written texts. Interpretation is fundamental to both.

Human teleology. An account in which it is held that humans act for the sake of intended goals, purposes, etc.

Humanism. A theory in psychology based on the autonomy of humans but allowing for the constraints of biology and social structures in which humans find themselves.

Hypothesis. The idea that guides a scientific experiment expressed in the form of a testable prediction.

I

Implication. The consequences and ideas that logically follow from a theory.

Implicit ideas. In relation to theories, hidden assumptions about the world that are crucial to a theory's formulation and use.

Independent variable. In an empirical study, the treatment variable that we expect to have an effect on the variable we observe (the dependent variable).

Instantaneous. A causal relation in which no time interval is required for the cause to have an effect.

K

Kant, Immanuel. An 18th-century philosopher who asserted another form of rationalism based on innate *categories of understanding* for structuring and organizing experience.

L

Learning theory. An explanation of the way the environment conditions and shapes one's behavior across time.

Locke, John. A 17th-century British empiricist philosopher who asserted that knowledge originated from sensation and reflection.

Logos. A Greek word meaning, among other things, discourse.

M

Material causation. Aristotle's notion of cause, which depends on the material or substance of which a thing is composed.

Materialists. People who believe that matter is the fundamental reality.

Metaphysics. The study/search for the fundamental thing(s) that make up reality. The term is also used to refer to those fundamental things themselves.

Metatheoretical. The idea that there are theories above or behind the theories used to describe human behavior. Theories are always based on other theories. A metatheory is a theory about theories.

Method. The particular activities used to achieve research results, including experimental designs, sampling procedures, and statistical treatment of data. In general terms, a method is any procedure for investigating that we believe will yield knowledge or truth.

Methodological pluralism. The idea that the choice of a particular method of study should be based on the nature of the problem we are investigating, the way in which the problem is framed, and the relevant strengths and weaknesses of possible methods.

Models of memory. Cognitivist explanations of how and what we can remember.

N

Natural teleology. An account in which it is held that nature itself acts for the sake of goals, or purposes, or that all of nature is moving toward some meaningful end.

Naturalistic explanation. An account in which phenomena are explained in terms of things presumed to be part of the natural world. Often contrasted with supernatural explanation.

Necessity. The idea that events must occur as they did, and things must be what they are. It is often contrasted with possibility.

Negating (denying) the consequent. A valid syllogistic argument in which the consequent (i.e., the *then* portion of the *if-then* statement) of the syllogism is denied, or shown to be untrue, and therefore the antecedent (i.e., the *if* portion of the *if-then* statement) must also be rejected.

Neuron. A specialized nerve cell that carries impulses.

Neurotransmitters. Chemicals located in the nervous system that enable neural impulses to be passed from one nerve cell to another.

Nihilism. The idea that there is no solid foundation for the behavioral sciences or anything else.

Noumena. In rationalist epistemology, the external world to which individuals never have direct access.

O

Objectivity. In some usages objectivity refers to the outer world consisting of the world of public objects and things. In many treatments of science it refers to a particular way of making observations or judgments in which the person making them is presumably uninfluenced by biases or subjectivity. It thus refers to a perspective from which it is thought to be unlikely that one could be wrong.

Ockham's razor. A theory that phenomena ought to be explained in ways that invoke few unsupportable constructs or assertions.

Operational definition. A translation of some theoretical construct into observable or measurable terms.

Operationalization. The process of letting something we can observe represent something we cannot, for the purpose of scientific study. The process of making operational definitions.

P

Paradigm. Implicit view of the world that scientists hold, that communities of scientists share, and that influences the way science is done.

Phenomena. In rationalist epistemology, experience that is the result of a combination of the a priori structure of the mind and the world. In many postmodern theories, "phenomenon" is used as roughly equivalent to experience. In common usage, "phenomenon" is a fancy synonym for "thing."

Positivism. A philosophy in which it is held that the purpose of science is to help scientists formulate a coherent view or model of the world. There are many different versions of positivism, but common and important to most of them are the notions that scientific understanding takes the form of laws or propositions, and that these propositions must be closely tied to observations.

Possibility. The idea that events could have occurred in a way other than the way they did.

Post hoc, ergo propter hoc. Latin phrase meaning "after that, hence because of that"; also a logical fallacy. The fallacy is to claim that because A follows B, A must have been caused by B.

Pragmatism. A philosophical position in which it is emphasized that the best way to decide questions of truth or reality is by examining the practical results of the ideas. If something successfully solves a problem, it can be taken as "true." It should be noted that because so many different positions are claimed to be pragmatic, any definition will likely be unsatisfactory to someone.

Present-at-hand. A hermeneutic mode of engagement characterized by reflection and detachment from ongoing practical involvement with the world.

Q

Qualitative methods. Procedures for investigating human action that do not involve measurement and quantification, but allow subjects to describe their own behavior and experience in the language native to their experience, and investigators to undertake the analysis of human phenomena in conversational language rather than numbers.

R

Rationalism. An epistemology in which it is assumed that the source of knowledge is the mind and its capacity for reasoning.

Ready-to-hand. A hermeneutic mode of engagement characterized by active involvement in practical activities in the world.

Realism. A philosophy of science in which it is held that the scientific method allows an investigator direct access to the real world.

Reductionism. A strategy for explaining phenomena by positing that when properly understood, seemingly complex phenomena are "really just" manifestations of seemingly simpler ones. Reductionism posits that X is "really just" Y.

S

Simultaneity. A type of causality in which the cause is not required to occur before the effect, but instead must be present at the exact time of the effect.

Skepticism. An approach to understanding in which one begins by doubting the truth of all theories or postulates. Doubting generally.

Social constructionism. An alternative to traditional theories of human nature and behavior in which it is emphasized that people "construct" for themselves their identities and the meanings of their experiences. This is possible because each person is involved in one or more "societies" that provide meanings and definitions for use in the constructions.

Soft sciences. Sciences, like most of the behavioral sciences, which deal with a subject matter not easily predicted, controlled, or quantified. In soft sciences, researchers have not achieved the same level of success as natural scientists in technology or ability to control and predict.

Subjectivity. The inner world of private emotions and thoughts. This inner world is most often seen to be unique to each individual person. It is also often seen to be illogical and unreliable as a source of knowledge.

Supernatural explanation. An explanation of the phenomena of the world in terms of gods, spirits, or other things that are not part of the natural world.

Syllogism. The logical argument consisting of a major premise; a minor premise; and the conclusion, which is the logical consequence of the relation between the major and the minor premises.

T

Technology. The products or practices that result from scientific knowledge applied to the solution of real-world problems. People may attempt to derive a technology not only from science, but from any theory.

Teleology. Any explanation in which a final cause is invoked as explanation is a teleological explanation. Literally, the word can be taken as referring to the study of the *telos,* or end toward which things lead.

Theory. In its most basic form a theory is an idea, a statement of relationship between two or more phenomena. Theories serve as explanations in that one phenomenon is believed to account for another.

U

Unconscious. The area of the mind, postulated by psychodynamic theorists, to which people commonly have no direct access, or of which they have no direct awareness.

V

Validity. The extent to which a measurement procedure faithfully represents the phenomenon it is intended to measure. The term is also used to refer to experiments. An experiment is said to be valid if we can be confident the results came about because of the variables and theories we were studying, and not other causes.

Variable. Any aspect of the world of interest to a scientist that can be observed, manipulated, or measured. Observations or measurements may vary from time to time, place to place, subject to subject, or method to method.

Verificationism. The belief that the role of science is confirming the truth of its theories or hypotheses. It is also assumed that scientific methods have the ability to do so. The term is often used in opposition to falsificationism.

W

Weltanschauung. A German term that means "worldview." As used in Chapter 6, it refers to the notion that scientific work is imbedded in the ideas and practices of the larger culture, and therefore not as objective and free from cultural influences as realists and positivists have thought (see Paradigm).

Wittgenstein, Ludwig. An influential linguistic philosopher of the 20th century who noted the importance of social agreements as a foundation for language.

References

Adams, D. K. (1937). Note on method. *Psychological Review, 44,* 212-218.

Ashcraft, M. H. (1989). *Human memory and cognition.* New York: Scott, Foresman.

Averill, J. (1985). The social construction of emotion: With special reference to love. In K. J. Gergen & K. E. Davis (Eds.), *The social construction of the person* (pp. 89-109). New York: Springer-Verlag.

Ball, M. S., & Smith, G. W. H. (1992). *Analyzing visual data.* Newbury Park, CA: Sage.

Bandura, A. (1977). *Social learning theory.* Englewood Cliffs, NJ: Prentice Hall.

Bandura, A. (1986). *Social foundations of thought and action: A social cognitive theory.* Englewood Cliffs, NJ: Prentice Hall.

Bohm, D. (1980). *Wholeness and the implicate order.* London: Routledge & Kegan Paul.

Bohman, J. (1991). *New philosophy of social science.* Cambridge: MIT Press.

Brand, M. (1976). *The nature of causation.* Chicago: University of Illinois Press.

Brookfield, S. (1987). *Developing critical thinkers: Challenging adults to explore alternative ways of thinking.* San Francisco: Jossey-Bass.

Bunge, M. (1959). *Causality.* Cambridge, MA: Harvard University Press.

Bunge, M. (1963). *The myth of simplicity.* Englewood Cliffs, NJ: Prentice Hall.

Chomsky, N. (1957). Review of *Verbal behavior* by B. F. Skinner. *Language, 35,* 26-58.

Churchland, P. S. (1986). *Neurophilosophy: Toward a unified science of mind-brain.* Cambridge: MIT Press.

Coulter, J. (1979). *The social construction of the mind.* New York: Macmillan.

Crabtree, B. F., & Miller, W. L. (1992). *Doing qualitative research.* Newbury Park, CA: Sage.

DeGeorge, R. T., & DeGeorge, F. M. (1972). *The structuralists: from Marx to Levi-Strauss.* Garden City, NY: Anchor.

Denzin, N. K., & Lincoln, Y. S. (Eds.). (1994). *Handbook of qualitative research*. Thousand Oaks, CA: Sage.

Dilthey, W. (1976). The rise of hermeneutics. In P. Connerton (Ed.), *Critical society* (pp. 104-116). New York: Penguin. (Original work published 1900)

Dreyfus, H. S. (1979). *What computers can't do*. New York: Harper & Row.

Edelman, G. M. (1987). *Neural Darwinism: The theory of neuronal group selection*. New York: Basic Books.

Ellis, H. C., & Hunt, R. R. (1989). *Fundamentals of human memory and cognition* (4th ed.). Dubuque, IA: W. C. Brown.

Faulconer, J. E., & Williams, R. N. (1985). Temporality in human action: An alternative to positivism and historicism. *American Psychologist, 40,* 1179-1188.

Faulconer, J. E., & Williams, R. N. (Eds.). (1990). *Reconsidering psychology: Perspectives from continental philosophy*. Pittsburgh, PA: Duquesne University Press.

Feyerabend, P. (1975). *Against reason*. London: Verso.

Feyerabend, P. (1987). *Farewell to reason*. London: Verso.

Fox, J., & Slife, B. D. (1995). *Newton's clock: Crumbling paradigms in the social sciences*. Unpublished manuscript.

Gadamer, H. G. (1982). *Truth and method*. New York: Crossroad.

Gelven, M. (1989). *A commentary on Heidegger's "Being and Time"* (rev. ed.). Dekalb, IL: Northern Illinois University Press.

Gergen, K. J. (1982). *Toward transformation in social knowledge*. New York: Springer-Verlag.

Gergen, K. J. (1985). The social constructionist movement in modern psychology. *American Psychologist, 40,* 266-275.

Gergen, K. J., & Morawski, J. (1980). An alternative metatheory for social psychology. In L. Wheeler (Ed.), *Review of personality and social psychology* (pp. 326-352). Beverly Hills, CA: Sage.

Gilgun, J. F., Daly, K., & Handel, G. (Eds.). (1992). *Qualitative methods in family research*. Newbury Park, CA: Sage.

Giorgi, A. (1970). *Psychology as a human science: A phenomenologically based approach*. New York: Harper & Row.

Giorgi, A. (Ed.). (1985). *Phenomenology and psychological research*. Pittsburgh, PA: Duquesne University Press.

Goetz, J. P., & LeCompte, M. D. (1984). *Ethnography and qualitative design in educational research*. Orlando, FL: Academic Press.

Gulley, N. (1962). *Plato's theory of knowledge*. London: Methuen.

Heelas, P., & Lock, A. (Eds.). (1981). *Indigenous psychologies*. London: Academic Press.

Heidegger, M. (1962). *Being and time* (J. Macquarrie & E. S. Robinson, Trans.). New York: Harper & Row.

Hempel, C. (1965). *Aspects of scientific explanation and other essays in the philosophy of science*. New York: Free Press.

Hilgard, E. R., & Bower, G. H. (1975). *Theories of learning* (4th ed.). Englewood Cliffs, NJ: Prentice Hall.

Howard, G. S., & Conway, C. G. (1986). Can there be an empirical science of volitional action? *American Psychologist, 41,* 1241-1251.

Johnson, D. P. (1981). *Sociological theory: Classical founders and contemporary perspectives*. New York: John Wiley.

Jung, C. (1960). The structure and dynamics of the psyche. In H. Read, M. Fordham, & G. Adler (Eds.), *The collected works of C. G. Jung* (Bollingen Series, Vol. 8). New York: Pantheon.

Koch, S. (1959). *Psychology: A study of science* (Vols. 1-3). New York: McGraw-Hill.

Kohut, H. (1978). *The psychology of the self* (A. Goldberg, Ed.). New York: International Universities Press.

Kuhn, T. S. (1970). *The structure of scientific revolutions* (2nd ed.). Chicago: University of Chicago Press.

Lakatos, I. (1970) Falsification and the methodology of scientific research programmes. In I. Lakatos & A. Musgrave (Eds.), *Criticism and the growth of knowledge* (pp. 91-196). Cambridge, UK: Cambridge University Press.

Leahey, T. H. (1992). *A history of psychology: Main currents in psychological thought* (3rd ed.). Englewood Cliffs, NJ: Prentice Hall.

Lee, D. (1950). Lineal and nonlineal codifications of reality. *Psychosomatic Medicine, 12,* 89-97.

Lee, V. L. (1988). *Beyond behaviorism.* Hillsdale, NJ: Lawrence Erlbaum.

Lewin, K. (1936). *Principles of topological psychology.* New York: McGraw-Hill.

Lutz, C. (1982). The domain of emotion words in Ifaluk. *American Ethnologist, 9,* 113-128.

Maslow, A. H. (1954). *Motivation and personality.* New York: Harper & Row.

Maslow, A. H. (1968). *Toward a psychology of being* (2nd ed.). New York: Van Nostrand Reinhold.

Maslow, A. H. (1970). *Motivation and personality* (2nd ed.). New York: Harper & Row.

McDowell, L., & Pringle, R. (1992). *Defining women: Social institutions and gender divisions.* Cambridge, UK: Polity.

Merleau-Ponty, M. (1962). *The phenomenology of perception* (C. Smith, Trans.). London: Routledge.

Messer, S. B., Sass, L. A., & Woolfolk, R. L. (1988). *Hermeneutics and psychological theory: Interpretive perspectives on personality, psychotherapy, and psychopathology.* New Brunswick, NJ: Rutgers University Press.

Ollenburger, J. C., & Moore, H. A. (1992). *A sociology of women: The intersection of patriarchy, capitalism, and colonialism.* Englewood Cliffs, NJ: Prentice Hall.

Overton, W. F., & Reese, H. W. (1973). Models of development: Methodological implications. In J. R. Nesselroade & H. W. Reese (Eds.), *Life-span developmental psychology: Methodological issues* (pp. 65-86). New York: Academic Press.

Packer, M. J. (1985). Hermeneutic inquiry in the study of human conduct. *American Psychologist, 40,* 1081-1093.

Packer, M. J., & Addison, R. B. (Eds.). (1989). *Entering the circle: Hermeneutic investigation in psychology.* Albany, NY: SUNY.

Patton, M. Q. (1990). *Qualitative evaluation and research methods* (2nd ed.). Newbury Park, CA: Sage.

Piaget, J. (1973). *The child and reality: Problems of genetic psychology.* New York: Viking.

Polkinghorne, D. (1983). *Methodology for the human sciences: Systems of inquiry.* Albany, NY: SUNY.

Popper, K. (1959). *The logic of scientific discovery.* New York: Basic Books.

Rakover, S. S. (1990). *Metapsychology: Missing links in behavior, mind and science.* New York: Paragon.

Reynolds, A. G., & Flagg, P. W. (1977). *Cognitive psychology.* Cambridge, MA: Winthrop.

Robinson, D. N. (1985). *Philosophy of psychology.* New York: Columbia University Press.

Robinson, D. N. (1989). *Aristotle's psychology.* New York: Columbia University Press.

Robinson, D. N. (1995a). *An intellectual history of psychology* (3rd ed.). New York: Macmillan.

Robinson, D. N. (1995b). The logic of reductionist models. *New Ideas in Psychology, 13,* 1-8.

Rogers, C. R. (1951). *Client-centered therapy.* Boston: Houghton Mifflin.

Rogers, C. R. (1959). A theory of therapy, personality, and interpersonal relationships, as developed in the client-centered framework. In S. Koch (Ed.), *Psychology: A study of a science. Study I. Conceptual and systematic. Vol. 3: Formulations of the person and social context.* New York: McGraw-Hill.

Rogers, C. R. (1970). Toward a modern approach to values: The valuing process in the mature person. In J. T. Haar & T. M. Tomlinson (Eds.), *New directions in client-centered therapy* (pp. 430-441). Boston: Houghton Mifflin.

Rosaldo, M. (1980). *Knowledge and passion: Ilongot notions of self and social life.* Cambridge, UK: Cambridge University Press.

Ross, A. O. (1987). *Personality: The scientific study of complex human behavior.* New York: Holt, Rinehart & Winston.

Russ, R. (Ed.). (1987). Special issue: Teleology and cognitive science. *Journal of Mind and Behavior, 8,* 179-350.

Russell, B. (1971). Descriptions. In J. F. Rosenberg & C. Travis (Eds.), *Reading in the philosophy of language* (pp. 166-175). Englewood Cliffs, NJ: Prentice Hall. (Original work published 1919)

Rychlak, J. F. (1981). *Introduction to personality and psychotherapy: A theory-construction approach* (2nd ed.). Boston: Houghton Mifflin.

Rychlak, J. F. (1988). *The psychology of rigorous humanism* (2nd ed.). New York: New York University Press.

Rychlak, J. F. (1994). *Logical learning theory: A human teleology and its empirical support.* Lincoln: Nebraska University Press.

Ryckman, R. M. (1989). *Theories of personality* (4th ed.). Belmont, CA: Wadsworth.

Schaffer, H. (1988). Child psychology: The future. In S. Chess, A. Thomas, & M. Hertzig (Eds.), *Annual progress in child psychiatry and child development* (pp. 89-112). New York: Brunner/Mazel.

Schweder, R. A., & Bourne, E. (1982). Does the concept of the person vary cross-culturally? In A. J. Marsella & G. White (Eds.), *Cultural concepts of mental health and therapy* (pp. 97-137). Boston: Reidel.

Skinner, B. F. (1957). *Verbal behavior.* New York: Appleton-Century-Crofts.

Skinner, B. F. (1971). *Beyond freedom and dignity.* New York: Knopf.

Skinner, B. F. (1974). *About behaviorism.* New York: Knopf.

Slife, B. D. (1981). Psychology's reliance on linear time: A reformulation. *Journal of Mind and Behavior, 1,* 27-46.

Slife, B. D. (1987a). Telic and mechanistic explanations of mind and meaningfulness: An empirical illustration. *Journal of Personality, 55,* 445-466.

Slife, B. D. (1987b). The perils of eclecticism as therapeutic orientation. *Theoretical and Philosophical Psychology, 7*(2), 94-103.

Slife, B. D. (1992). *Cognition, memory, and Plato's "Meno."* Paper presented at the meeting of the American Psychological Association, Washington, DC.

Slife, B. D. (1993). *Time and psychological explanation.* Albany, NY: SUNY.

Slife, B. D. (1994a). Free will and time: That "stuck" feeling. *Journal of Theoretical and Philosophical Psychology, 14,* 1-12.

Slife, B. D. (1994b). The possibility of possibility. *Journal of Theoretical and Philosophical Psychology, 14,* 96-101.

Slife, B. D. (1995a). *The ethicality of an eclectic orientation to psychotherapy.* Paper proposed for the meeting of the American Psychological Association, New York.

Slife, B. D. (1995b). An introduction to "The Legacy of Newton." *Journal of Mind and Behavior, 16,* 1-7.

Slife, B. D. (in press). Information and time. *Theory and Psychology.*

Slife, B. D., & Lanyon, J. (1991). Accounting for the power of the here-and-now: A theoretical revolution. *International Journal of Group Psychotherapy, 41*(2), 145-167.

Smith, J. (1981). Self as experience in Maori culture. In P. Heelas & A. Lock (Eds.), *Indigenous psychologies* (pp. 145-160). London: Academic Press.

Solso, R. L. (1991). *Cognitive psychology* (3rd ed.). New York: Allyn & Bacon.

Tageson, C. W. (1982). *Humanistic psychology: A synthesis.* Homewood, IL: Dorsey.

Turing, A. M. (1950). Computing machinery and intelligence. *Mind, 59,* 433-460.

Valentine, E. R. (1992). *Conceptual issues in psychology.* London: Routledge.

Van Inwagen, P. (1983). *An essay on free will.* Oxford, UK: Clarendon.

van Manen, M. (1990). *Researching lived experience: Human science for an action sensitive pedagogy.* Albany, NY: SUNY.

van Zuuren, F. J., Wertz, F. J., & Mook, B. (1987). *Advances in qualitative psychology: Themes and variations.* Lisse, The Netherlands: Swets & Zeitlinger.

Watson, J. B. (1913). Psychology as the behaviorist views it. *Psychological Review, 20,* 158-177.

Webster's new collegiate dictionary. (1981). Springfield, MA: Author.

Wheelwright, P. (1960). *The presocratics.* Indianapolis, IN: Bobbs-Merrill.

Williams, R. N. (1987). Can cognitive psychology offer a meaningful account of meaningful human action? *Journal of Mind and Behavior, 8,* 209-222.

Williams, R. N. (1992). The human context of agency. *American Psychologist, 47,* 752-760.

Williams, R. N. (1995). Temporality and psychological action at a distance. *Journal of Mind and Behavior, 16,* 63-76.

Wilson, E. O. (1975). *Sociobiology: The new synthesis.* Cambridge, MA: Harvard University Press.

Wittgenstein, L. (1953). *Philosophical investigations.* Oxford, UK: Blackwell.

Wolf, F. A. (1981). *Taking the quantum leap.* San Francisco: Harper & Row.

Yalom, I. (1980). *Existential psychotherapy.* New York: Basic Books.

Yalom, I. (1985). *Theory and practice of group psychotherapy* (3rd ed.). New York: Basic Books.

Index

About the Authors

Brent D. Slife is Professor of Psychology at Brigham Young University. He is an active psychotherapist and was until recently Director of Clinical Training at Baylor University. He is also editor of *Taking Sides: Clashing Views on Controversial Psychological Issues* (7th ed.), editor-in-chief of the *Journal of Theoretical and Philosophical Psychology,* and a member of the editorial board for the *Journal of Mind and Behavior.* His most recent book is *Time and Psychological Explanation* (1993).

Richard N. Williams is Professor of Psychology at Brigham Young University. He is a Social Psychologist, but currently the Chair of the Theoretical and Philosophical Psychology Program at Brigham Young University. He serves in editorial capacities on several journals and publishes empirical and theoretical work in the areas of human agency, postmodern approaches, and stereotyping. He most recently coedited the book *Reconsidering Psychology: Perspectives From Continental Philosophy* (1990).

Lightning Source UK Ltd.
Milton Keynes UK
UKOW031159181212

203789UK00002B/137/A